SIXTY-ONE

The Team / The Record / The Men

Tony Kubek & Terry Pluto

A FIRESIDE BOOK • PUBLISHED BY SIMON & SCHUSTER INC.
NEW YORK • LONDON • TORONTO • SYDNEY • TOKYO

FIRESIDE
Simon & Schuster Building
Rockefeller Center
1230 Avenue of the Americas
New York, New York 10020

First Fireside Edition 1989
Published by arrangement with Macmillan Publishing Co., Inc.
FIRESIDE and colophon are registered trademarks
of Simon & Schuster Inc.

Designed by Jack Meserole
Manufactured in the United States of America

1 3 5 7 9 10 8 6 4 2 Pbk.

ISBN 0-671-67539-7

To my Dad, "Poosh 'Em Up Tony,"
and all the other great minor league players
who never got the chance I did

CONTENTS

ACKNOWLEDGMENTS

The authors would like to thank the following members of the 1961 Yankees for their help with this book: Ralph Houk, Frank Crosetti, Johnny Sain, Wally Moses, Yogi Berra, John Blanchard, Moose Skowron, Bobby Richardson, Bob Hale, Jack Reed, Joe DeMaestri, Clete Boyer, Hector Lopez, Tom Tresh, Bob Cerv, Mickey Mantle, Whitey Ford, Bill Stafford, Bud Daley, Ryne Duren, Rollie Sheldon, Ralph Terry, Luis Arroyo, Bob Turley, and Jim Coates.

Others who contributed to the section of the book about the late Roger Maris were Jim Ogle, Hoyt Wilhelm, Whitey Herzog, Pat Maris, Big Julie Isaacson, and Mike Shannon. Arlene Howard offered many insights into her late husband, Ellie Howard.

Roberta Pluto and Pat McCubbin waded through the countless hours of taped interviews and took an active part in preparation of the final manuscript. A final thanks goes to Macmillan editor Jeff Neuman, for his support of this project.

—Tony Kubek and Terry Pluto

I

Roger

1

THE LAST TIME I talked to Roger Maris was about two months before he died. It was one of his good days when the pain wasn't so bad, and he was able to talk with an old friend for about ninety minutes.

For a while, we asked about each other's families and some friends we had in common, but it wasn't long before our conversation turned back to the 1961 Yankees. That's how it usually went with us.

That year, Bobby Richardson led off, I batted second, Roger hit third, and Mickey Mantle was fourth. Roger liked to talk about the lineup, how I used to dig a hole with my back foot in the batter's box. We kept our back feet in the same spot, and Roger's swing was in such a groove that season he could tell if the hole was just a little off. He'd come back to the dugout and ask me why I was standing in the wrong place.

It's kind of crazy the things you end up remembering and talking about after twenty-five years. It's also strange that Roger's one home run I remember the most was not his sixty-first, but his fifty-eighth. We were playing in Detroit, and I was on second base. Roger was at the plate and stepped out of the batter's box. He seemed to be staring at the upper deck in right field. I looked out there, but I didn't see anything. Suddenly, a flock of about 250 Canadian geese appeared on the horizon, flying right over the right-field roof in Tiger Stadium. Roger took off his cap, wiped his brow, and just watched the geese. I know it couldn't have been more than a minute, but it seemed like about ten before he put his cap back on and got into the batter's box. Nester Chylak was the umpire, and I could see he was getting a little nervous because Roger was holding up the game, but Chylak let Roger stand there looking at the geese. Terry Fox was the Detroit pitcher, and he wasn't thrilled with the delay. He stood on the mound, rubbing up the ball and wondering what Roger was doing. But like Chylak, Terry never said a word. The game just stopped because Roger Maris wanted to watch some geese.

Finally, Roger was ready to hit. Fox threw him a pitch that was about a foot outside and six inches off the ground. I could see it perfectly from second base. Roger went out and got it, pulling a four-hundred-foot homer into the upper deck in right, just under where the geese had flown.

I mentioned this to Roger, and he said, "Tony, I can still see those geese. Watching them was so peaceful."

In 1961, I think the only place Roger felt any peace was at home plate. In the outfield, he was in danger of having some jerk rip out a chair and throw it at him, as happened in Detroit. In the clubhouse, there were countless reporters with endless questions. In the hotels, there were fans wanting time and autographs. But at home plate in 1961, Roger Maris could do anything he wanted.

"I always loved to hit," Roger would say. "I loved everything about playing baseball. As for the other stuff, well, you can have it."

"Roger was in such a groove in sixty-one," said Ralph Terry. "He really had that three-and-one shot down pat. Roger would be at the plate, and some poor guy on the mound would be pitching him carefully. Then the count would run to three-and-one, and the pitcher would look at the on-deck circle and see Mickey Mantle. So what is he supposed to do, walk Roger and get to Mickey? He had no choice but to come in there, and Roger was ready. Roger hit 61 homers and didn't draw one intentional walk. That shows you how strong our lineup was and how much the pitchers feared Mickey."

During the last few months of the 1961 season, Roger was getting about three thousand letters a week. I received about one hundred, a lot of them admonishing me not to make the last out of a game, depriving Roger Maris and Mickey Mantle of a last at bat and another shot at a record.

I was twenty-five, the starting shortstop for the New York Yankees. I used to walk out of the park three hours after a day game and see over one hundred kids wanting to know if Roger and Mickey had left the dressing room. I used to go to a place called The Dutchman's, which was really Daube's Steak House, with Roger and Mickey. It was just off 161st Street, over a hill from Yankee Stadium. Babe Ruth and Lou Gehrig used to eat there, and so had a lot of old National League players since the Polo Grounds wasn't far away. Supposedly, the Gas House Gang would come into the place, literally tear it up, and then leave a pile of cash on the table to pay for the damages. The place raised rustic to an art form with sawdust floors and a couple of Dobermans guarding the door. One of the waiters told us that Babe Ruth would have a few beers and start sliding headfirst into the tables.

You ordered your steak by the ounce and felt as though you had stepped back in time.

Ruth seemed to be everywhere in 1961. For most of the season, he haunted Roger and Mickey as they chased his home run record. After Mickey was hurt, it was Roger versus the Babe, a duel neither man would have ever imagined. And in many ways, it was just one of many ironies. For example, not only did Ruth lose his home run record to Roger, his record for consecutive scoreless innings in World Series competition was topped by Whitey Ford.

Our team won 109 games. We hit a record 240 homers without the benefit of a designated hitter and playing in a much bigger Yankee Stadium than exists today. Also, there weren't the homer havens that have opened since, such as the Kingdome, the Metrodome, and Exhibition Stadium. It was the first time Whitey won twenty games and the last time a hardheaded pitcher named Jim Coates ever insulted Ellie Howard. It was the end of Casey Stengel and the beginning of Ralph Houk. For Luis Arroyo and Rollie Sheldon, it was the beginning and end of their careers, all in one year. It also was the last time a shortstop named Tony Kubek would play a big-league season without suffering from back problems.

"All I can tell you about the 1961 Yankees," said former Detroit manager Bob Scheffing, "is that they had the best infield in the league, and they had so much power that a guy like Moose Skowron hit seventh, and that seemed to be the right spot for him."

Bud Daley came to the Yankees on June 14, 1961, one day before the trading deadline. He had been with Kansas City and in last place. "What struck me about the Yankees was the confidence. The hitters would tell us to keep the score within a run in the last three innings and the other team would crack. The other team usually did because one of our guys was cracking a home run."

"The 1961 Yankees may have been the best team of all time," said Johnny Sain. "We had defense no one knew about. We had pitching no one knew about. We had a manager in Ralph Houk no one knew would become a great one. And we had Roger hitting 61 homers. You know that no one ever expected that to happen."

"The year belonged to Roger and Mickey," said Clete Boyer. "Those guys were just such great players. I remember a doubleheader in Chicago where I hit two home runs. That was pretty good, considering the White Sox' pitching. What the hell, you hit a couple of homers, and you expect to see your name in the paper. But Roger hit four that day. His name was in the headlines and mine was only in the box score. But no one was jealous of Roger and Mickey getting all the publicity because they deserved it."

It also was the story of three men—Roger, Mickey, and Babe Ruth. And in the end, it came down to two men—a very human Roger Maris versus Babe Ruth, who had become so great that even his very human failings became legendary.

Sixty-one.

That's the number of home runs Roger hit, and it was a year when we all wore crew cuts. Roger always preferred to have his hair cut near his home in Kansas City, because "New York barbers give you that glamour-boy look I can't stand."

Sixty-one was when I lived at a place called The Stadium Motor Lodge, a two-story motel about eight blocks from Yankee Stadium. It was a place fans would spend a night or two when they came to town to catch a game. I shared a room there with an infielder named Joe DeMaestri and, early in the year, pitcher Johnny James. Bill Stafford, Clete Boyer, and Moose Skowron also spent some time there. For us, it was a place to hang our clothes and watch television. It was close enough to the park so we could walk. When we went on the road, we'd check out of all the rooms but one, throwing all of our stuff in there. Hey, it saved a few bucks. As for Roger, he lived with Mickey and Bob Cerv in an unpretentious apartment in Queens. That's where Roger cooked breakfast for the three of them. They would spend hours in their living room, playing for pennies by putting a golf ball into a little tin hole that sat on top of the carpet. They rode to the Stadium in Roger's convertible, the top down and the wind in their faces serving as the air conditioner.

At the park, Roger kept to himself. Between innings early in the game, Roger sometimes went into the clubhouse, smoking one of his Camels or sipping coffee. The Yankees also had a television in the clubhouse, and Roger used it to get a better look at what the pitcher was throwing. You could hear the scraping of his spikes against the concrete as he came down the runway just before it was his turn to bat or to go out and play right field. He prized the quiet you find in an empty clubhouse during a game.

Before the game, Roger often sat at the huge oak table that was in the middle of the clubhouse. That table went back to the days of Ruth and Gehrig, and clubhouse man Big Pete Sheehy would never let the front office replace it. As usual, his coffee and Camels were near. He had this game, it was a box about a foot wide and three inches deep. Inside, there were two small wooden platforms with forty holes. The idea was to maneuver a little steel ball from one hole, through a maze, and one level to another. Roger was fascinated by it and would play the game for hours. He had a routine in which he could smoke his Camels, drink coffee, and play the game all at the same time.

The first things I thought about when Roger died were him staring at those Canadian geese and him playing that labyrinth game. Then I started to think about the team, and I remembered a picture we had taken by *Look* magazine. They dressed us in suits and handed us briefcases. The theme of the photo was that the Yankees were like U.S. Steel—cold, corporate, businesslike. That wasn't the Yankees I knew, and it was Roger's death that convinced me to contact the guys who were a part of sixty-one. Most of us are in our fifties, and some are over sixty. In our last conversation, Roger said, "You know, Tony, we're all getting kind of old. There were some pretty good guys on that club. Not too many people know that."

And Roger was one of them. It was easy to get the wrong impression of Roger. He was suspicious of strangers and could care less about his public image. He didn't crack many jokes, and when he did, they often came out wrong when he was in the company of strangers. The first time people met Roger, it wasn't surprising if they came away with the misconception that Roger was one morose guy.

But Roger had his moments. In Baltimore, he loved to order hard-shelled crabs and have them delivered to his room. His roommate, Clete Boyer, would fill their bathtub with ice and a couple of cases of beer. A lot of guys would come up to the room, and Roger would have a little party.

Once, they ordered three bushels of crabs instead of the usual two, meaning we had plenty left over. Then Roger went out for a while and returned with a live lobster. One of our trainers, Joe Soares, was known to have a couple beers at night, and when you saw him, you knew he had made a pit stop at the bar. While Soares was out, we got a key to his room. Roger brought the lobster while Clete and I took the crabs into his room. We put the crab shells under the covers of Joe's bed, and Roger dumped the lobster in the toilet. The place smelled something awful. We left the room, and nothing happened for a while. But about midnight, we heard this scream, and there was Joe running down the hallway, babbling about a lobster in his toilet. Apparently he had drunk too much to smell the crab shells.

"Roger liked a good time as much as anyone," said Clete Boyer. "But once he got going in 1961, he was under the gun all the time, and that was bound to change his personality. Roger was a country boy from Fargo, North Dakota. He never understood how great he was. And the guy was a great player. They like to say that 1961 was a fluke, but Roger hit 39 homers and was the American League MVP in 1960. Not too many stiffs become back-to-back MVPs. See, Roger thought he was a good ballplayer, a complete ballplayer. But he never thought of himself as a forty or sixty home run guy. In 1961 he got on this unbelievable roll, and the press made him out to be nothing but a home-run hitter. Roger knew he couldn't hit forty or fifty homers year after year, but he found himself in the position of trying to be something he was not. And there was the press, asking him about being another Babe Ruth. Then they made Mickey out to be the good guy and Roger the bad guy because it gave them good stories. What a bunch of crap. He was twenty-six, just a kid. Some guys say he didn't handle everything the best. Well, how could anyone handle it? Roger was like the rest of us. What he wanted to do the most was win. He wanted to get into the World Series for two reasons—the prestige and the check. Believe me, that eight-thousand-dollar World Series check came in handy every Christmas."

When I think of sixty-one, I first think of Roger Maris.

2

ROGER MARIS arrived in New York wearing a crew cut and a pair of white Pat Boone buckskin shoes.

That's what Big Julie Isaacson told me. Big Julie ought to know, because he was at the airport to meet Roger when he came to New York for the first time as a member of the Yankees.

"I knew Bob Cerv pretty well, and he said that Roger was a friend of his and he needed a ride from the airport and somebody to help him get settled in the city," said Big Julie. "I have a lot of connections around New York, and I'm always willing to help out a new guy. So what the hell, I figured I'd go out to the airport to meet this Maris kid.

"I was standing by the gate and watching all these people get off the plane. I knew who Roger was because he played for Cleveland and Kansas City, but I'd never met him. I knew who he was, but I didn't know his face. Anyway, I'm watching all the people get off the plane, and I don't see anyone that looks like a Yankee ballplayer to me. Then I saw this young guy looking sort of lost. He was wearing a polo shirt, some kind of corduroy jeans, and white Pat Boone shoes. He was a young guy with a crew cut, so I figured that must be Maris. And from looking at him I figured this guy must be some piece of work.

"Roger spotted me and said, 'You Julie?'

"I said, 'You're Maris?'

"He said, 'That's right.'

"I said, 'Listen kid, Yankee ballplayers don't dress like you. You got these Pat Boone shoes, they gotta go.' Then I saw that Roger was looking at me real hard. Hey, I didn't know what to say to the guy. I'd never seen a ballplayer dressed like that. Remember, this was 1960 when people dressed real nice, you know? Finally, I said, 'I don't know, kid, I don't think the Yankees are gonna like this.'

"Roger said, 'The hell with them. If they don't like the way I look, they can send me back to Kansas City.'

"We didn't say much in the car as I drove him to this hotel on Forty-third and Eighth Avenue. I kept asking myself, who is this guy?

I mean, this guy was supposed to be the new Yankee rightfielder? We got to the hotel, and I asked Roger if he wanted something to eat.

"Roger said, 'Is there a Thom McAn shoe store around here?'

"I said, 'Yeah, there's one on Forty-second Street.' We started walking in that direction, and I'm wondering what this guy wanted with Thom McAn's. Nobody buys shoes from Thom McAn's unless you're a kid or something. So I ask Roger what he's going to do in the store.

"Roger said, 'I'm going to Thom McAn to get two more pairs of these white shoes.'

"I said, 'Come on, Roger, nobody in New York wears them kind of shoes.'

"But Roger walked right into the store and bought two more pairs. That's just the way he was. You couldn't tell Roger what to do or what to wear. The next day, I picked him up at the hotel to drive him to his first game. Roger was wearing the same shirt, pants, and the Pat Boones on his feet. The only difference was that he had put on some kind of Sears Roebuck seersucker jacket. What could I say? He looked like a hillbilly. I started to tell him how the Yankees had a tradition of great dressers from DiMaggio to Mantle. Mickey even had a whole wardrobe he kept at the Stadium. But Roger, he didn't care, and I just shut up. From all that, you'd never believe that we'd have become great friends, would you?"

But that's exactly what happened between Big Julie and Roger. Big Julie is the international president of the Novelty Workers Union. He is about six foot three, and as for his weight, well, it's a lot. There is a reason he's called Big Julie. He has managed boxers, including Ernie Terrell, and says he played seven years of minor-league baseball. All I know is that Big Julie always had friends on the Yankees and among the New York sportswriters. When Roger was in New York, no one was closer to him than Big Julie Isaacson.

"We were as opposite as you could get, me and Roger were," said Big Julie. "He was a country kid from North Dakota; I grew up in Brooklyn and I own New York. I'm a Jew, he was German. When Roger was in a room, he didn't want no one to know he's there. When I'm in the room, people know. I don't think there is one guy in North Dakota like me. But Roger and I, we both didn't have any time for crap. If we didn't like something or somebody, we told them. That's why we got along. Also, I was the first guy Roger got to know in New York and I helped him out. Roger was always loyal to those who were there in the beginning. I was Roger's friend before he was *Roger Maris*, know what I'm saying? I was there way before the sixty-one homers, and I was there after the sixty-one homers when everybody wanted to hang the poor kid. And I'll tell you something else, Dan Topping could never understand why Roger had me for a friend. He couldn't figure out why Roger liked a guy in the labor movement, a guy who managed fighters. Topping hired a private eye to follow me around and investigate. I found out from friends that this private eye was impersonating an FBI agent. I had some friends in the FBI, and I called them. They took care of the private eye, because posing as a federal agent is some kind of crime. Next, I found out who the private eye's immediate superior was. I went up to that guy, punched him out, and threw him in a trash can. Roger thought it was hilarious when I told him what happened."

Big Julie was right; Roger was never a New York kind of guy. He was Fargo, North Dakota, through and through. The son of a railroad worker.

"Roger worshiped his father and his older brother," said Big Julie. "Both were named Rudy. The old man, he used to go out and pound railroad ties into the ground when it was forty below zero. Roger talked about that, how his father was tough and had to fight those North Dakota winters. Roger used to tell me about his brother Rudy, saying what a great athlete Rudy could have been. Then there was Pat. They met in high school and got married after they graduated. What I'm saying is that Roger Maris was a family man. He cared about and respected his parents and his brother. He loved his wife and kids and was always loyal to them."

Pat Maris met Roger while she was a freshman and he a sophomore at Shanley High in Fargo. It was Roger who took her to her first prom, and he was the one who first bought her a corsage. He wore a suit to the prom because few high school kids in Fargo could afford a tuxedo.

"Roger was always very thoughtful," said Pat Maris. "That's one of the first things I noticed about him."

"I never knew that Roger was a great athlete in high school until I went to his funeral," said Mike Shannon, a former teammate and St. Louis third baseman who is now a broadcaster for the Cardinals. "That's not something guys talk about. I was the St. Louis city high school player of the year in football and basketball, but was that something I was going to tell Roger Maris? Everybody who gets to the majors was a pretty good athlete in high school. But when I was up there in North Dakota, I couldn't believe the things they were telling me about Roger in high school. His old coach said Roger returned four kickoffs for touchdowns in a state playoff game. They said it's still a national record. From how Roger talked, I always thought Rudy was more of a star than Roger."

Roger was offered a football scholarship to Oklahoma.

"I remember Roger telling me about that," said Bob Cerv. "Oklahoma did give him a scholarship, and Roger said he got on a bus in Fargo and went to Oklahoma City. Now, Oklahoma is in Norman, which is still pretty far from Oklahoma City. Roger said he stayed around Oklahoma City for a couple of days waiting for someone from the university to meet him. No one showed up, so Roger got back on the bus to Fargo."

Roger's next step was to attend tryout camps run by Cleveland and the Cubs. For some inexplicable reason, the Cubs told the six-foot, 175-pound Roger Maris he was "too small." The Indians quickly signed him. He made it to Cleveland in 1957, was traded to Kansas City in 1958, and went to the Yankees in 1960 along with Joe DeMaestri and Kent Hadley for Hank Bauer, Don Larsen, Marv Throneberry, and Norm Siebern. In the newspapers, the trade received very mixed reviews, and the comments turned bitter when Roger said, "I really don't know if I want to go to New York. Sure, I have to go, but I like Kansas City. I have a home here."

Yankee ballplayers were not supposed to wear Pat Boone shoes, and they weren't supposed to say that given the choice between Kansas City and New York, well, I'll take Kansas City. Roger was an interesting contradiction. He stuck out in New York the way Big Julie would have in Fargo. But Roger was the ideal Yankee ballplayer. He was tough, hard-nosed, and smart. He broke up double plays, always took the extra base, and I can't remember him missing the cutoff man. He was a left-handed pull hitter, with the perfect swing for Yankee Stadium. The Yankees were aware of all this, and that's why they jumped at the deal. I also think that the front office was more worried about Mickey Mantle than it would ever let on. Everyone knows that Mickey talked a lot about not living until he was forty. But I think the Yankees didn't know how long Mickey would last, and they weren't just thinking about his knees. They wanted to groom Roger just in case something happened.

The Yankees knew Roger could play. In 1959, he went into July leading the American League with a .344 batting average. Then he had an appendicitis attack, missed a month, and hit .165 for the rest of the season and ended up at .272. "That year I went 6 for 110 and never got booed once in Kansas City," said Roger. "People asked me why I liked playing for Kansas City. Well, they had good fans."

In 1960, Roger came to New York and hammered 27 homers in his first 70 games, putting him well ahead of Ruth's pace. Then he collided with Baltimore's Billy Gardner, who later played for us in 1961. Roger severely bruised a few ribs. He finished the year with 39 homers, one fewer than Mickey. But Roger led the league in RBIs and slugging, and it was Roger, not Mickey, who was the MVP in 1960.

Certainly New York agreed with Roger Maris the ballplayer. And the way he could best survive in a city that was so shockingly different from his home in Kansas City and his youth in North Dakota was to draw a rigid line between baseball and the rest of his life. I think that's really why Roger didn't bring his family with him to New York during the season.

"There were a couple of reasons Roger wanted us to stay in Kansas City," said Pat Maris. "He didn't think New York was the best place to raise four children. We had a nice home in Kansas City, and the children were in school. Roger didn't want to uproot everyone. Besides, it's hard to find someplace nice in New York with enough room for our children. We had four at the time of the trade and ended up with six. I think he felt more comfortable knowing we had a stable home in Kansas City."

The absence of his family also explains why Roger's friendship with Big Julie bloomed so quickly.

"When Roger first got to the Yankees, he stayed at a couple of hotels downtown," said Big Julie. "He even lived above the Stage Deli for a while, but he just didn't like life in Manhattan. So I got him an apartment off the Van Wyck Expressway in Queens, not far from Kennedy Airport. At first, he just lived with Bob Cerv. Mickey didn't move in until 1961. Roger used to like to cook me breakfast. He would fry the bacon first, and then he'd make the eggs in the same fat from the bacon. The eggs always came out black. I used to tell him this wasn't North Dakota, that no one in New York makes eggs like that. But Roger did, and I ate them. I'll say this, they weren't bad."

"Roger just liked to eat," said Clete Boyer. "The guy really went at food, and it disappeared from his plate so fast that you would have thought he had three hands."

"You should have seen the first time Roger ever ate stone crabs," said Big Julie. "We were at this place in Florida, and we were eating with this monsignor friend of mine. Roger had one order and liked it. Then he had another, and another, and another. After two hours, Roger was still eating stone crabs, and the monsignor was making the sign of the cross because he was worried about Roger's stomach."

By the end of his time with the Yankees, Roger's stomach would be tested. Not by food, but by that kind of pressure that gives you ulcers.

3

WHEN Big Julie Isaacson tells the story, his voice stays strong, sometimes even angry, but there are tears in his eyes. Like the rest of us, Big Julie understood the complex relationship between Mickey Mantle and Roger Maris, and how it was distorted in 1961 and still confuses some people.

"The day Pat Maris called me to say Roger had died, she asked me to get in touch with Mickey," said Big Julie, his voice rising. "That's right, Mickey Mantle, the guy who Roger supposedly hated and the guy who supposedly couldn't stand Roger. Pat wanted to call Mickey herself, but he was out of town and she couldn't find him. So I made a bunch of calls and tracked down Mickey in Fort Lauderdale where he was making a commercial.

"When I got him on the phone, I said real quietly, 'Mickey, this is Julie. I have bad news. Roger died.'

"Mickey screamed, and it was one of the worst screams I've heard in my life. Then he said, 'What?', screamed again, and slammed down the phone. I knew it really bothered him, and that he had no idea where I was and he didn't want to hang up. So I waited a couple of minutes and called him back. He apologized for hanging up, and we started to talk about the funeral.

"A couple of days later, I saw Mickey at the funeral in North Dakota. He had gone through all sorts of hell. I mean, this is a man who was living with death all his life, and he just buried a good friend. Yes, Roger Maris and Mickey Mantle were good friends, and only an idiot would think otherwise. At the funeral Mass, the priest asked if anyone wanted to say anything. Bobby Richardson gave his beautiful eulogy. I wanted to get up and say that my fondest wish in this life is that my grandsons grow up to be like three people—my father, Gil Hodges, and Roger—but my feet couldn't move. I was paralyzed. Then Mickey tried to stand up, but he was shaking so much he couldn't make it. He just put his hand on my shoulder and sat back down. He opened his mouth to say something, but there were no words. We were pallbearers, and you could see Mickey's hands trembling as he carried the casket. After the funeral, we were sitting around and talking. Mickey had a few drinks and didn't say much. He just had this terrified look on his face. When he did speak, I remember Mickey saying quietly, 'I'm scared. I'm really scared. The last funeral I was at was my father's thirty-four years ago. The next one will be my own.' "

Mickey expressed those same feelings to me.

"When Roger died, it really hurt," he said. "I mean, I never thought I'd outlive Roger Maris. I was asked the other day who was the best all-around player I'd seen, and I said Roger. I really believe that the sixty-one homers was the greatest feat in baseball history. I used to think that I might do it, but I never could. Roger did. That year, we were so close because we roomed together."

"It was Roger's idea that we go get Mickey," said Big Julie. "We were riding to the park one day, and Roger said, 'We gotta get Mickey out of town. That life is killing him.' "

Cerv and I agreed that Mickey would be better off if he got more rest.

"Roger said, 'I'm going to talk to Mickey, see if he wants to move in with us.' That's how it ended up that the two guys who hit more home runs than anyone else in baseball history lived in the same apartment in Queens."

In the dressing room, we'd read these stories about Roger and Mickey feuding and laugh. I guess the writers hoped that Mickey and Roger would be at each other's throats because Ruth and Lou Gehrig supposedly didn't get along. It's as though they wanted to draw this ridiculous historical parallel, and they were frustrated when there were no facts to back up that theory. The *New York World*'s Dan Daniel never wrote about a fight between Roger and Mickey, but he didn't seem to really know them, either. "Both Mickey Mantle and Roger Maris like movies, but in a mild way," wrote Daniel.

Most good hitters feel that flickers might hurt their eyes. Mickey is a good sleeper. Rog also likes to pound the hay, but not so ardently as the other Mr. M. Neither has established the reputation as a reader of books. Rog occasionally gets a hold of an interesting paperback. If Mickey goes in for the classics, he does it in privacy. Maris never says anything unless he is spoken to. I never heard him give vent to a belly laugh. In that respect, no club ever had two such quiet sluggers. . . . They say little and laugh seldom. . . . Writers have found Maris not quite as responsive as they have hoped and say he is surly. Roger himself has pleaded guilty to the charge and has said he was born surly and intends to go on being that way. If Maris has gone surly, it must have been just recently. I haven't found him that way and I have the impression he is perpetrating a hoax to get the writers off his neck. . . . As for Mantle, he cannot understand that a player can laugh even if he happened to strike out, as Ruth did. Mantle heard my comment and inquired, "What did he laugh up, big chunks of blood?" If you refer to a player having a sense of laughter, Mantle thinks you are taking a crack at him. But Mickey has mellowed. He now can be interviewed for five minutes, but the Oklahoma Kid still appears to regard conversation as boring.

Well, make that conversation with writers, to whom Mickey and Roger were not about to reveal the extent of their friendship. Even though I knew they were close, it wasn't until I talked to Big Julie that I heard it was Roger's idea to invite Mickey to the apartment. I also think that Mickey accepted for two reasons. First, he knew that he was going broke staying at the St. Moritz. Second, Mickey also knew that this would be a difficult season for Roger in that the press and fans were putting a lot of pressure on him. Mickey had been through it so many times that I really believe he thought he could help Roger by moving in and giving support.

Roger and Mickey were in the same situation because neither of their wives were in New York. Merlyn Mantle hated to fly, and she would ride a train for three days with their four boys from Dallas to New York. For a while, they had a home in New Jersey, but Merlyn was never very comfortable there. She was very worried that someone would rob them when Mickey was on the road. One night, there was a severe storm, and Merlyn was upstairs feeding the baby. She heard something downstairs and was convinced it was a burglar. She grabbed the baby in one arm and had a .45 in the other, and she walked down the stairs. The pistol accidentally went off, blowing a hole in the wall. There was no robbery, but that was the end of Merlyn's living in New Jersey. So Merlyn and her children stayed in Dallas, and Pat Maris and her family were in Kansas City, while their husbands lived together in New York.

"It was amazing how Mickey lived at the St. Moritz," said John Blanchard. "The year I made the team as a rookie out of spring training, I didn't have a place to stay in New York, and Mickey liked to take in a young guy and get him squared away. When we checked in at the St. Moritz, the desk clerk said, 'That will be $125 a night.' I had about forty bucks on me, so I knew this place wasn't for me. I picked up my suitcase and started out of the lobby. Mickey looked at me and I said, 'Hey, Mick, I better ease down the street a ways because this place is kind of heavy for my blood. I can't afford anything around here.'

"Mickey said, 'Tell you what. I'll pay the $100 and you pay $25.'

"That's how I got to stay at the St. Moritz. When we got up to our rooms, it was an adjoining suite. Mickey said he was hungry, and we ordered a couple of hamburgers, some french fries, and two large milks. I figured this couldn't cost too much, so I offered to pay for the food. The room service guy came up to the room and wheeled in the cart. I pulled out a ten-dollar bill and gave it to the guy. He just stood there, staring at the bill in his hand. And then I glanced at Mickey, and he was on the couch laughing so hard that tears were coming out of his eyes.

"Then the room service guy said, 'That will be $22.50.'

"Mickey was laughing even harder. I thought he was going to fall on the floor. Mickey then tells the guy not to worry about it, he'd take care of the tab. Meanwhile, I was turning red and purple, and I don't know what else. I couldn't figure out if I was more mad or embarrassed. But that was Mickey. He thrived on the high life."

The guys in the locker room used to joke about Mickey's thousand-dollar tabs, and that was for one weekend in 1961. Mickey would invite guys from both teams for a party. In 1961, Mickey was earning sixty-five thousand dollars, and he was going to be in the hole by July at that rate. When Mickey first came to the Yankees at nineteen, he was interviewed by a writer named Joe Trimble, who wasn't thrilled with the brevity of Mickey's answers. Trimble should have known that a nineteen-year-old from Commerce, Oklahoma, was not about to stand up and give the Gettysburg Address. Instead, Trimble wrote, "Mickey Mantle is a hillbilly in a velvet suit." That label stuck with Mickey for a long time, and I think it bothered him. In his dress and his life-style, Mickey seemed to try to work against that cliché. By 1961, Mickey was a serious clothes horse, but Roger never changed.

"I was with Roger when he talked to Mickey," said Big Julie. "Roger said there were some nice little restaurants around the apartment, and that they wouldn't allow any reporters out there. It would be a nice quiet place away from the Stadium. Now Roger and Mickey were two opposites. Mickey had the tailored suits and the Copacabana. Roger bought his clothes off the rack and liked to eat at good restaurants, but he didn't stay up all night. But Mickey knew Roger had a good idea, so he went along with it. In fact, me and Roger drove over to the St. Moritz, loaded Mickey's stuff into our car, and took him to the apartment."

"I liked it in Queens," said Mickey. "The press couldn't find us. We had an icebox full of sandwiches and pizza. Roger liked his privacy. When we went out to eat, Roger didn't like to be bothered for autographs during the meal. He'd ask the person to come back when he was finished eating. Usually, I just signed to get it over with. But if I was with Roger, I followed his lead. Outside the park, Roger would stand there and sign as long as anybody, but he had a thing about being bugged in restaurants. That's why the apartment was perfect for him, and it was good for me. He wanted to get away from everything, and I needed to get away from it all, too."

Big Julie and Mickey didn't say much about Cerv, but I think he was a kind of link between Mickey and Roger. As I said before, Mickey was from Oklahoma, Roger from North Dakota. Well, Cerv fit in because he was from rural Nebraska. Cerv kept things light. Probably on some nights, Mickey and Roger wouldn't have had anything to talk about if Cerv hadn't been around. It wasn't that there was a barrier between them, but that they weren't especially talkative.

"It was nothing for an hour or so to go by when no one said a word," said Cerv. "That didn't mean they were mad at each other. Mickey and Roger liked the quiet."

With Cerv around, the silence couldn't have lasted long. He loved to talk about everything and anything. Roger and Mickey used Cerv for comic relief. Let's just say that Cerv had a fairly high opinion of himself. But his ego was really entertaining.

A couple of guys would be on a bus about two in the morning, talking about fishing, saying they caught some two-pound bass. Suddenly, Cerv would be in the conversation, saying the last time he went fishing, he caught a couple of three-pounders.

One day, Mickey was saying, "We were hunting in Colorado using a high-power thirty-ought-six with a scope. We glassed the side of a mountain, and I saw this big elk about five hundred yards away. I shot and the elk starts falling . . ."

Before Mickey finished, Cerv had jumped in and said, "I remember the last time I went elk hunting and it seemed to me that the elk I got was about six hundred yards away . . ."

Cerv's "Can You Top This?" routine reached its absurd conclusion during one bus ride when Roger, Joe DeMaestri, and Mickey started talking about tomahawk throwing. These guys had never thrown a tomahawk in their lives, but they talked about it enough so that Cerv was soon saying he'd heaved one farther than Mickey, Roger, and maybe Sitting Bull, too. But Cerv made everyone laugh, which was especially important in their apartment.

"Roger usually woke up first," said Mickey. "Then he'd shake Cerv and say something like, 'Hey Cerv, get up. Me and Mickey are gonna have a fight.' Those kind of jokes were big around the apartment."

According to Big Julie, Roger and Mickey were like any two guys sharing an apartment in Queens.

"One day, we went shopping at a supermarket in Queens," said Big Julie. "Roger and Mickey were pushing around shopping carts, loading up with ham and beer, things like that. There were these two stockboys; one was on a ladder, and the other was handing him cans to stack on the top shelf. The kid on the ground said, 'Hey, there's Maris and Mantle.'

"The other kid said, 'Man, you're crazy. No Mantle and Maris is gonna be in a supermarket in Queens.'

"Those kids went on and on like that for quite a while. Finally, Roger and Mickey came up their aisle. The kid on top of the ladder spotted them and started to yell. Then he got so excited he fell down and cans went everywhere. Mickey and Roger started laughing, and they took off, leaving me with their carts. I got stuck for a $140 tab.

"The apartment was in my name, and I spent a lot of time over there. Roger and Mickey loved country music. I couldn't stand it, and I used to take my Jewish records and play them. If you're not Jewish, those songs will drive you crazy. Even if country music stinks, at least you can understand the words. Mickey and Roger would humor me for a while before they would change the record. But one day, Roger really surprised me. I took him to a friend's bar mitzvah, and Roger stood up and sang "Hava Nagila." He had learned the whole thing from listening to my record when I wasn't around. It really meant a lot to me, Roger singing that song like he did. He didn't do it as a joke, but as something to please a friend."

Big Julie and Roger didn't share every interest. Big Julie likes the horses, and at least once a week he goes to the barber and then to the track.

"In North Dakota, they don't have any horse players because there's no tracks," said Big Julie. "It's no secret that I've been known to place a bet. I used to tell Roger he should go with me, watch the ponies run. I think it's a good way to relax. So he finally went with me, and he wouldn't bet more than two bucks a race. I won big that day, and Roger came out fourteen bucks ahead. A few weeks later, we went back. Roger did the same thing, betting a couple bucks a race. At the end of the afternoon, Roger was down six bucks and he said to me, 'The hell with this. I'm not coming out here to throw my money away.' And that was it, he never went to the track with me again.

"Roger didn't come from money, and he respected money. My third daughter, Barbara, would always ask Roger for his autograph when he came to my house. After she did this about six times, I asked her what she was doing with all those autographs. Roger jumped right in and said, 'She's like you, Jules, she's hustling.' It turned out that Barbara was selling Roger's signature. Roger called her 'The Little Gangster,' but he always signed extra autographs for her. I guess Roger liked the idea that she had a little business going."

Mickey said, "Roger loved to play hearts at the apartment, but we never played for money. He wasn't the kind of guy to throw his cash around."

Listening to Mickey and Big Julie, I realized that it took two trips to the track for him to learn that you can't beat the house. Certainly, Roger loved to compete.

"No matter what sport we'd mentioned, I used to say I was the Oklahoma state champion," said Mickey. "There was a day during the 1961 season when we were at Bob Turley's house in Baltimore. We were sitting around the pool, and some of the guys were saying that Roger was a great swimmer. So I piped up about being the state champion. Then Roger said, 'Let's get into the pool and do a few laps.'

"All that sounds okay except for one thing—I can't swim. Whitey Ford was there, so I told Roger that Whitey is my coach and I have to consult with him. Whitey said, 'Don't worry, Mick, when you jump in the water I'll hand you the pool sweeper and pull you along.' Roger and I dove into the pool and Whitey handed me the sweeper. Whitey ran along the side of the pool, dragging me along. But Whitey was running sideways, and I was scraping my shoulder against the side of the pool. When I got to the end of the pool, I jumped out and sat on the side. Then there was Roger, looking like Johnny Weissmuller, you know how you turn your head to the side to breathe and all that? I mean, Roger was looking great. He got to the end of the pool, and he couldn't believe I had beaten him. He wanted a rematch. He was mad. Then he saw that my shoulder was scratched, and he saw Whitey leaning on the sweeper, laughing like crazy. That's when he knew we cheated. He wanted to try it again, but I finally told him I couldn't swim."

Roger seldom went into great depth about his relationship with Mickey. Yes, they were friends. And yes, they respected each other's ability. But there was even more to it than that. One of the people he did discuss it with was Mike Shannon.

"He started talking about it while we were out playing golf," Mike told me. "First, Roger gave me the background, how they used to boo Mickey because he had replaced DiMaggio. Mickey was still hearing a few boos when Roger showed up in New York. But then they got off Mickey and made Roger their whipping boy. Roger couldn't figure out what was with the fans. He was having an MVP year in 1960, and a few people were starting to boo him. I mean, all of a sudden Mickey was the hero and Roger was the bad guy. Mickey never deserved to get booed. And Roger sure as hell never should have been booed.

"Then Roger said to me, 'That's when I decided I was going to outdo Mickey. At the end of 1960, I figured I was going to hit more homers than Mickey. It was nothing against Mickey. It was the damn writers and the fans booing. I just got sick of it, and I wanted to shut everyone up.'

"Roger took that anger, frustration, and spite and turned it into the greatest year a power hitter ever had.

"Roger said, 'It was something. Mickey would hit a home run, then I'd hit one. Mickey'd hit two, I'd hit a couple. The SOB would hit three in a doubleheader, and I'd do the same. I loved Mickey, but I wanted to outhomer him.' "

Mickey said, "I don't think Roger ever understood why the fans booed him. I doubt that I could have if the tables were turned. We never talked about it, but I think Roger was aware that the fans wanted me to break the record."

Mickey was right. The fans were obviously pulling for him. But so were most of the Yankee players, and I was as guilty as the rest.

Whitey Ford explained it best when he said, "We wanted Roger and Mickey both to break Ruth's record, but I think the majority of the players wanted Mickey to hit more home runs than Roger. It was nothing against Roger. We just knew Mickey longer, and we knew him better."

In the back of our minds, at least it was in the back of my mind, was the thought that Mickey was the one who deserved to break the record. He had earned the right because he came up through the Yankee farm system, and he had hit over fifty homers before. To us, Mickey Mantle *was* the New York Yankees. You had to see Mickey day after day, year after year, and watch him play on days when his knees hurt so bad that he could barely walk to fully appreciate his greatness as a player. I just figured Mickey would be the one to break the record because he was a switch-hitter and because of his immense talent. Roger was one of only two players in the starting lineup who was not a product of the farm system, the other being Clete Boyer. It was almost as if he were an outsider. But once Mickey got hurt, we rallied around Roger, and I think Roger felt better about going for the record. And even before that, we were behind Roger because of the pressure he endured. One of the clearest memories I have of 1961 is Roger Maris at the plate and Mickey Mantle cheering for him in the on-deck circle, and prior to that season Mickey had never said much on the field. Roger and Mickey were fighting for the home run record, but it was the healthiest form of competition because they drove each other to excellence.

"I'm a New Yorker all the way, and I understand the psyche of this city," said Big Julie. "You have to remember that the Yankees always had their man. Ruth. DiMaggio. Mantle. When Roger came along and hit 61 homers, it was like he crashed the party. Of course Roger wanted to break the record once he got close. But he never wanted to be the Yankee franchise. He had no interest in replacing Ruth or Mickey in the hearts of the fans. But that was Roger's legacy with the Yankees: that the wrong guy hit 61."

Whitey Herzog expanded on this theory: "The press always tried to protect Mickey. If Mickey came in too hung over to play, the Yankees would say Mickey's leg was hurting, and that's what the press would write. But when Roger was injured, the Yankee front office, Ralph Houk, and the trainers *never* protected Roger. They hinted he was jaking it, and that got into the papers. That's why Roger sometimes felt Mickey got special treatment."

A *New York Times* story reflected this attitude: "Yankee fans fervently trust Maris's recent leg injury will not derail him. The medical report at hand is it's nothing serious. But then, although Roger's a fine fellow, he's a bit of a worrier. He frets to no end when the slightest muscle twinge throws off the delicate mechanism of his perfect timing. On the other hand, Mantle, though far more prone to injury, seems impervious to pain. No matter what is wrong with his leg, he's satisfied when trainer Gus Mauch tapes him from ankle to hip."

That story was written on August 1, 1961. At that point, Roger had yet to miss a game.

"I suppose it's possible that Roger resented the fact that Mickey got a lot of good publicity," said Bob Turley. "But if Roger did, he kept it down deep and never showed it. I know that Roger thought he should get good ink because he was Roger Maris having a great year, not because he was trying to be another Mantle or Ruth. When he was compared to those guys, Roger would first become frustrated, then get doggone mad."

The lineup was another source of controversy, not between Mickey and Roger, but among the fans and writers. Roger batted third and Mickey was fourth. It had been the other way around in 1960.

"Most of my mail was about where Mickey and Roger were batting," said Ralph Houk. "My only consideration that year was winning the pennant. It seemed to me that we won a lot of games with Maris third and Mantle fourth, so why change? The fans forgot we had a lot of power behind Mickey—Moose Skowron, Ellie Howard, and Yogi Berra. The pitchers had to respect them. I don't see a reason to juggle the lineup when it's working."

"One thing I liked about Casey Stengel was that he batted me third," said Mickey. "It's not that I had any real gripe about batting behind Roger. Ralph is right when he said I had some good hitters behind me. In 1961, I led the league with 126 walks [compared to 94 for Roger], and Roger never got an intentional walk. The main thing is that Ralph told me why he was switching me and Roger before he did it. Ralph said my being behind Roger would get Roger more good balls to hit. Roger would see a lot of fastballs when he was ahead in the count because the pitchers wouldn't want to walk him to get to me. Hey, that sounded all right. Ralph, Roger, and me all wanted the same thing—to win the pennant."

That didn't stop the fans and writers. The pennant race got lost in the endless debates about the lineup, the liveliness of the balls, the lightness of the bats, the effect of expansion, and the number of games Roger had in which to officially break the record.

"No matter what you say, Roger still had to hit all them home runs," said Mickey. "Cut through all the crap, and that's the important thing. No one hit those home runs for Roger, and no one has ever hit as many before or since.

"I'll tell you, I felt bad about what some people wrote and said about Roger. You could see him holding it all inside, see his hair falling out. He had rashes all over the place. And Roger would never really drink. I mean, he'd have a few beers, but that's not the kind of drinking I'm talking about. I remember telling Roger, 'You can't hold all this inside you or you'll blow up. You gotta release it somehow. Let's go get a few drinks.' But on the road, Roger stayed in his hotel room. At the apartment, he'd just sit around the house and maybe have a couple beers, but never let loose."

Big Julie remembered one night when Roger ran with Mickey. It was the first and last.

"I think it was in 1962," he said. "That was when the press was really on Roger. One Saturday night, Mickey convinced Roger to go out with him. Sunday morning they showed up at my house. Roger was kind of drunk, and Mickey was ossified. I mean, Mickey couldn't even stand up. Roger could walk around, but he really wasn't in the best shape to play. I poured coffee into them and did the best I could to sober them up. I had to drive them to the park. Roger got into the dressing room all right, but I had a cop help me with Mickey. We took Mickey to the door and handed him to the trainer. I remember telling Gus Mauch, 'Take him, he's all yours.'

"During batting practice, I didn't see Mickey or Roger, but they were announced in the starting lineup. I thought to myself, 'Houk must be crazy. Roger can't stand up and Mickey can't see.' In the first inning, Roger went to right field and Mickey to center. During the national anthem, Roger had his head down and Mickey was swaying. If a ball was hit to either one of them, they would have been killed. In the top of the first, the other team hit three grounders, so Roger and Mickey were safe. In the bottom of the inning, a couple of guys got on and Roger took a called third strike. Then Mickey was up and he was still swaying, only now he was doing it in the batter's box. I prayed he wouldn't get hit. The first pitch was a changeup, and Mickey started to swing and then stopped. Then he swung again and hit it into the center-field bleachers, 460 feet away. Mickey started trotting around the bases. He hit first base and looked like he was going to keep running down the right-field line. The umpire was Ed Runge, and he said something to Mickey and sort of pointed to second. Mickey finally made the turn and got around the bases. Houk took Mickey and Roger out after that inning. The reason he played them was to punish them. But that was the only time I ever knew Roger not in shape to play. And I do remember Roger promising never to go out all night with Mickey again."

4

DURING the 1961 season, everything was Maris & Mantle, the M&M Boys. The sales of M&M candies skyrocketed, and Mickey and Roger didn't endorse the product, they just went by the same initials. There was a line of Maris & Mantle mens and boys clothes, which earned both players forty-five thousand dollars annually for three years. They signed with Columbia Pictures to appear in a movie called *Safe at Home*, about a Little Leaguer running away from home and right into Roger and Mickey, who helped the kid straighten out his life. For two weeks' work, Roger and Mickey made twenty-five thousand dollars each. Roger also got an extra role for Big Julie, and Mickey did the same for Whitey Ford. In Fargo, a street was named Roger Maris Road. Mayor Herschel Laskowitz passed out business cards that read, "Fargo, the hometown of Roger Maris."

For Mickey, nothing much changed after the season. He was a celebrity when the year began, and he remained one when it was over. But for Roger, nothing was ever the same after sixty-one.

It really wasn't until after the season that Roger had serious problems with the press. After Roger's death, Dick Young wrote in the *New York Post*, "I thought Roger was a helluva guy, the way he handled the press down the stretch in 1961. The thing to remember is that new newspapermen were joining the pack every day. Many of the questions were the same ones he heard day after day and I kept waiting for Roger to blow his top. . . . But he didn't. He just sat there, propped in his locker, sucking on the beer and answering them."

Sixty-one was unique in a lot of ways. The Dodgers and Giants had left New York, and the Mets had not started. That left seven newspapers and one team. None of us understood the press as well as a lot of the modern players such as Pete Rose, Gary Carter, and Steve Garvey. There were no formal press conferences for Roger, as was the case when Rose was chasing Ty Cobb's all-time hit record.

"If I only knew then what I know now," said Bob Fishel, the Yankees' public relations man in 1961 who now is executive vice president for the American League. "The Roger Maris watch was the first of its kind in baseball history. We didn't have daily press conferences because we had never been confronted with the problem before. That would have been ideal for Roger because he could have gotten all the questions taken care of at once. But public relations was not nearly as advanced as it is today."

The Yankees' statistician, Bill Kane, said, "I talked to writers who covered Ruth when he hit sixty homers. It was no big deal. They figured he'd hit sixty-two the next year."

I remember Roger showing up at the park at 9:00 A.M., and that was for night games. He had interviews morning, noon, and night. And the questions; they never stopped, and a lot of them were far from original. You had seven New York papers looking for seven different angles, and you had a guy like Roger Maris who wasn't especially glib. Ask him a question, you get an answer. But he didn't have seven different answers for seven different guys. Roger was a literal person, and there were no long-winded speeches or bizarre theories from him. He preferred to answer a question with a yes or a no. Roger also took what was written about him very seriously, and if he didn't like it, he told the writer. This candor surprised a lot of writers, who took the view that Roger was a country bumpkin who had no right to tell them how to do their business. Joe Trimble was the first guy to ask Roger if he would break Ruth's record. Remember that Joe was the guy who got on Mickey about dressing like a hick from Oklahoma. Well, Joe used to dress like an unmade bed. Anyway, when Trimble asked Roger about the record, Roger answered, "How should I know?" That was Roger's typical answer. Besides, it was the end of the June, so how would he know about breaking the record? In terms of logic, it made sense. As for public relations, quotes like that don't exactly cause papers to put out an extra edition.

I can remember a lot of the questions:

"Roger, is the ball more lively?"

"Roger, can you break the record?"

"Roger, what did you eat for breakfast?"

"Roger, how does it feel to hit all these homers?"

It was Roger this and Roger that. As Bud Daley told me, "It is no exaggeration when I say that I saw Roger go take a crap, and five reporters followed him right up to the stall."

Bob Turley said, "It was funny to watch the writers. They would go to Mickey and somebody would ask a stupid question. He'd smile or laugh and not say much of anything. After a while, they'd get tired of Mickey and go to Roger. Also, Mickey had been around for a long time, and Roger was relatively new. So he gave them some different material."

After a game, one of the things to do in the dressing room was to sit around and watch the press interview Roger. We were curious about who was asking what and how many guys were around Roger's locker. I remember the reporters coming at him in waves. They got Roger when he first came near his locker, they got him after he had stripped off his uniform, and they got him when he came out of the shower. It was only after the writers had talked to Roger and Mickey that they might interview us, and then you had the feeling it was done as an afterthought. This could have been an explosive situation, except that Roger and Mickey handled it so well. There were so many games when Roger would say, "Why don't you guys talk to Ellie Howard, he's hitting .350. Talk to Whitey, he's won twenty games. Talk to Luis Arroyo. Talk to Bobby Richardson, he never plays a bad game." The important fact was that we knew Roger was sincere. He didn't enjoy the attention, and he believed it should be spread around. He played the game the same way. Sure, there were the home runs. But he was selfless, as he broke up double plays and even bunted runners over.

"There was a game where we won 5–3, and Ellie Howard had 2 homers and 5 RBI," said Jack Reed, who was a reserve outfielder with the Yankees in 1961. "All the reporters were around Roger, and Ellie was sitting on the stool in front of his locker all alone. Roger had popped out twice and struck out twice. Finally, Roger said, 'Listen, guys, Ellie won the game, not me. Go talk to him.' All the reporters' heads turned in Ellie's direction, stared at him for a moment and then turned right back to Roger to ask him the same old questions."

For the most part, Roger stayed out of the gossip columns. But once he was linked to Ava Gardner. She used to go to the park and sit by the Yankee dugout. Ava Gardner was definitely not a baseball fan. The Yankees had become a glamorous team, and a lot of celebrities went to the games, just in hopes of getting their names in the paper. I know there was nothing to the Ava Gardner story because you won't find a stronger family man than Roger. But that kind of story upset Roger, and who could blame him?

"My locker was next to Roger's," said John Blanchard. "As soon as the game was over, I'd rush to my locker, grab my clothes, and move a couple of lockers away to dress by Hector Lopez. Roger would sit back in his locker, the sides of which were wire mesh like a fence. Some writers would literally be in my locker and talking to Roger through the screen. It reminded me of Roger in a confessional."

Bob Cerv said, "If only Roger hadn't taken the questions to heart. He would say, 'Bob, what I am supposed to tell these guys? They keep coming at me. One guy even asked me if I screw around on the road. I can't do any more for these guys.' Roger was so honest and sincere, he couldn't just brush off a question with a shrug. I told him to lie, tell the writers what they want to hear. But Roger said he couldn't do that."

Joe DeMaestri said, "There was a real contrast between Roger and Mickey with the press. The press would be around Roger, and everyone knows that not all of Roger's answers were the greatest. Meanwhile, Mickey would be watching the whole thing, laughing. And when a reporter would ask Mickey something stupid, he'd say, 'Hey, Rog, you take this one.' Mickey could defuse the press with a smile."

In August, a Japanese reporter from a paper called the *Hochi Shimbun* descended on Roger. In the *Sporting News*, Dan Daniel wrote as only he could:

Here were the 18 questions from the Nipponese Newsman:

1. How does it feel for you to go after Babe Ruth's record?
2. What method of attack do you think is best to break any home-run hitting slump?
3. What is giving you strength in your home-run race today?
4. Are opposing pitchers deliberately walking you?
5. Is the deliberate walking upsetting your equilibrium and your co-ordination?
6. What remedial methods do you use in such cases?
7. How are you tackling lefthanded pitchers?
8. What do you do to maintain your playing condition?
9. How heavy is your bat?
10. Are you particular about the weight and quality of your bat?
11. How are you reacting to the fuss your friends, writers, and baseball officials are making over your home-run race?
12. Are you the type that gets worried about a record to break?
13. What is your biggest worry today?
14. What is your happiest experience today?
15. What is your present batting average and why?
16. Do you think Mantle will catch and pass you?
17. What is Houk's attitude toward your homer-record challenge?

18. If 162 games are to be played, do you think you will exceed Ruth's record and by how many?"

From that list, you would have thought they were ready to ask Roger if he was breathing and why. Roger looked at the questions, shook his head, and said, "Tell them Mantle will pass me. That should take care of all this."

"I thought Roger had the patience of a saint," said Johnny Sain. "I think Roger never realized what a big story he was. Like it or not, he was the big man in New York in 1961, and if he sneezed, it was news. What he ate, how much he slept, what he wore . . . those were all big stories. I know Roger hated losing his privacy and thought much of what went on was idiotic, but that's how it was. If Roger wasn't such a firm person, he never could have withstood everything."

Roger drew even closer to Big Julie during the stretch drive in 1961. Since Julie knew many of the writers, he helped Roger schedule interviews.

"One thing you could count on, if Roger said he would talk to someone at three o'clock, he was there," said Big Julie. "That's why I was surprised with what happened between him and the *New York Post*'s Milt Gross, who wrote one of the first negative stories about Roger. I had set up an interview between Roger and Milt. Roger had 59 homers and he was in Baltimore. At 8:30 that night, Milt called me and he's screaming and swearing because Roger didn't show up. Milt said he was going to rip Roger from one side to the other. I asked Milt to give me a few minutes to find Roger. I called the hotel in Baltimore and Roger wasn't in his room. I got in touch with Cerv and Bob said, 'I know where he is, but Roger made me promise not to tell anyone.' So I started screaming at Cerv, but he wouldn't say anything.

"Three hours later, Roger called me and I asked him what happened and if he had made an appointment with Milt.

"Roger said, 'I did.'

"I said, 'Where were you?'

"Roger said, 'I can't tell you.' We started yelling at each other, and I hung up. The next day, the *Post* comes out and Milt had taken Roger apart, saying he was nervous, sassy, and all that crap. When the team got back from Baltimore, I picked up Roger at the airport, and I showed him Milt's story. Finally, I got Roger to tell me what happened. He and Whitey Herzog were good friends because they had been teammates with the A's and lived near each other in Kansas

City. When Roger was supposed to be talking to Milt Gross, he was with Whitey at a hospital giving a sick kid an autographed ball and a bat. It turned out the kid had cancer and he died two days later. But Roger refused to have any publicity about it, and he wouldn't let me tell Milt where he was, not even off the record. Roger went to a lot of hospitals, but he didn't call a press conference like some of these guys today. In fact, if Roger thought the press knew he was going somewhere, Roger made a point to skip it. That's just how he was. I knew this, but I still had to try and make it up to Milt. So on the night before the day Roger hit number sixty-one, I happened to mention to Milt that Roger and I would be eating at the Spindletop. Milt just happened to show up, and he got an exclusive. Roger's relations with the press were good until after 1961. I really think his problems began during the winter when he had to go to banquets and while he was trying to negotiate his new contract."

The first decisions Roger made at the end of the season was for Jim Ogle to write his biography. Jim was with the Newark *Star-Ledger,* and he was the sportswriter covering the Yankees whom Roger trusted the most.

"Everybody wanted to do Roger's book," said Big Julie. "I'm talking about all the heavyweights in New York, but Roger was loyal to Jim Ogle, so he went with Jim. It didn't matter that one of the New York guys could have gotten more money for Roger. Jim Ogle was Roger's friend. But the other New York writers didn't like the idea that Roger had picked a guy from Jersey to do his book."

Jim Ogle is now the editor of *Yankee Magazine*. Twenty-five years later, Jim still wasn't sure how and why Roger and the press went to war.

"In 1961, everything was great," said Ogle. "Then everything fell apart, and it was all during the winter. How can you get in trouble when you're not playing? I suppose what started it was when Roger had to go to Sacramento for a banquet. Sal Durante, the kid who caught Roger's sixty-first home-run ball, was to get a five-thousand-dollar check from a restaurant owner in Sacramento in exchange for the ball. Roger didn't want to go to California, and he told the people there he would not make a speech. The only reason he did go was because the kid was getting married and Roger wanted Durante to get the money. Roger had this plan—the kid would get the five thousand dollars, Roger would get the ball, and everyone would get out of there. But when he arrived, there were a bunch of reporters expecting a press conference. Roger said he wasn't going to give a speech, and he stuck to it. That started the anti-Maris stuff."

The next trouble spot was Roger's 1962 contract. I'll never understand why the Yankees decided to play hardball with Roger. In the last month of the season, he had made them millions by drawing extra fans at home and on the road. But this was 1961, and in 1961, every team fought you for every penny. During the season, Roger earned $42,500 and Mickey was at $75,000.

"Once in a while, Roger and I would talk about his contract," said Clete Boyer. "You would have thought the front office would have come to Roger during the year and given him a bonus. Or at least you'd think they would take care of him the next season. He had to put up with so much and had done what no player had ever done before. The press was calling what he did a fluke, and the Yankees were acting like the press was right. Roger was the greatest draw in the game, but the Yankees refused to make an attempt to reward him. Considering how the Yankees handled his contract, it seemed to Roger that they were saying the hell with him."

Roger consulted with Big Julie about his contract.

"All winter, the Yankees refused to be serious," said Big Julie. "They wouldn't move from around $60,000. Roger went to spring training without a contract. He had a meeting with Dan Topping, Roy Hamey, and Houk. In 1961, Mickey had made $75,000, and the Yankees had given him a raise to $100,000. But the Yankees never said what Mickey was making, and a lot of people thought he got only $85,000 for 1962.

"Anyway, Roger came to me after a meeting and said, 'We're not going to get a hundred thousand dollars.'

"I said, 'What did they offer?'

"Roger said, 'Nothing. It was a joke, something like a fifteen-thousand-dollar raise. They said they gave Mickey the hundred and they couldn't give it to me because no one was going to make more than Mickey.'

"I asked, 'So what did you say?'

"Roger said, 'I told them that I would take ninety thousand dollars, but they wouldn't even consider it.'

"For a few days, Roger stayed in Florida, but he had no real meetings with the Yankees. Ralph Houk came to see me and said, 'What's wrong with your friend?'

"I told Houk about all the people Roger had put in the ballpark.

Ralph stopped me in the middle of a sentence and said, 'We can't pay him as much as Mickey.'

"I said, 'So give him ninety.'

"Houk said, 'Can't do that either.' We talked some more, and then Houk set up another meeting between Roger, Topping, and Hamey.

"So Roger went to see those guys and after a few minutes, Roger was back with me and he said, 'That's it, we're going home.'

"I said, 'Wait a minute. You got four kids and a wife. How are you gonna feed them?'

"Roger said, 'They're just being ridiculous. I dropped down from a hundred to ninety to eighty-five to eighty and they still wouldn't go for it. Their best offer was sixty-seven thousand dollars.'

"I talked Roger into going upstairs one more time. What else could he do? There was no free agency. No arbitration. No one had an agent. Finally, he settled for $72,500 plus he got another $5,000 in living expenses."

The spring of 1962 was very stormy. During the 1961 season, Roger had been criticized by Rogers Hornsby and Ty Cobb. Hornsby said that Roger "couldn't carry Ruth's jock," and Cobb said, "The only thing Maris could do like Ruth was run." Asked about old-time players, Roger said, "A lot of them looked like banjo hitters to me. They had those little gloves, they only played during the day, and the travel was nothing. When I say things like this, people think it's Roger the Redneck talking, but that's how I feel."

As the spring went on, the Maris stories grew meaner and the booing all the more fierce.

Clete Boyer said, "Roger refused to respond to the booing, but he heard it. He wasn't like some guys who lie and say they don't hear the boos. Roger told me, 'I heard the boos, and I know why I'm getting booed. The fans still think I want to be another Ruth and all that crap. I'm sick of it and it hurts, but there isn't anything I can do.' Then there was the incident with Hornsby. Some photographer wanted Roger and Hornsby to pose together for a picture, the two Rajahs and all that. After Hornsby hammered Roger in the papers, why should he pose with that guy? So he told Hornsby and the photographer to take a hike, and the press got ahold of that and took it all out on Roger."

Joe DeMaestri said, "I played for Hornsby with the St. Louis Browns. He was the meanest guy I ever met. There are very few people I don't like, but he's one. When Bill Veeck fired him, the players got together and bought Bill a trophy. You couldn't please Hornsby unless you went out and spiked somebody."

Big Julie said, "Roger was getting nailed left and right. I had spent the early part of spring training with Roger, and then I went to New York. When I got home, I looked at the newspapers, and there seemed to be a million stories knocking Roger. I was home about a week when someone from the Yankee front office called me and asked if I'd go back to Florida and 'settle Roger down.' So I showed up in Fort Lauderdale to see what was going on.

"Roger saw me and asked, 'What are you doing here?'

"I said, 'I came down for a few days, do you mind?'

"Roger said, 'You were just here. I don't know why you're here again.'

"I said, 'Look, if you don't want me here, the hell with you. I'll stay somewhere else.'

"Roger was sort of disgusted, but he said, 'Don't sweat it, stay with me.' We went out to eat at a Hawaiian joint and when we got back to his room, Roger said, 'Okay, Jules, what's going on?'

"I opened my suitcase, and there must have been fifty articles from papers all over the country ripping Roger. Guys who never knew him, guys who never had even said hello were taking shots at Roger. He was a redneck, he was surly, he was everything bad you could think of.

"Roger looked at the stories and said, 'So?'

"I said, 'So what are all these stories? Why is everybody taking shots at you?'

"Roger explained it to me like this. He was at this banquet in Fort Lauderdale, and a kid walked over to Roger and handed Roger a ball. The kid said, 'Mr. X, will you sign this?' Roger takes the ball and signs it 'Mr. X.' It turned out the kid's father was the mayor of Lauderdale, which really meant he was a nobody. What the hell is the mayor of Lauderdale? It's just like a pebble on a beach. But the mayor had a friend on the newspaper, and the next day there was a story in the Fort Lauderdale paper saying Roger was rude and how he had signed the ball 'Mr. X.' "

That story was by UPI's Oscar Fraley, who never talked to Roger, but wrote, "If either of my sons has a hero, I hope it's John Glenn. Guys like Roger Maris bat a round zero with me."

"The next day, Jimmy Cannon wanted to talk with Roger," said Big Julie. "It was during infield practice, and Frank Crosetti expected everyone to be on the field, or you didn't get to play. Roger and

Cannon were good friends. They used to eat breakfast together. But Roger was mad about what was in the Fort Lauderdale paper. He told Jimmy, 'I'm not talking to anyone, and that includes you.' A few minutes later, Roger cooled off and said he'd talk to Jimmy after practice, but Jimmy was upset."

Jim Ogle said, "Cannon wrote two of the most vicious columns I've ever read. [One was titled "Roger the Whiner," and the other was "Maris Envies Mantle."] Cannon said that Roger was fighting with Mickey and that he was destroying the morale of the team. It was so bad that Houk had to call a press conference to deny the charges. The whole thing just snowballed, and Roger stopped giving interviews. It all got crazy. That spring, we had an autograph party for Roger's book at Jordan Marsh. I was sitting next to Roger as people lined up in front of him for autographs. He signed everything—scraps of paper, pictures, postcards, gloves, and napkins. A reporter stood about ten feet away and watched the whole thing. The next day, the guy came out with a story saying, 'If you make the cash register ring, you get Maris's autograph. The only way he would sign is if you bought his book.' That was a bald-faced lie, but ripping Roger was the thing to do in 1962. They said Roger didn't take it well. I want to know what you're supposed to do when that stuff is in the papers day after day."

In *The Miami News,* Tommy Devine wrote, "If it weren't for sportswriters, Roger Maris would probably be an $18-a-week clerk at the A&P back in Missouri."

"It was getting bad," said Big Julie. "I was with Roger a couple times when middle-aged men came up to us in a restaurant and said something like, 'Hey, Maris, I don't much like you, but my kid wants your autograph.' Then they wondered why Roger told them go to hell."

The Roger Maris we were reading about was not the Roger Maris we saw in the dressing room. The world wanted a hero, a golden boy, not a hard-working guy from North Dakota. When he didn't measure up, some writers insisted he had changed. "Roger Maris has turned," a few of them wrote. Turned from what to what? All I know was that Roger was pretty much as he had always been. He played aggressively, got along with the guys, and more than anything else, he wanted to win. Inside, I'm sure Roger had changed. No one could have endured what he had without some scars. Roger had to think about all the pressure and the criticism, and he had to wonder if it was worth it. By 1963, Roger started getting hurt, especially suffering from a severe wrist injury. I'm sure that cut down his power. He used to attack the ball and was one of the most feared pull hitters in the game. But more and more, I saw Roger going to the opposite field. He was feeling for the ball, just making contact. After sixty-one, the expectations about Roger were so high, and there was no way he could do anything but fail. He had to realize this. The players never mentioned it, and it never crossed my mind until I retired, but perhaps Roger subconsciously didn't want to hit that many home runs again. He had achieved greatness, but the price he paid was immense, and I doubt that he ever wanted to go through it again.

"After sixty-one, Roger Maris wanted to go back to being a ballplayer," said Mike Shannon. "He told me that when we played together in St. Louis. He was proud of the record, but he didn't want to cope with all that pressure of trying to outhomer Mickey and Ruth. Day after day, it just wore him down. And when he did it, people acted like Roger kicked the pope between the teeth. Why have the press following you everywhere? Why get thousands of letters telling you that you're a bum? Why would anyone want to have to hide at friends' houses just to get away from everything? And no matter what he did, he got ripped and booed. Yeah, I think Roger just wanted to go back to being a good, all-around player. That's the only way he ever thought of himself, anyhow."

5

IN 1962, Roger Maris was indeed a good ballplayer. Thirty-three homers, which was fifth best in the American League. One hundred RBI, sixth best. The Yankees won another pennant, and Roger played his usual superb right field. But it was written off as a disappointing season, one in which Roger Maris hit "only 33 home runs."

Actually, 1962 turned out to be Roger's last healthy season.

For five seasons ending in 1962, Roger averaged 33 homers and 100 RBI, and remember that the only men at the time who played right field as well were Roberto Clemente and Al Kaline. Anyone who played with Roger Maris knew the 61 homers was a once-in-a-lifetime thing, but Roger was consistently productive. But also keep in mind that when you play like Roger, you often get hurt. In 1963, he pulled several leg and back muscles and bruised his shoulder running into a wall. Roger appeared in only 90 games and hit 23 homers. Roger rebounded in 1964 with 26 homers and 71 RBI, but the fearsome swing was gone.

"Roger still had some good times after sixty-one," said Big Julie. "One winter he invited me to Kansas City to show me his town. He wanted me to know that Kansas City wasn't a cow town. We went to where President Truman lived, to some nice restaurants and places like that. But I told Roger, 'This is still a cow town to me. You got no Jews here. What do you have? Forty people living here?' Roger laughed, and it was those moments when he seemed the happiest.

"Something else Roger loved to do was give a rookie the business. In the spring of 1965, Roger and I played a trick on Bobby Murcer that Roger always loved to talk about. Bobby was nineteen and still had all that Oklahoma dirt under his skin, if you know what I mean. Roger and I picked up Murcer at the team hotel. Roger had told Murcer a lot of stories about me, how I was a big union guy in New York.

"Roger told Murcer, 'Julie is so tough, he buries people alive.'

"When Murcer came out to the car, he put out his hand. I didn't shake it, I just glared at him. At the restaurant, Murcer ordered a beer.

"I screamed, 'Listen kid, you don't order until I order first.'

"Murcer looked at Roger, who said, 'When I go out with Julie, he's the boss.'

"I ordered a Scotch and then looked at Roger. He ordered a beer. Then we let the kid order. When the menu came, I told Murcer, 'You better not order anything more expensive than I do.'

"You could see a lump in the kid's throat, and all he did was nod. Meanwhile, Roger was doing all he could to keep a straight face. When dinner was over, Roger said to Murcer, 'You better tell Jules what Houk has in mind.'

"The kid said, 'Well, I'm coming to New York. The Yankees are bringing me up.'

"I yelled, 'You? They're bringing you up?'

"Murcer got quiet and sort of worried. He nodded.

"Roger said, 'About the passport.'

"Murcer said, 'What passport?'

"I yelled, 'The passport to New York. Rog, can you tell this snot-nosed kid has never been to New York.'

"Roger asked me, 'Didn't Houk tell you about Bobby?'

"I said, 'Unless I hear something official, the kid doesn't get a passport.'

"Roger said, 'I don't know, Bobby. I don't think you can go to New York unless Jules gets you a passport.'

"Murcer said, 'Maybe I should talk to Houk.'

"Roger said, 'You better.'

"The next day, Murcer went in and told Houk, 'Last night, I went out to eat with Roger and this union guy, Julie. Roger said this guy Julie runs New York and unless he helps get me a passport, I can't get in.' Houk laughed so hard that he almost fell on his ass. Roger got the biggest kick out of setting up those gags."

But there was little laughter for Roger in 1965. In May, he slid back into second base and appeared to jam his left wrist. At least, that's what the Yankees said Roger did. They listed his injury under the infamous category of "day-to-day."

"The dang thing was busted, and they kept telling Roger he had a bruise," said Bob Cerv. "He kept trying to play, but his swing wasn't the same. The whip was gone."

Clete Boyer remembered the incident bitterly. "I love that day-to-day crap. That's a terrible thing to do to a ballplayer like Roger. All they did was play games with him, hinting to reporters that the only pain was in Roger's head. How could anyone say Roger was dogging it? But that's what the front office basically said."

When a player is listed as "day-to-day," the onus is on him to determine when he can play. If a day-to-day injury becomes week-to-week, as was the case with Roger, it looks as though the player lacks guts and can't tolerate pain. All the Yankees said was "there's something wrong" with Roger's wrist. It was mysterious, because no one knew what the "something" was, not even Roger. But it also was an indictment of Roger's attitude, full of implications that a lot of guys have played with injuries that were much worse.

Big Julie was with Roger during the trips to the doctors, and he said, "The Yankee team physician, Sidney Gaynor, couldn't find anything wrong with Roger. Two other doctors looked at it, and they couldn't find anything, either. Ralph Houk was then the general manager, and he couldn't figure out what was going on. Roger said it was killing him, the doctors said nothing was wrong, and the papers were saying Roger was jaking it. Even some of Roger's teammates were starting to wonder about him. I could understand how Roger felt. What the hell, he knew there was something wrong. And I can understand Ralph Houk. The doctors told him Roger was fine. And Johnny Keane was the manager. Poor Johnny, a nice guy, but he had no chance. The job was too much for him. It got to the point that I had some doubts. They sent the guy to three doctors, and all the doctors said the same thing. How was I supposed to know the doctors were a bunch of damn shoemakers?

"One day, Roger and I came out of the Spindletop, Roger was rubbing his wrist and he had a grimace on his face. I said, 'Now what's wrong with you?'

"Roger just looked at me, real hard.

"I said, 'Roger, is the world nuts and you're the only sane one, or what? There's nothing wrong with you.'

"Roger said, 'Are you one of those jerks, too? So even you don't believe me.'

"In a minute, we were yelling at each other. You see, it was even getting to me, and Roger was my best friend. But it was like Roger was the only voice in the wilderness.

"Finally, the Yankees got sick of hearing Roger complain, and on the Q.T. they sent him to a specialist on Park Avenue. I wanted to go into the office with the doctor, but he made me stay in the waiting room. Then the doctor took the X rays of Roger's wrist from a bunch of angles. The door opened and Roger came out. He said to the doctor, 'You tell Jules, he's my buddy.'

"I said, 'Tell me what?' They made it sound like Roger was going to drop dead on the spot.

"The doctor said, 'The X rays show a bone chip hitting against a nerve in Roger's left wrist. Every time Roger hits the ball, he gets a shooting pain up and down his arm.'

"Then I started to think, well, Roger was right and the world was wrong.

"Next, the doctor said, 'Roger, you have two choices. You can leave the wrist alone and you'll have to stop playing, or we can operate. If there is surgery, there is no guarantee it will be successful. But an operation really is the only way you'll have a chance to continue your career.'

"As we were driving home, Roger said, 'The hell with it, I'm not having any damn operation.' I told him to calm down and call his wife in Kansas City. The next day, Pat flew to New York. Roger and I picked her up at the airport, and we went walking the streets, talking about his wrist.

"Then Roger said, 'The hell with it, I'm still not getting the operation.'

"I said, 'You get the operation or you don't play. It's that simple.'

"Roger said, 'Like I said before, the hell with it.'

"I said, 'So what are you going to do?'

"Roger said, 'I don't know, Jules. I just don't know.'

"For years, Roger talked about getting a beer distributorship, but he was no closer to having one in 1965 than he was when he first had the idea. And what else could he do but play ball? Roger signed out of high school. It's not like he couldn't do anything else, but baseball was all he had done since he was eighteen. But that didn't stop Roger from calling Houk and telling him there would be no operation.

"After he hung up with Roger, Houk called me and said, 'I don't know what we're going to do. Roger won't have the operation, and if he doesn't have it, he can't play.'

"I suddenly got an idea and I said, 'Listen, Ralph, I'll make you a deal. I'll get him to have the operation if you guarantee his salary for next year.'

"Ralph said, 'No way we can do that. Teams don't do that.'

"I said, 'If you want him to get the operation, guarantee him the same money for next year.'

"Ralph said, 'Can't you talk to him?'

"I said, 'I have talked to him. He needs the guarantee or he won't do it.'

"There were three or four more calls back and forth before Houk agreed to the deal. Then I went to see Pat and Roger. I had just cut a deal for Roger without talking to him.

"Roger, Pat, and I went out for another walk. I remember it perfectly. We stopped at the corner of Fiftieth and Broadway and I said, 'Roger, you're going into the hospital because I made this deal with Houk.'

"Roger said, 'What are you talking about?'

"I told him about the deal and his guaranteed money. This was 1965, and no one guaranteed a player anything in 1965.

"Roger said, 'You're crazy.'

"I said, 'You got no choice. You get the operation or you quit. No way you can keep going like this.'

"We argued some more, and Roger finally agreed to do it. He went into the hospital in the morning and had the surgery. The doctors removed the bone chip, but they were worried about damage to the nerve. Pat and I visited Roger that night. Pat was staying with me and my wife, so after the hospital we went to my house.

"At 7:00 A.M. the next morning, my doorbell was ringing. I answered it, and there was Roger in his pants and a hospital shirt.

"I said, 'What's this?'

"Roger said, 'Pay the cabbie.'

"I said, 'You're supposed to be in the hospital.'

"Roger said, 'Jules, just pay the guy.'

"I said, 'What about the operation?'

"Roger said, 'Pay the guy, the meter is running.'

"So I went out to the street and paid the cabbie. When I got back into the house, Roger was telling Pat that he left because the Yankees had set up a press conference for him that afternoon.

"Roger said, 'They didn't ask me about it. They just said they were bringing some writers over, and I was to talk to them. I said, the hell with this. I checked out and came over here.'

"Roger never did go back to the hospital. He stayed at my place and went to a doctor's office for treatment. At that point, Roger didn't trust the Yankees or Houk, and he was going to do things how he wanted."

After the wrist injury, Roger was never the same player. Nor did he ever feel the same way about the Yankees.

Mike Shannon said, "When Roger and I were with the Cardinals, he told me about the wrist. He was convinced the damn thing was broken and the Yankees wouldn't tell him. He thought someone had seen the problem on the X rays and they were holding back the information. Roger couldn't believe that three doctors were unable to see something was wrong. He felt the Yankees wanted to keep him playing because he still brought a few more people into the park."

Bob Cerv said, "Roger said that Houk didn't level with him about the wrist. I don't think those two ever resolved their problems. But Roger wasn't bitter about it. He used to tell me, 'What's gone is gone. I don't have time to worry about it now.' "

My last season with the Yankees was 1965, and I can understand Roger's frustration, but I was never able to figure out what happened. I find it hard to believe that Houk would lie to Roger about his wrist, but it's also hard to imagine three doctors not finding anything. Clearly, Roger was hurting. Anyone could see that. I don't know why the Yankees would want Roger to play if he was jeopardizing his career. I do know that Roger and Houk weren't communicating. When I looked up the guys from sixty-one, I asked Ralph about Roger's wrist, and he acted as if nothing was wrong. It wasn't something he cared to discuss. Part of the problem was that Roger and Houk were so much alike. They had a stong relationship, especially in 1961 when Houk helped Roger deal with the pressure of Ruth's record. Houk also called that press conference in 1962 to take some of the heat off Roger when the press was after him. Roger and Ralph were big men, very physical men, and very stubborn. They valued integrity and loyalty and were very candid. But neither man was willing to make the first move to sit down and talk over what had happened. And over the years, the misunderstanding grew and festered until it was impossible to really know the truth.

6

THE 1966 YANKEES weren't much of a team. Why hedge about it? They were a terrible team. What else can you say about a New York club that finished dead last in the American League? I had retired because of a back injury, Bobby Richardson was in his last season, and Mickey was literally on his last legs. Mel Stottlemyre was the best pitcher, and he lost 20 games. Johnny Keane opened the season as manager and twenty games later he was gone, taking a 4–16 record with him. Ralph Houk came back down from the front office to manage. I believe that Ralph was a great manager and a terrific handler of people. But he was completely miscast as a general manager, and a lot of the guys felt betrayed by him. When he was the manager, the players thought he fought with the front office for them. But when he moved upstairs, Ralph was the front office. Suddenly, Ralph was the one giving you a hard time over a thousand-dollar raise. So naturally, when Ralph returned to the dugout, a lot of the guys who had tried to run through outfield walls for him no longer had that intense loyalty.

The game was changing. With the coming of the amateur draft, the Yankees could no longer corner the market on young talent. Topping and Webb saw the draft as the beginning of the end of the Yankee dynasty. They also were cutting corners in preparation to sell to CBS. Severe cuts were made in salaries, scouting, and the farm system. So the ball club was showing its age, it no longer had the deep farm system, and to top it all off, the front office had made some suicidal trades.

After the wrist surgery, Roger played in 1966, but his swing had no resemblance to the sixty-one model. Most of Roger's hits went up the middle or to left field. In 348 at bats, he hit .233 with 13 homers.

"It was a combination of things bothering Roger that season," said Big Julie. "Recovery from surgery was no picnic. The team was brutal, and that got him down. He was also disillusioned by the front office because of all that happened before the operation. A lot of Roger's fire was gone.

"That season, Roger did something that really surprised me. When he had broken the record, he was invited up to Grossinger's Hotel in the Catskills. He was supposed to make appearances for a week and pick up five grand. Roger went up there and found out it was a benefit for the Yonkers Police Department, so he did it and didn't take any money. Like I said, that was Roger. Just like all the hospital visits he made, he did this but wouldn't let anyone know he had refused the five grand. Anyway, Paul Grossinger owned the hotel, and he got to be a friend of Roger's. It was a Sunday afternoon and Roger had a doubleheader at the Stadium. It also was Grossinger's birthday, and they were having a big party at the hotel.

"Roger told me, 'Jules, let's go to the park and right after we'll head up to Grossinger's.'

"I said, 'Roger, it's a doubleheader, remember? We'll never get there on time.'

"Roger said, 'Don't worry about it.'

"In the first game, Roger gets into an argument with the umpire and is tossed in about the fifth inning. I was sitting in the stands thinking, okay, that's it for game one, but. . . . Then an usher came up to me and said, 'Mr. Maris is waiting for you in front of the Yankee clubhouse.' I asked the usher if he was sure, and he said Roger had sent him. So I went to the clubhouse, and there was Roger, out of uniform in his regular clothes.

"Roger said, 'Let's go.'

"I said, 'Roger, what's all this?'

"Roger said, 'Let's not waste time. Let's go to Paul's party.'

"I said, 'But what about the second game?'

"Roger said, 'Ah, Keane will never miss me.'

"So we went. That was the only time in his entire career that Roger did something like that, but it showed how bad things had gotten for him and the Yankees. He just didn't have the same desire. His wrist didn't hurt as much after the operation, but it was so weak. The surgery wasn't a success. They took out the bone chip, which relieved some of the pain, but there was damage to the nerve. Roger talked about quitting after the season and more or less told Houk that was his plan. But the Yankees didn't want him to make any public statements. As it turned out, they wanted to keep him quiet because they were trying to trade him.

"In December, I got a call from the *Post*'s Milt Gross. He told me that Roger had been traded and no one could find him.

"I said, 'Traded to who?'

"Milt said, 'St. Louis.'

"I said, 'For what?'

"Milt said, 'Charley Smith.'

"I said, 'Who's Charley Smith? . . . Ah, I don't even want to know.'

"I hung up with Milton and called Roger in Kansas City. He had an unlisted phone number, and that's why the reporters called me. When I got Roger on the phone, the first thing he said was, 'Jules, I'm quitting.'

"I said, 'Roger, you can't quit.'

"Roger said, 'I can do whatever the hell I want.'

"I said, 'You can't quit now.'

"Roger said, 'Why not?'

"I said, 'Roger, don't you see? You're finally gonna get that beer distributorship. Think about it. Who owns the Cardinals. Old man Busch, right? Busch, Budweiser, Michelob. For years, all you talked about was getting a beer business. Now you can do it.'

"Roger said, 'Then I might be interested.'

"After I hung up with Roger, I called [St. Louis general manager] Stan Musial and told him what Roger had in mind. Stan said that Gussie Busch would never sell a distributorship to a player. I said if he wanted Roger, he might have to make an exception. Stan agreed to see what he could do, and eventually they made a deal so Roger could buy one after he retired."

Pat Maris was excited about the trade.

"We were still living in Kansas City, so St. Louis was relatively close to home," she said. "The important thing was that Roger could have us in St. Louis during every homestand. He was so tired of being away from the family. The trade to St. Louis could not have come at a better time. I think Roger was happiest playing baseball when he was with the Cardinals."

The trade brought Mike Shannon and Roger together, forming a friendship that would end only with Roger's death. Interestingly, Mike used almost the same words as Big Julie when he said, "Roger had a lot of friends, and I don't know who was his best friend. But I knew he was mine."

In 1966, the Cardinals were assembling a young team that included Orlando Cepeda, Julian Javier, Bob Gibson, Curt Flood, and Lou Brock. By dealing Smith to the Yankees, they could move Shannon from right field to his natural position at third base. Roger took over for Mike in right.

"When we got Roger Maris, no one was sure what to think," said

Shannon. "The Cardinals were a close-knit team with a delicate chemistry. We had one star, Bob Gibson, and a lot of good players who blended together. In New York, it was a star system—Mantle, Maris, Ford. And we had heard the stories about Roger fighting with the press, being moody and unhappy. I thought back to the 1964 World Series. That was when Mickey was having leg problems so they put him in right and Roger in center field. I was impressed by the way Roger played center and how he ran the bases. Roger knew how to knock a second baseman on his ass to break up a double play. All of that ran against his reputation. But it only took a week for us to realize that Roger Maris was a heckuva guy."

Then Mike said the same thing we did in the Yankee clubhouse: "Roger didn't seem anything at all like the guy we read about."

Ironically, the Cardinals' spring headquarters was in Saint Petersburg. The last time Roger trained there was sixty-one. The Yankees moved their spring base to Fort Lauderdale in 1962. Roger did not exactly terrorize the Grapefruit League, hitting .225 with 1 homer. But he was usually the last player in the clubhouse, as he did some extra hitting or running.

The Cardinals opened the 1967 season at home, and Roger opened in right field.

"He was really apprehensive before the game," said Mike Shannon. "I think he was worried that the fans would boo him. After New York, we all could see that Roger was really burned, baby. I'm talking about a guy who was badly singed. He had taken some serious knocks and it showed. Hey, who could blame the guy if he was a little gun-shy of the fans? But as Roger found out, he didn't know the St. Louis fans."

The opening day lineup was announced, and when Roger Maris popped out of the St. Louis dugout, the fans cheered. They rose and cheered. Roger stood along the first-base line, hands on hips, staring at the crowd. Amazed. Shocked. Then a fan in right field unrolled a sign that read, "Welcome Roger Maris."

"You should have seen that game," Mike Shannon told me. "The first time he came to bat, Roger tried to bunt a one-and-one pitch and fouled it off. That made the count one-and-two. There were runners on first and third, and Juan Marichal was pitching. Roger hit a line drive to left. It looked like a single, but Roger hit the bag and took off for second. He caught the leftfielder napping and went into second with a headfirst slide. It was the damndest thing you ever saw."

In the top of the second, Roger jogged out to right field, where the fans greeted him with another standing ovation.

"But the best was later on in the game," said Mike Shannon. "Roger was at the plate, and they were all shifted way around to right field, playing Roger to pull. It was a one-run game, and we needed a baserunner, so Roger dropped a bunt down the third-base line and beat it out. When he went out to right field next inning, the fans went crazy. It sounded like they were going to tear the place down. In St. Louis, they understand that kind of baseball. And I'll tell you something else, that bunt did more to win Roger respect than about anything else he could have done. He could have tried to be a big man, swing from the ass for a home run. But the foremost thing in Roger's mind was getting on base and winning the game.

"Roger loved St. Louis, and he relished the two pennants we won while he was there. In New York, they wrote him off. Said he was finished. He came to St. Louis and got in two more World Series, and where the hell were the Yankees those two years? New York had problems, but they weren't Roger Maris. Roger was on pennant winners in seven of his last nine years in the majors. That tells you something right there. Roger didn't care about personal stats. His wrist was shot. He had no strength whatsoever, and that pretty much took care of his power. But Roger was the best I have ever seen when it comes to driving in a runner from third with less than two outs. A lot of times, he did it with a ground ball to second base, but he did it. Roger gave himself up to move runners. When I think about it, it makes me mad. Those guys in New York had Roger figured all wrong. All he needed was for people to get off his back. And the St. Louis fans, man, they could see what was going on. They never booed Roger in two years. See, the fans in St. Louis come to the park to see the Cardinals win, and they want to help the team. Sure, they'll jump on a guy's back if he's loafing or if the team is playing stupid. But generally, these people have a real positive attitude. They recognized Roger for what he was—a damn good ballplayer. They didn't care about all the 61 home runs and Babe Ruth crap. In St. Louis, he got along with the fans, press, the players, everybody. The only time he would get discouraged was when he couldn't hit the ball like he used to, then he'd swear at his wrist and that would be it."

In 1967, Roger batted .261 with 9 homers and 55 RBI.

"Even though his wrist was done, Roger still frightened pitchers," said Mike Shannon. "He got 20 intentional walks that year, and Orlando Cepeda was hitting behind him, leading the league in RBI.

Roger was a singles and doubles hitter, but he loved those two years, savored every minute. He showed the world that his ass wasn't done, especially in the World Series."

Roger batted .385 in the 1967 World Series as the Cardinals defeated Boston. In 1968, Roger played his last season, hitting .255 with only 5 homers in 100 games.

"I know his numbers didn't look that great, but the Cardinals wanted Roger to play again in 1969," said Mike Shannon. "Roger had told Gussie Busch that sixty-eight was his last year, but we won another pennant, and Roger was still doing the little things that win games. Toward the end of the sixty-eight season, Frank, Mr. Busch's valet, appeared in the dressing room. He told Roger, 'The boss wants to see you.'

"Roger said to me, 'This is it.'

"I said, 'What do you mean?'

"Roger said, 'Gussie is going to want me to play another year.'

"I said, 'So what are you going to do.'

"Roger laughed and said, 'I just don't know.'

"So Roger went upstairs and talked to Mr. Busch. Roger was right, Mr. Busch wanted him to keep playing. Roger said, 'I'd really like to be home with my wife and kids and run the beer business for you. But if you really want me to play again, I will.'

"All Mr. Busch had to do was tell Roger he was needed for another year. Roger felt a lot of loyalty to Mr. Busch and the Cardinals, and he would have done it. But Mr. Busch told Roger, 'I see that it is important to you that you be with your family. Since that's the case, I want you to be with them.' That showed you what kind of guy Gussie Busch is. He treated Roger like a man."

So after twelve years and 275 home runs, thirty-four-year-old Roger Maris moved to Gainesville, Florida, ostensibly to retire, but really to start over as a rookie in the beer business.

"We had hoped to get a distributorship in Kansas City," said Pat Maris. "But the only one that came open was in Gainesville, and Roger jumped at it. They are very hard to get."

For some athletes, the retirement dream is owning a night club, a four-star restaurant, or being in the broadcast booth.

"During the five years I roomed with Roger, all he wanted was a beer distributorship," said Clete Boyer. "Early in his baseball career, he had met a guy who had one, and the guy was doing well. And once Roger decided what he wanted, that was what he wanted. He didn't care what kind—Miller, Coors, you name it. He just wanted one, and he was lucky he ended up with the Cardinals, because Busch is the top of the line. The key to the business was Roger's brother Rudy. Not that Roger wasn't willing to work, but Rudy was the one who understood how to run a business. Let's face it, most of us can't go from baseball to business and be a success. We know life on the outside is tough and that we're not trained for it."

Mike Shannon said, "Roger worked his butt off when he opened that business. The competition was going around to all of Roger's clients saying, 'Now that Busch has that big-shot ballplayer running the business, you'll never see him.' But for the first six months, Roger rode the delivery trucks and went to see all his clients. He would show up in bars, buy everyone a Bud, and talk up his product. After a while, Roger's clients told him, 'Those other guys said we'd never see you, but you're around more than anyone else.' Roger's territory is eight counties, and business tripled when he and Rudy ran it."

Early, Roger did face a crisis.

"Right after he and Rudy bought it, the workers went on strike," said Big Julie. "They figured the Maris brothers had no idea what they were doing. Now, I'm a union man, but those guys were trying to hold Roger up. Roger and Rudy, they had none of it. One brother was as stubborn as the other, and they let those guys walk off the job. The Maris family loaded and drove the trucks, not missing any deliveries. I mean, the kids were out there throwing cases onto the back of the trucks. It wasn't long before the workers settled."

Clete Boyer said, "I visited Roger in Florida at least once a year. Rudy and Roger made a great team. Rudy had the business sense, Roger had the name. Roger would go out to meet new clients, and Rudy made sure the orders got there on time. After a couple years, they had it going so well that Roger didn't have to be in the office that much. He went around to golf tournaments and did some other public relations things for Busch. Mostly, he spent time with his kids."

Roger's six children became the focal point of his life.

"We followed the kids everywhere," said Pat Maris. "Between golf, basketball, and baseball, we probably averaged six games a week. I remember going to as many as three games in one day with Roger. It was a great time for him to be out of baseball, because he got a chance to see the children grow up. I'm very serious when I say watch, because Roger didn't say anything during games and never pushed the children into sports. The thing he hated the most was Little League mothers and fathers. He said they took the fun away from the kids."

During his retirement, the friends from baseball Roger kept in contact with the most were Clete Boyer, Mike Shannon, Big Julie, and Whitey Herzog.

"When I was player personnel director for the Mets, every June we had a rookie camp down in Florida," said Whitey Herzog. "Roger would come down with me to look at the first-year players. He got a kick out of watching young talent. One summer, Roger had his four sons and my two boys with him. He took them to a diamond and threw batting practice to those kids for almost two hours. Florida in June is always over ninety. Roger was sweating his tail off, but he just kept throwing and throwing. He knew that the best way to be a father is to spend time with your kids."

Pat Maris said, "Because of his hand and shoulder injuries, Roger was never able to play for long periods with the children. He really couldn't swing a bat and throw very well. His idea was to be around if he was needed."

Mike Shannon said, "Roger bought a house on a lake about thirty miles outside of Gainesville. He also built a guest house on the lake, and my family used to stay there. Roger never fished a day in his life until he retired. I loved to fish, and I used to invite him along when we were with the Cardinals, but Roger would say, 'I ain't no fisherman.' Roger liked to play golf, and his regular house was on a golf course. But one day we were staying on the lake and Roger said, 'I think I'll go fishing.'

"I asked Roger, 'What's this about?'

"Roger said, 'Some of the kids are fishing, and I think I'll go along.'

"I said, 'Since when did this start?'

"Roger said, 'Nothing has started.'

"I went out to the pier with him, and it turned out that Roger knew a lot of the fishermen. It used to bother him to go to some public places because he didn't like being recognized. But he found out that fishermen were different. The president could be throwing a line into the water about five feet away, and a fisherman wouldn't say two words to him unless it was to ask what kind of bait he was using. Roger found out that he was just another guy on the pier to the fishermen, and it was Roger who went to them to talk about fishing. Roger hated pretension. That's why he liked the fishermen on the pier or the guys in the neighborhood bar. The writers liked to portray him as this bitter guy down in Florida. Well, the only thing he was bitter about was the asterisk or whatever they put by his record. But the rest of it, he wouldn't have traded a minute of what he did in baseball or after. If anyone should be bitter, it's the writers. They're the ones who missed the damn boat when Roger was making history."

That may have been the case, but Roger was very reluctant to go back to New York. He rejected countless invitations to Yankee old-timers' games. The first time Yankee owner George Steinbrenner met Roger, he asked, "Roger, why don't you come to New York?" and Roger supposedly said, "No, they might shoot me."

"There were a couple of problems," said Big Julie. "We all know that Roger felt the Yankees and Ralph Houk screwed him around with his wrist injury. The fans and writers had beat him up pretty good, too. Roger was worried about getting booed. He liked baseball and used to go to games in Atlanta and St. Louis, but after he retired he only went to New York once. That was on beer business."

Roger learned he had cancer during the Christmas holidays of 1984. That, combined with Steinbrenner's persistence, led to his return to Yankee Stadium.

"Every winter, Roger and his boys and me and my boys would go hunting," said Mike Shannon. "We had some outstanding goose hunts, and Roger liked being outside in the woods. But right after Christmas, Roger called to tell me he couldn't make it.

"I said, 'We always go this time of year.'

"Roger said, 'I don't know, I've got this thing. I don't know what the hell it is. It's mono or something. I went to see a doctor, and he took some tests, and he's supposed to know something in a week. I just feel tired right now.'

"About a week later, Roger called, and I asked about the doctor's report.

"Roger said, 'Well, I just got back from the doctor's office, and I've got some good and bad news. The good news is that I don't have mono.'

"I said, 'What's the bad news?'

"Roger said, 'I've got cancer.'

"I said, 'Oh, God.'

"Then Roger said again, 'I've got cancer.'

"I said, 'Man, you gotta be kidding me. What did the doctor say?'

"Roger said, 'I've got lymphoma.'

"I said, 'Okay, what's that?'

"Roger said, 'All I know is that they say it's 80 percent curable.'

"I said, 'Roger, that's great.'

"Roger said, 'What if I'm in the other 20 percent?'

"I said, 'Listen, you don't go thinking like that. A guy gives you eighty-twenty, you gotta jump on the eighty.'

"Roger said, 'I hope you're right.' "

It wasn't long after his conversation with Mike Shannon that Roger had another meeting with Steinbrenner.

"Roger and Steinbrenner got to know each other fairly well because George would visit Roger when the Yankees were training in Florida," said Big Julie. "For years, Steinbrenner talked to Roger about New York, and for years, Roger said he wasn't interested. But that last winter, they were together and Roger was telling Steinbrenner about a Little League field near his house.

"Roger said, 'You know, George, those kids could really use some lights.'

"Steinbrenner said, 'You got it.'

"Roger said, 'I don't know, George, the turf isn't that great either.'

"Steinbrenner said, 'Okay, we'll put in some artificial turf for the kids. How does that sound?'

"Roger said, 'I really appreciate it.'

"Steinbrenner said, 'Now I got a favor I want from you.'

"Roger was quiet.

"Steinbrenner said, 'Come to New York for the opener. We'll retire your number. You and Mickey throw out the first ball. What do you say?'

"Roger said, 'I'll do it.'

"That night, Roger called me and said, 'Hey, Jules, I need a passport.'

"I knew exactly what he meant.

"Roger said, 'Jules, I'm coming to New York for the opener.'

"I said, 'I don't believe it.'

"Roger said, 'It's because of Steinbrenner.'

"I said, 'Steinbrenner. Don't you know what kind of guy he is?'

"Roger said, 'You ever meet him?'

"I said, 'No, I only know what I read.' Then we both started to laugh because it could have been me talking to a stranger about Roger Maris. Maybe that's part of the reason Roger and Steinbrenner got along."

Clete Boyer and Mike Shannon both understood why Roger accepted Steinbrenner's invitation.

Mike Shannon said, "George Steinbrenner made Roger a very happy man. Down deep, Steinbrenner thinks the world of the Yankee tradition, and he knows that Roger Maris was a big part of that tradition. George sat in his box at the Stadium and looked out at the monuments and said, 'We have Babe Ruth out there. We have Lou Gehrig and Mickey Mantle. But where is Roger Maris?' George knew that the Yankees had alienated Roger over his wrist. But he kept telling Roger, 'I don't care what happened in the past. I don't care what the Yankees did to you. Those guys who hurt you are gone. They were just a small part of the Yankees. You're a big part, and we want you back.' It not only meant a lot to Roger to go to New York, it was important to Steinbrenner to bring Roger back."

Clete Boyer said, "The last time Steinbrenner asked Roger, he was ready. I don't think George had to do that much of a selling job. Roger was near the end, and he wanted to be back in baseball, if only for a day."

Roger also talked to Whitey Ford about Steinbrenner's invitation.

"He was still afraid of the fan reaction," said Whitey. "Mickey and I both talked to him for a long time. I guess he couldn't take the idea that he might be booed one more time. But Mickey and I convinced him the fans would cheer so loud they'd shake the Stadium when he stepped on the field."

Because he had lost a lot of weight after contracting cancer, Roger had a new wardrobe made up for his New York trip. He was met at the airport by Big Julie.

"The day of the opener, Steinbrenner sent a limo to the Essex House," said Big Julie. "That's where the Yankees put up Roger, his family and me. When we got to the Stadium, Roger was real nervous, and he didn't say a word. He did a lot of pacing around. You know, he never would admit that the thing keeping him out of New York was the fear of getting booed. I always thought that was it, but the way he acted that day convinced me. There was no other reason for him to be acting afraid. And when he stepped on the field, the place just went crazy. He had tears in his eyes, and he was laughing at the same time. He was happy and relieved all at once."

Whitey Ford said, "Seeing Mickey and Roger riding around the Stadium in that convertible, waving at the fans and hearing the ovation . . . it got my heart pounding just to watch it."

The day after the opener, Big Julie made an appointment for Roger to see a specialist at Mount Sinai Hospital.

"I always thought the best doctors were in New York," said Big Julie. "So I wanted them to check out Roger. He was examined thoroughly. They took blood tests, went over his records, did everything you could do. At the time, Roger was feeling very good. Anyway, the doctor told us that the cancer was in remission, and Roger could live another twenty years. All the doctor did was change Roger's medication. We went straight from the hospital to the Plaza Hotel and had a champagne breakfast to celebrate. That night, we were going to celebrate again. I set up a big dinner for us at Elmer's. My friend owns it, and they flew in some stone crabs from Florida just because they knew it was Roger's favorite. Roger was a real eater. Anyway, they brought out the crabs, and Roger barely touched them. Then he turned white and broke into a cold sweat. It turned out that his remission had ended, and that was why the hospital couldn't detect how sick he was. The next day, Roger got on a plane back to Florida."

Roger spent most of his last year watching baseball.

"We bought a satellite dish so Roger could see more games," said Pat Maris. "He liked the games, no matter if it was Little League or major league. For a while, we had had cable, so he got to see a lot of the Braves. But after we got the dish, Roger was excited because then he could pick up the Cardinals."

"I talked to Roger about five times a week," said Mike Shannon. "He always wanted to know our satellite coordinates so he could follow us. He paid close attention to what was going on. Roger and I liked the same part of the game, the intangible aspects of baseball. He'd watch our games and then talk about what guys were doing the fundamental things and what guys weren't. He knew who was in position, who moved up the runners, and who didn't."

Whitey Herzog said, "The last time I talked to Roger was during the World Series. I was worried about how he was feeling, and Roger was more concerned because my team wasn't hitting against Kansas City. He kept telling me that he was feeling fine, not to worry."

Other friends checked on Roger.

"During the last month, Roger had trouble getting to the phone," said Mickey Mantle. "After a while, I didn't like to call because it was so sad. Instead of bothering Pat, I started calling Rudy. But I'm not a very good talker on the phone and neither is Rudy. Both of us would hold the phone, knowing the other was there, but not saying anything."

"I was with Mike Shannon in St. Louis for the World Series," said Big Julie. "Mike and I took turns calling Roger. After the World Series, Mike and I both called Roger, and then we would talk to each other. We knew he was going down and there wasn't anything we could do, but we wanted to try something. It was such a helpless feeling.

"One day, Mike called and said Roger was in very bad shape. I called his house, and I couldn't get anyone to answer. I finally got in touch with Roger's daughter, Susan, who said Roger and Pat had gone to a hospital in Tennessee. In Tennessee, they changed his medicine, but that didn't help. Next, he went to a hospital in Houston. On the morning of the day he died, I called Pat in Houston, and I could tell from the tone of her voice that something was really wrong, and I wanted to fly down.

"Pat said, 'He's very sick. I don't think he can see anyone.'

"I started to break down.

"Pat said, 'Julie, there is no sense in coming. They're trying this other medication. I'll call you tomorrow and tell you how it works.'

"It turned out that Roger was already in a coma and Pat didn't want to tell anyone. It wasn't long after that when Pat called me and said, 'Julie, we lost him.' That was it. I remembered screaming, and then I remembered Pat telling me that the medicine they used on him was really an experiment. They didn't think it would cure Roger. It was too late. But they thought it might tell them something that would help their research. They told Roger all this, and he wanted them to try it, even though it might cause him even more pain."

Big Julie and Mike Shannon made the calls to Roger's friends and teammates to inform them of his death. I was down in the Dominican Republic watching some winter ball games when I heard. I was scheduled to go on a television talk show, but when the news came a half hour before we were going to start taping, I got too upset to go on. I knew he had cancer, and I knew he didn't have long to live, but it still really hit me. I called Pat Maris a little later because I was having all kinds of problems getting a flight from the Dominican to Fargo, and I couldn't make the funeral. Pat said she understood, and she started talking about how she and Roger had spent their honeymoon in the Dominican, while Roger was playing winter ball there. They had just gotten married, and Roger was playing winter ball down there. It was a pleasant, nostalgic conversation, and I know I'll never be able to go to the Dominican again without thinking of Roger.

"What always impressed me was how Roger took that last year," said Mike Shannon. "You know, he loved to play golf. He always said it was a good game, a clean game where no one got hurt. He liked the idea of being out on the course with a guy for three hours, just getting to know him as you talk between shots. When I called him, he used to watch the guys playing golf from out his window as he talked to me. The only time he ever mentioned anything about dying was one day when he said, 'Mike, there are these four old geezers coming down the fairway. I'm looking at them, and it pisses me off, Mike, because I know I'll never get to be like the old guys out there playing golf.' "

II

The Season

7

WHAT MAKES a great team? Where does it come from, and what's the most important element? If the Yankee dynasty proved anything, it's the value of long-range planning every step of the way. To understand the sixty-one Yankees, you have to know how they got their players and who those players were. It was no accident that they could lose Joe DiMaggio, and then along would come Mickey Mantle. People would say that Phil Rizzuto's gone, so the dynasty is over. They'd say Yogi Berra is getting older, so who's going to catch? Well, how about Ellie Howard or John Blanchard? It seemed there was a never-ending supply of talent ready to step in. Believe me, there was this amazing pool of young players just waiting for a chance. I know because I was part of it.

When I was a kid in Milwaukee, it seemed that everyone wanted to grow up and play for the Yankees. I bet it was like that just about everywhere in the country. This was before the amateur draft, so the team with the best scouts and the most money could corner the market on the top prospects. Supposedly, there was magic to the Yankee operation. There was magic, all right—because they controlled so many ballplayers. When they signed me in December of 1953, they had at least sixteen farm clubs and about five hundred players in their farm system. They didn't just sign a guy and release him after a year or two because he didn't produce immediately. They gave their players time to develop, and they had the right kind of minor-league instructors to bring them along, thanks to the far-sightedness of farm director Lee MacPhail.

I signed with the Yankees for a fifteen-hundred-dollar bonus and a fifteen-hundred-dollar annual salary. I could have gotten more than three thousand dollars that first season, but baseball had a rule that said players signing for over three thousand dollars had to spend their first two years on the big-league roster.

"Take less and go out and play every day."

That's what my father told me. He would know. For five years, he played every day in the minors, one season hitting .357. The Yankees already had two bonus babies when I signed, Frank Leja and Tommy Carroll. Leja was supposed to be the next Lou Gehrig. His ultimate big-league career consisted of 23 at bats and an .043 average over three seasons. Carroll ended up with 30 big-league at bats. I'll never know whether Carroll and Leja didn't make it because of the two years they had to spend sitting on the Yankee bench or whether they didn't have the talent in the first place. But I do know what it meant to have to cut your way through the Yankee farm system.

Right after I signed with the Yankees, I was invited to Casey Stengel's accelerated spring training program. Basically, it was an instructional league for the organization's top prospects held before the start of regular spring training.

As I mentioned, my father was a minor-league player. So were three of my uncles. One of them, John, was a grizzled old catcher, and I'll never forget what he said before I got on the train for that first spring training: "Kid, if you don't make it, don't come home."

Then I got to Forida and saw that I was one of nine shortstops. I was taking grounders with guys like Woodie Held, Bobby Richardson, Billy Hunter, and Jerry Lumpe. You had a feeling that if you booted a couple grounders, you were gone. That wasn't the case, but the group illustrates the talent the Yankees had stockpiled.

It also showed why the Yankees could afford to be so selective. This was baseball's version of Darwinism, and only the best and the brightest survived. For years, Lumpe was stuck in the Yankee farm system because he wasn't quite as good a second baseman as Richardson. Norm Siebern was an outfielder/first baseman, and he had Moose Skowron standing in his path. A right-handed hitter, Deron Johnson had a lot of power, though perhaps not enough for Yankee Stadium, and he lacked the speed and defensive skills the Yankees wanted. It wasn't until these guys were traded that they made the majors. They also became fine big leaguers, all of which is a further testimony to the richness of the Yankee farm system. Those guys were traded, and the Yankees never missed them.

I had one advantage—right from the start, Casey knew who I was and liked me. During that first spring training, he grabbed me by the arm and said, "I remember your father from the American Association. Your dad was a nice hitter, ran like hell, good fielder, but couldn't throw. He hit .350 that one year. They ruined him because they wanted him to pull the ball. I'm not going to let them do that to you."

My father quit the game in 1935, the year I was born. In his five years in the minors he never hit under .281 and hit over .300 three times. The St. Louis Browns offered him a contract for 1935, but the money didn't make it worth his while to keep playing. At the time, my father was responsible for ten people—myself, my two sisters, my mother, and her brothers and sisters. He worked in a tannery, wearing boots that almost went up to his neck because he had to wade through dangerous chemicals as he tanned leather products.

I think my background was like that of a lot of the 1961 Yankees. We didn't come from money, and we grew up at the tail end of the depression. I was raised in Milwaukee, and there were times when I pulled a red wagon through Kosciusko Park to pick up some food because we were on welfare.

My father had a fourth-grade education, and he was like a lot of guys in the 1930s, a hard worker who was willing to take about any job so he could support his family. The problem was finding a job—there weren't that many. The tannery folded, then my father went to work in a tool-and-die plant. He also went to night school and became a foreman. Then the tool-and-die plant died. Next stop was a brewery. He finally got a position at the post office. That meant a lot to us, because civil service jobs have security.

During the 1957 World Series when we played the Milwaukee Braves, I took some of my old Yankee teammates and the batboys to my house in Milwaukee on Fifth Place for a Polish dinner. We rode around the neighborhood, which was a Polish ghetto. I mean very Polish, very Catholic, and a lot of bars. A corner wasn't a corner unless it had three taverns and a bunch of guys sitting there, sipping beer and shots and listening to games on the radio.

My parents bought a house with a thirty-five-year mortgage. It was a small two-bedroom place, yet it was where my mother, Jennie, raised eight kids, counting all the relatives who stayed with us. Some of us would sleep in the attic, others in the basement. All the comfortable chairs and sofas were taken, and every bed had two people. Three kids would sleep in the one big double bed.

There were parks in my neighborhood, and there were always baseball games going on. Just as sports was a natural part of my family, it was second nature to the neighborhood. It was what guys did with their time. Hey, nobody even owned a television set. I remember standing with about twenty people in front of an appliance store, watching the "Milton Berle Show" through the window.

I was a pretty good all-around athlete at Bay View High, but I was also terribly shy. That's kind of strange when you consider that

I now make a living doing the baseball "Game of the Week" on NBC, but in high school I wouldn't even raise my hand in class if I knew the answer. I didn't want to be noticed. If I was called upon, I would sometimes say I didn't know the answer even if I did. If I had a good game, I would sometimes stay home from school the next day because I knew people would want to talk about it, and I hated the attention.

I was like a lot of guys who played baseball in the 1950s and early 1960s. We weren't molded at baseball factories like Southern Cal, and we didn't play Little League ball in which every kid over the age of five had a uniform with his name on the back.

The Yankee scouts found players everywhere. Whitey Ford grew up in a New York saloon, and Mickey Mantle was pulled out of a Commerce, Oklahoma, zinc mine. Ellie Howard was born in urban St. Louis, and Ralph Terry was weaned in a log cabin.

The first major-league game I saw was in Yankee Stadium. I was sixteen and playing in an amateur all-star event called the Hearst Sandlot Game. After that game, we watched the Yankees. They were the only team I wanted to play for, although I was scouted by every other clubs. In my family, pro baseball was just a natural progression. My father went out, my uncles went out, and when it was my turn the Yankees signed me.

I always thought that my Uncle John was deadly serious when he told me that I had better stick with the Yankees or forget about coming home. Fortunately, I never had to find out.

Casey Stengel brought me to New York in 1957 because I could run and play everything but pitcher and catcher. I played all the outfield positions, short, and third base, hitting .297 and winning the American League Rookie of the Year Award. I was twenty years old.

For nine years I played in the majors, but I'm still known as the guy who got hit in the throat. I suppose everyone is known for something, and I guess everyone is supposed to be famous for at least ten minutes. The throat incident took about ten seconds, but that's what people remember. I meet a stranger, and the guy might say something about having seen me on the NBC "Game of the Week." Then he'll say, "Aren't you the guy who got hit in the throat?"

And what can I say? That it was a bad hop? Well, it was. But it happened in the World Series; the seventh game, no less.

It was a ground ball that cost the Yankees that Series and probably cost Casey Stengel his job. It was a ground ball that made the sixty-one Yankees perhaps the greatest team of all time because without

Ralph Houk as manager, I don't think everything would have clicked as it did in sixty-one.

Casey was not at his best in the 1960 World Series.

"I still can't figure out why he didn't start Whitey in the first game," said Mickey Mantle. "Whitey Ford was still our best pitcher. He deserved three starts, because we would need a guy like him if there were a seventh game."

Whitey Ford said, "That was the only time I was ever mad at Casey. I always pitched well in the Series. I know I had some arm trouble in 1960, but still . . ."

The Series opened in Pittsburgh, and Casey wanted to save Whitey for Yankee Stadium. So Art Ditmar started and didn't get out of the first inning. Whitey didn't start until the third game. Then he pitched again in Game 6, both times throwing shutouts.

That seventh game was crucial, not just to the 1960 season, but because it set the tone for sixty-one. Pittsburgh jumped on Bob Turley, knocking him out in the first, and had a 4–0 lead after two innings. But we kept pounding away to take a 7–4 lead. Despite everything, it looked like we were going to get by. When we had a lead in the late innings, Casey had been making several defensive changes. I usually went to left field for Yogi Berra, and Joe DeMaestri took over for me at short.

"With us hitting in the top of the eighth, I went down to the bullpen to get loose," said DeMaestri. "I was sure I was going into the game. That's what Casey had done all season and during the Series."

In the bottom of the eighth, I asked Casey about the change before running on to the field, but Casey just waved his hand as if to say he wasn't worried. Gino Cimoli opened the inning with a pinch single. Bill Virdon followed with a ground ball to me that looked like a double play until it took a vicious hop and nailed me in the throat.

"That Pittsburgh infield was like a cement airport runway," Casey said later.

The ball was going to hit me between the eyes or in the nose, but I threw my head back. I collapsed and Casey came on the field to see how I was. I was trying to tell Casey that I wanted to stay in the game, but I couldn't talk. My windpipe had begun to swell, and doctors later told me that it was closing from the size of a quarter to a dime. When the World Series ended, I was in the hospital.

Later in the eighth, there were two outs, with Jim Coates pitching, and Roberto Clemente hit a grounder to Moose Skowron at first, but Coates forgot to cover the base. Hal Smith followed with a three-run homer.

That gave Pittsburgh a 9–7 lead, but we scored two runs in the top of the ninth to make it 9–9. Then Bill Mazeroski homered off Ralph Terry to win it in the bottom of the ninth.

"To this day, I can't see how Mazeroski's home run got out of the park," said Yogi Berra. "I was in left field, and I was ready to play the ball off the wall. I figured it would be a double. But the ball actually skimmed the top of the wall, and instead of bouncing back into play, it went over."

Ralph Terry was in a tough spot when he finally got into the game in the bottom of the eighth.

"I warmed up five times before I finally got in," said Terry. "I warmed up in the first inning when Turley was pitching. Then Bill Stafford came in, and I warmed up again with Bobby Shantz. When Shantz got in trouble, I warmed up again, but Bobby got out of it. Then Jim Coates and I warmed up, and Casey went to Coates. I finally got into the game after Hal Smith hit the three-run homer. By the time I got to the mound, I didn't have much left, but I know there were days when I'd sneaked by with less. Don Hoak was the first hitter I faced. I hung a curve, and he should have hit it a mile. Instead, he was overanxious and popped out.

"The great thing was that we came back to tie the game in the top of the ninth, and I can still hear Casey saying, 'All right, let's go get these National League phonies.' We charged onto the field, and two pitches later, it was all over. A high slider to Maz. I didn't think it was gone at first, but it was a dry, fall day, and the ball kept carrying and carrying.

"After the game, I saw Casey. We had a feeling that this might be his last year. Before that seventh game, Casey told us, 'Win or lose, it's been a good year, and I want to thank you for everything.' It sounded like a farewell speech to me. But it wasn't until Maz's homer that the significance struck me. I started to say something to Casey, and he asked me, 'How were we trying to pitch Maz?'

"I said, 'I wanted to give him sliders low and away, but I hung one.'

"Casey said, 'Well, that's what we were supposed to pitch him. That's all I'm concerned about. If you weren't doing what you were supposed to, I wouldn't sleep too good tonight. But just forget it.' "

While Ralph Terry was talking to Casey, Mickey was crying in the clubhouse.

"I just felt so awful," he said. "We had the game and screwed it up. Has anyone ever figured out why Casey didn't use Whitey in the opener? I can't imagine having Whitey Ford on my team and not trying to get three starts out of him in the Series. I don't know. I loved Casey, I really did. He was one of the great managers of all time, and he did a lot for my career, but I really believe that Casey blew the 1960 World Series."

Whitey Ford said, "I suppose I'm still shocked that I didn't start the opener. I pitched the third and sixth games. We won those games by scores of 10–0 and 12–0, and Casey let me throw nine innings even though both games were blowouts. I could see that the seventh game was going to be a wild one, and I tried to warm up, but my arm was so stiff from pitching nine innings the day before that I couldn't even get the ball to home plate on a fly."

Bobby Richardson had a tremendous series, winning the MVP award even though he was on the losing team. He batted .367 and drove in 12 runs. Mazeroski was considered the best defensive second baseman of that era, but the only difference between Maz and Bobby was at the plate, not in the field. Maz had more power, but Bobby was a great defensive second baseman.

"When I drove home to Sumter [South Carolina] after the World Series, they had a parade for me," said Bobby. "I was honored because the people in my town went to such an effort for me, but I felt hollow. Losing the Series took the excitement away, and it wasn't a happy time."

Bobby was one of the young players Casey didn't understand, as this quote points out: "Richardson doesn't drink, he doesn't smoke, he doesn't swear, he doesn't run around, and he still can't hit .250."

"Casey was a good manager, and he got a lot out of his players," said Bobby. "But he didn't have much patience, especially with young players. He also tended to be very sarcastic when you'd make a mistake. He used to make me so mad. It's hard to knock his results, but I just wasn't too fond of his methods."

Casey used the needle in print to motivate his players. He was a great showman, a kind of funny man who spent a lot of time entertaining the writers. He gave the press terrific material, but sometimes it was painful for the guys to read the paper. Once, after Moose Skowron had come back from an injury but was struggling at the plate, Casey said, "The way Moose is hitting, he'd be better off hurt again."

Bob Turley reminded me of another incident when Casey was rough on a young player: "I lost a no-hitter because a fly ball fell in front of Norm Siebern. Norm made a good effort, but he didn't dive, and that bothered Casey. After the game, the writers went straight for Norm, but his head was down, and he was choking back the tears. When they saw he couldn't talk, the writers went to Casey, who said, 'If that dumb clod had dove for the ball in left field, Turley would have had his no-hitter.' I was feeling kind of bad about not getting the no-hitter, but what Casey said made me feel even worse. Norm was just a young player, and something like that could ruin his confidence. I went over to Norm and said, 'Listen, partner, there's no way you could have caught that ball, and don't ever let anyone make you feel bad because you didn't.' By knocking guys to the writers, Casey wanted to make them mad so they would be more determined to prove him wrong. But when it came to young players, that just wasn't the best approach."

Casey's treatment of Clete Boyer in the 1960 World Series also caused a few people in important places to wonder.

"One of the things I'll never forget is how Casey batted for me in the first game," said Clete. "It would have been something else if it were the late innings, but it was the second inning, and we were losing 3–1. We had a couple of guys on base, and Casey yelled at me from the dugout. I went over to see him, figuring he wanted me to bunt or something. I never thought I was done for the day in the second inning, but Casey said Dale Long was going to bat for me. Long popped out, but that wasn't the point. I was so hurt and embarrassed. Imagine being in your first World Series game and you get batted for in your first at bat. My brother Ken had come to Pittsburgh for the game, and that's what he got to see. I felt so awful, I couldn't even go into the clubhouse. For seven innings I sat in the little bathroom that's in the dugout.

"I owe Casey some thanks because he brought me to the majors. But I also know that he never liked me. He left me at third because I made a lot of good plays for him, and once in a while, I'd hit a homer. I don't think he could decide if I was going to be a good player or not, but he used me basically because he had no one else. But that thing in the World Series . . . I mean, who gets hit for in the second inning? You don't treat people like that, and then I didn't play again until the sixth and seventh games. But in that first game,

I went from my biggest thrill to my biggest disappointment in baseball all in one inning."

Hector Lopez told me, "You can tell a lot about a manager when you see how he handles the guys on the bench. When I played for Casey, he was older, and he didn't pay much attention to us. When he wanted me to pinch-hit, Casey would say, 'Hey, you, grab a bat.' He never used my name. Ralph Houk always went out of his way to talk to me. With Casey, the guys on the bench were never sure if he remembered we were there."

I think Hector made a good point. As the years passed, Casey became more conservative, preferring to play veterans over rookies. The strain of managing all those years had to take a mental and physical toll on anyone.

Casey did have a big fan in Jim Coates: "Casey was a man's man. There was a game in 1960 when Early Wynn had thrown at Mantle, Howard, and Moose. Wynn was coming to bat, and Casey told me that I had four shots at Early and I had better not miss. I didn't. It was just like the time I was warming up against the Red Sox, and Jimmy Piersall was standing about two feet from the batter's box. Piersall had four bats on his shoulder. I didn't like him so close to the plate while I was warming up, so I threw at him. Piersall then heaved the four bats at me. Casey liked that sort of stuff. All Houk cared about was winning the game, not some of the other things that happen in baseball. I don't know, I think the guys might have played harder for Casey."

That may be Coates's opinion, but I'm not sure it was shared by many other players. And the front office obviously didn't agree with Coates because five days after the World Series, Casey was fired and Ralph Houk took over. Casey was seventy that season, and as he was fond of saying, "Most people are dead at my age, at the present time at least." After he was fired, Casey said, "I'll never make the mistake of being seventy again."

Dan Topping and Del Webb held the same opinion as many of the players—the Series was lost because Whitey didn't pitch the opener. They also felt that Casey was holding back some of the young players such as Clete, Bobby, and John Blanchard. And it was no secret that Topping and Webb were fond of Ralph Houk and were grooming him as the future Yankee manager. He was an organization man, a backup catcher in New York and later a coach. He also managed at Class AAA Denver, where he had Ralph Terry, John Blanchard, Bobby Richardson, and myself. The front office was not pleased with Casey's handling of young players. Also, a few other clubs had expressed interest in hiring Houk to manage.

But I still don't think they could have fired Casey if we had won that World Series. He was so popular with the fans and writers, to fire him after winning would have been a terrible public relations blunder. Win or lose, the change to Ralph was one that had to be made, but losing made it much easier on the Yankee front office.

Ralph Houk told me he didn't have the job until after the season.

"The front office told me to sit tight and wait until the Series was over," he said. "I knew they were interested in me, but they didn't make any commitments until after the World Series."

8

I'M ABSOLUTELY CONVINCED that Ralph Houk was the ideal man to replace Casey and handle the Yankees. As Bobby Richardson told me, "There just was something about Ralph. We had tremendous confidence and faith in him. I think part of it was because he was in the war. He is a big man who looked and talked like a leader. If Ralph Houk said something, you believed him because you knew it was true."

Casey had managed the Yankees for twelve years, winning ten pennants. It seemed as though no one in the New York press ever wrote a bad word about him, and he was worshiped by the fans.

"Perhaps the greatest pressure I felt all year was at the press conference where I was named manager," said Ralph. "I knew we had to win the pennant. In New York, that was expected. No one would stand for a loser. But I also knew I had great talent to work with. Basically, we had the best team in the league, and if you are the best, you should win. It's that simple. But I could never compete with Casey when it came to dealing with the press or public speaking. The New York writers loved Casey, and for good reason. My style was going to be different than Casey's, and the writers had to accept that."

The front office had actually tipped its hand that Ralph was the manager of the future when Casey went into the hospital for two weeks in June of 1960 with a bladder infection. Frank Crosetti would have been the natural pick to run the team in Casey's absence. Cro had been with the Yankees as a player and third-base coach since the time of Babe Ruth, but Dan Topping and Del Webb put Houk in charge.

Houk did have daily conversations with Casey, who was recovering at Lenox Hill Hospital. But he also made some changes, installing Clete Boyer at third and giving John Blanchard and Hector Lopez more playing time. The team went 6–6 without Casey, but the Yankees front office saw that Houk was willing to use the young players.

In spring training, the *Sporting News*'s Dan Daniel asked Ralph about his rules, and he said the following: "I have nothing against a round of golf on a day off, but there will be trouble if I find out that any of my players was on the course the day of a night game. . . . There will be a midnight curfew after day games and 2 A.M. after night games, but they won't be spied on by detectives or have to check with someone before they go to their rooms. . . . I'm not opposed to a player having a can of beer after a game, but I don't want my players guzzling beer in the clubhouse. Nor do I want my players drinking hard liquor in public. . . . There will be no card playing for high stakes. Poker and dice are out. Hearts, bridge, and pinochle for low stakes can be fun. . . . To sum it up, I'm a reasonable man, no Puritan, no martinet, no guy looking for a chance to take things out on the players. I don't want to impose fines and I think we have about as well-behaved a bunch as you'll find in the majors."

Many people wondered how Ralph would handle Mickey Mantle. In 1960, Mickey failed to run out a ball, and Casey jerked him out of the game in front of fifty thousand fans.

Mickey and Casey liked each other, but it was a Vince Lombardi–Paul Hornung relationship. It was as though Casey thought Mickey might be running around a bit, but he also knew that Mickey was still producing. So every once in a while, Casey knew he had to discipline Mickey to make a point. If Mickey didn't run out a ball as hard as Casey thought he should have, he'd pull Mickey out of the game and say, "Hey, Mantle, you've got to show a little more hustle than that. Set an example for the young guys." In the process, Casey was making an example out of Mickey.

Mickey's philosophy was that he sometimes deserved to take it easy. He played hurt, and he played hard. But like the repentant bad boy, Mickey would promise to Casey that he'd never do it again. There were never any real problems or incidents between the two men. It was almost as if they were playing a little game.

"At a few team meetings, Casey got all over me and Mickey," said Whitey Ford. "And afterwards, he came over to us and winked. He did it for show, for the benefit of the other guys."

One day, Casey might say something to the press such as, "Too bad the guy in center field didn't go just a little harder because that ball might have been caught." Then a few days later, when Mickey started getting heat in the papers and from the fans, Casey would say, "I never saw a man booed so much before he even went to work."

Ralph's approach was much different. Roger and Mickey were both prone to pulled leg muscles, and over a 162-game schedule, there would be days when they played hurt. If they hit a fly ball to the outfield and didn't run hard to first base, Ralph didn't make it an issue. Not as long as they hustled to make catches in the outfield and put out 100 percent on the bases. Ralph came to the conclusion that pulling players out of games and zapping them in the papers was not going to work with this team. It also wasn't his style.

"I always refused to say anything bad about a player in public," he said. "If there is a problem, you settle it behind closed doors. It's a man-to-man thing, the proper way to act."

The idea of being treated with respect and as a man appealed to the guys on the team. Before, we'd lose a couple games and the detectives would show up. They would hang around for a week or two, just to make sure the team had straightened up its act. It was silly. One day, they followed Bobby Richardson and me to the YMCA, where we went to play Ping-Pong. When Roy Hamey became general manager and Ralph took over for Casey, that was the end of the detectives.

Casey loved to have team meetings, and they were pretty long. After a while, guys would get bored, and pretty soon they stopped listening. Sometimes, Casey would ask us how we thought a certain hitter should be pitched, and ten guys would speak up with ten different answers. Ralph had very few meetings. He delegated a lot of responsiblity to the coaches and veteran players. Guys talked among themselves. If Bobby and I had messed up a play, it was Frank Crosetti who'd talk to us, not Ralph. And usually he'd wait a day or two after it happened, and then Cro' would come up and say, "Remember that play the other day . . ."

The Yankees had a philosophy that discipline doesn't come from the top. We disciplined each other. The expression heard all the time, especially when a veteran was talking to a younger player, was, "Stop fooling around. You're messing with my money." They were talking about World Series money, which we all needed badly. We knew each other and had played together in the minor leagues. We were supposed to know how to play the game right.

Early in spring training, in sixty-one, Ralph went to Mickey and put the responsibility on his shoulders. He told everyone, "I want Mickey to be our leader." To a lesser extent, he said he wanted Whitey to be the leader of the pitching staff and me to be the leader of the infield.

Sportswriter Dan Daniel was not originally impressed with Houk's plan. Daniel wrote, "When told he was supposed to be the team leader, Mantle was about as jubilant as a centipede with gout. To fathom Mickey's mind is not always simple . . . but he likes to perform without fanfare, minus the spotlight."

"Ralph's secret was to figure out who were the big guys on the team and get them on his side," said Moose Skowron. "With the Yankees, it was Mickey and Whitey. Ralph won them over, and everyone else fell into line."

A little slower to fall in line was sportswriter Dan Daniel. To us, it seemed as though Daniel had been covering the Yankees forever. Maybe he had, since he had written about Babe Ruth, Joe DiMaggio, Mickey Mantle, Roger Maris, and everyone in between. He was a dapper, well-dressed man who was not immune to making up quotes to enhance his stories. That spring, Dan had a fortieth wedding anniversary party to which he invited all the members of the team. The event received five paragraphs in the *Sporting News*. But you'd think after all those years and all those stories that Dan Daniel would know a little about spring training. Dan took it hard when we lost our first eight games in Saint Petersburg and ended up with a 9–19 spring record.

The Yankees ended the spring with a dinner at the Desert Ranch, which was rather strangely named since it was located on Saint Petersburg Beach. Dan was asked to speak, and he said, "Men of the Yankees, get the lead out of your pants. Get started. Arouse yourselves. This stuff about not getting alarmed over exhibition defeats is the bunk. Don't work into a rotten habit. If you wait until the dough is on the table, there may not be any dough there for you."

And in case we missed Dan's pep talk he gave it again, this time in his *Sporting News* column.

No one took Dan's message seriously. In spring training, we didn't take much of anything seriously except getting in shape for the season, and it should have been obvious to anyone that Ralph wasn't playing those games to win. Ralph had a team of young veterans, guys in their middle to late twenties who had been around for four or five years. Being the scourge of the Grapefruit League wasn't exactly a high priority. It's not like the mentality the Yankees have now in which George Steinbrenner thinks about changing managers just because his team lost a spring game to the Mets that happened to be televised in New York. The only ones who were shaken up were Dan Daniel and a few other writers. Well, I supposed they had to act alarmed so they'd have something to fill up the space in the newspapers. But in retrospect, it all seemed pretty silly.

While looking through the newspaper stories from that spring training, I was amused by some of the things we supposedly said. For example, *The New York Times*'s John Drebinger quoted Ralph Houk like this: "If we can come up to opening day of the championship season in the same correspondingly sound condition that we're enjoying right now on the eve of the exhibition season, I certainly will be more than pleased."

Why do I have the feeling that Ralph didn't say that? At least not in that way. The guy was a baseball manager, not the chairman of the Senate Foreign Relations Committee.

What really happened in the spring of 1961 had little to do with what appeared in the papers. Like Hector Lopez showing up overweight and blaming his wife's good cooking for his putting on fourteen pounds. "She cooks rice dishes like a champ," said Hector. "She makes it a dozen different ways and I love them all." There also was talk of Babe Ruth's record being broken—not by Roger, but by Mickey. Ralph Kiner and Billy Martin both insisted Mickey would make a run at Ruth. And that was the spring when Moose Skowan got to be Mickey and Whitey's chauffeur.

"We had a lot of fun in spring training," said Moose. "My locker was between Mickey's and Yogi's. Mickey always said I should go out with him and Whitey, and I'd say, 'If I go out with you guys, I'll end up in headlines.'

"But one day in March, Mickey went to Houk, and Ralph gave him permission to take me out. Whitey and Mickey rented a big car, and they bought me a chauffeur's cap. I was the driver, and they rode in the back. We went from one bar to another. I'd park the car near the door, go inside, and tell the manager that I had Mickey Mantle and Whitey Ford outside. The manager would never believe me, but I'd keep talking, and finally the manager would go outside to see. I'd open the back door of the car, and Whitey and Mickey would step out. Then we'd get the best table in the joint. We went to four or five places until everything was closed. At five in the morning, the only place open was a bowling alley, so we went bowling. I didn't get back to my room until 6:30 that morning. I was really glad Houk let me have that day off."

Moose was also the reason I met Marilyn Monroe.

Joe DiMaggio was in camp with the Yankees as a guest hitting instructor. Marilyn went to Saint Petersburg to visit Joe. They had been divorced for some time, but it seemed as though they might have been trying to get back together. She was having some trouble in Hollywood and said she wanted to get away from the West Coast for a few weeks. To her, Joe represented security, and that was what she was looking for at that point. Joe's son was also in Florida, and that gave Marilyn a feeling of being part of a family.

"I was the one who set everything up," said Moose. "Tony, remember when you, Joe DeMaestri and Yogi asked me if I knew Joe D. pretty well? You guys wanted to ask him and Marilyn out for dinner, but no one would do it. So I went and talked to Joe D."

Joe D. invited several of the players to stay around after practice because Marilyn wanted to play baseball. Joe had a softball and some bats, and we took turns pitching to Marilyn. She hit the ball, ran around, and had a great time. Two straight nights, Joe D. invited me and some of the other guys out to dinner to an Italian place on the beach. We had a table way in the back. She was late both nights, and Joe D. would call every fifteen minutes or so to say they were coming, but Marilyn was still getting ready. Both times, they showed up about two hours late.

At dinner, Marilyn was very bubbly. I remember Joe D. not saying much, but sitting there with a big smile on his face. Yogi and Moose did most of the talking, asking her her questions like, "Do you really know Frank Sinatra?" And all Marilyn wanted to do was talk about baseball.

There were photographers all over the place, trying to get a shot of Joe and Marilyn together. They chased her up and down the beach. I was so excited to be at dinner with them that I didn't say much of anything.

A strange footnote to this story happened a few months later when we were playing the Angels in Los Angeles. After a night game, I was paged in the lobby of the L.A. Hilton. Bobby Richardson and I had just gotten off the team bus, and it must have been almost midnight. This was the first time I had ever been paged, and I thought something terrible must have happened. I picked up the house phone near the elevators and I heard this deep, throaty voice saying, "Tony."

I put my hand over the phone and whispered, "Bobby, I think somebody is imitating Marilyn Monroe on the phone."

Bobby and I both put our ears to the phone and I said, "Hello."

"Tony, this is Marilyn,"said the voice.

"Yeah . . . Okay," I said. I figured it was some of guys, maybe Mickey and Whitey, playing a joke on Bobby and me. They were always on us about being the Milkshake Twins, and they probably would have thought it was funny to get us going about Marilyn Monroe.

The next thing the voice said was, "Is Joe D. traveling with the club?"

I said, "No, he doesn't travel with us. He has a business in California and spends a lot of time in New York. He doesn't have time to be with us."

Then I started thinking that Marilyn ought to know all this. She asked again about Joe D., and I said sharply, "No, he's not here."

The voice said, "I wanted to find Joe because I just moved into this new apartment in Beverly Hills. I thought he might like to see it. I'm sitting here by myself. Would you and some of the guys like to come over and see my apartment?"

I put my hand over the receiver and whispered to Bobby, "I really think this is Marilyn Monroe."

Finally, I said, "Marilyn, I'll tell Joe you called if I ever see him. Listen, we've got a game tomorrow, and I've got to get some sleep. Thanks a lot for the invitation."

I hung up and Bobby said, "Why didn't we go, dummy?"

Actually, I'm not sure why I didn't at least talk to her some more. Sometimes, I wonder why she called me. I was single at the time, but I'm not saying she had an ulterior motive. I think she did it because she had met me in spring training and remembered my name. She sounded so lonesome, and I really believe she wanted to see Joe D. but couldn't find him. I think she wanted some of the players to come over and keep her company, but I was so shocked that I started to talk real fast, and then I hung up.

In between Moose being a driver and going to dinner with Marilyn Monroe, we were preparing for the season. Ralph Houk had the most on his mind.

"Going into spring training, I wanted to make sure all our key people were in condition and that no one got hurt," said Ralph. "Next, I had to sort through the young pitchers and find out who could help us. We had lost Eli Grba and Bobby Shantz in the expansion draft, and I was worried about Bob Turley's arm. The other things I had to do was convince Yogi to play left field and find a way to handle Ryne Duren."

Ralph was asking Yogi to make a major concession to age, something that's never easy for a ballplayer. But Yogi made it easy.

"I was worried about Yogi's reaction," said Houk. "He had been a great catcher for years, but we needed to get Ellie Howard and John Blanchard time behind the plate. Yogi could have made a real mess if he had said, 'No, I don't think I want to go to left field.' We would have had an established star, perhaps the most popular player on the team, challenging a rookie manager. But I explained the situation to him, and all Yogi said was, 'If that's best for the team, I'll do it.' "

Yogi said, "It was no big deal. Since that was what Ralph wanted, I was ready to do it. I came up as an outfielder, and I knew I could play out there."

Duren was another story.

"As soon as Houk was named manager, I expected to be traded," he said. "One of the factors was that Luis Arroyo had saved some games at the end of the 1960 season. He more or less had moved me out of short relief."

But there was more to it than pitching. Duren was a fearsome pitcher, well known for his fastball, his thick glasses, and his drinking, and not necessarily in that order. He came to the Yankees in 1958 and had two tremendous seasons, saving 34 games with a 1.91 earned run average. He struck out 183 hitters in 156 innings. As Casey Stengel said, "When Duren walks in from the bull pen, people stop chewing their peanuts."

By 1961, Duren wasn't throwing quite as hard, but he was drinking all the harder. There was an incident on an airplane when Duren pinched a stewardess, who doused him with champagne. Then he went to the front of the plane and approached a writer named Joe King, who had a thin moustache. Ryne grabbed it, ripping out about six hairs. King got up screaming and demanded that the Yankees trade Ryne. After the Yankees clinched the pennant in 1960, Ryne again had too much to drink on a plane, and he tried to put out a cigar in Ralph Houk's face. That was not a good idea.

"I know that the problem I had with the stewardess got back to Houk," said Ryne. "I was boozing and got fresh, and she threw a glass of champagne in my face. It created more trouble for me. Besides, I was thirty-two and my arm wasn't bouncing back like it should. Ralph talked about starting me that spring, but I really don't think it was much more than just talk. Some people have given Houk a lot of credit for making me a better pitcher because he had me at Denver in 1957. But I was a good pitcher when I got there. In my first game for Ralph, I threw a seven-inning no-hitter. I had no business being in the minor leagues in the first place. I was 13–2 that year, and the only thing Ralph Houk did was give me a chance to pitch."

The Yankees knew that Duren's drinking was out of control, and there was one night when, according to Dan Daniel, "Duren, certainly no lush, got gay around four in the morning and banged on the door of the Houk family suite at the Soreno Hotel."

Houk fined Duren two hundred dollars, but tried to keep it quiet.

"This was one instance when I tried to cover up something that I shouldn't have," said Ralph. "I thought the fine was between him and me, but it leaked out when Ryne mentioned it to some out-of-town writers. When the story ran, that didn't look very good for the guys covering our camp."

Dan Daniel wrote, "When the story broke on March 26, Duren went into hiding and did not appear until the following morning when he had a substantial breakfast and was quiet and contrite. He said he had locked himself in Room 244, ignoring the knocks and the ringing phone because he didn't want to talk to reporters about the fine. 'Yes, I do occasionally take a drink,' Ryne said. 'But when Houk fined me, he didn't say it was for drinking. It was for breaking the curfew rule.' "

No matter what the official word, that finished Ryne with the Yankees.

"Now I understand Houk much better than I did when I played for him," said Ryne. "I think I was more concerned about Ralph as a person than he was about me. I don't think he worried too much about me and my problems. I'll admit that I was an adolescent at the time and my outlook about the situation was immature, to say the least. I was in a state of suspended adolescence, and I wasn't going to get out of it until I stopped drinking. But I don't think that everyone around me was operating in the most mature fashion, nor were they operating completely free of alcohol. It did come down to the fact that I was anesthetized to the point where I had very bad judgment."

In 1961, teams did not use psychologists or help players enroll in drug treatment centers.

"Everything was under control as long as I was pitching well," said Ryne. "But when I began to slip on the mound, I started to drink even more. I was beginning to embarrass the club. If I was outstanding, they could tolerate me. But once I became mediocre, they handled me by trading me. Which was how baseball operated then—stick your problem guys with someone else."

Three weeks into the season, Ryne went to the Angels for Bob Cerv.

"My life continued to go downhill after I left the Yankees," said Ryne. "I had a progressive illness, and I often thought of suicide. I went through seven hospitals and four different treatment centers until I got into an out-patient center in Milwaukee that helped."

Duren later became the director of the alcoholism rehabilitation center at Stoughton Hospital in Wisconsin and is now a consultant on substance abuse rehabilitation.

Meanwhile, the season began on a grim note for Ralph Houk, and it wasn't much better for Roger Maris. The Yankees lost a home opener for the first time in seven years as only 14,007 fans showed up in the frigid weather to watch Pedro Ramos and Minnesota win 6–10. We managed only three hits and looked pretty feeble. Making matters worse, the bitter cold and rain made us wait five more days before playing another game. During that time, the writers went to work.

"The Cassandras got busy at once with their prognostications of woe," wrote Dan Daniel. "All assumed the stand that Casey had been thrown out of his job and most wondered if the right man had been picked for succession. The postponements gave the prophets of grief a lot of time to mull over the opening defeat, which in some places was magnified into a small catastrophe."

This story featured a picture of Ralph, under which was written "Fires Salvo."

Basically, Ralph said the Yankees were a great team and the world didn't stop spinning because we lost a game. "I said we'd win the pennant in November, I said it again in spring training and I'll say it again now," said Ralph in what I guess was supposed to be his salvo.

Anyway, there was a lot written about the Yankees getting fat and how dumping all those exhibition games might carry over into the season. A few writers pointed out that the 1960 club finished with fifteen straight wins, but Casey was the manager of that club. On and on it went, including a lot of gnashing of teeth because Whitey Ford was the loser in the opener.

Ralph wasn't worried and neither were we. But we were concerned.

We were a .500 team after the first ten games, and it could have been a lot worse if it hadn't been for Mickey, who already had five homers, 11 RBI, and was hitting .455. But Roger wasn't "hitting the size of his breakfast check, which usually comes to $1.70," according to Dan Daniel. Actually, Roger was 5 for 31 (.161).

That is what a lot of people forget about sixty-one. It was Roger who started slowly while Mickey carried the team. Houk was getting booed by the fans, and the writers were skeptical, but Mickey kept it from being a lot worse. We won back-to-back games against Detroit and Cleveland in which Mickey was sensational. In the first game, he hit two home runs—one left-handed and one right-handed. In the nightcap, he tied the score with a 400-foot sacrifice fly and won the game with a 410-foot triple. He also made a leaping catch that inspired Yankee announcer Phil Rizzuto to say, "Holy cow, Mickey's arm must have stretched twenty feet for that ball." His hot start bought time for both Roger and Ralph.

Houk was searching for a lineup. Bobby Richardson began the season as the leadoff hitter, with Hector Lopez second, Yogi third, Mickey fourth, and Maris fifth. Sometimes, I hit first, other times second, and occasionally seventh. And, as I mentioned before, Clete led off a few times, too.

It wasn't until the middle of May that Ralph settled on what everyone now remembers as the set Yankees lineup all season—Richardson, Kubek, Maris, Mantle, Berra, Howard, Skowron, Boyer, and the pitcher.

Probably the most consistent aspect of the team was the defense. Clete was sensational at third, playing tighter than anyone in the league, daring hitters to bunt on him (none could) and daring them to hit the ball by him (none did). It seemed that Bobby never made a costly error at second, and Moose worked hard at first. In the outfield, Mickey and Roger were as good as any center- and right-fielders in the league. Yogi ran surprisingly well in left field. Behind the plate, Ellie Howard was in a class by himself. He made catching and throwing look so easy.

Looking through my scrapbook, I discoverd the early season was even worse than I remembered.

On May 12, Detroit beat the Yankees 4–3 behind Frank Lary, who raised his career record against us to 25–8. In that game, Detroit outfielder and Bronx native Rocky Colavito was ejected when he ran into the stands to come to the aid of his father, who was being harassed by a fan. "What was I supposed to do, let my sixty-year-old father get beat up?" asked Colavito. Even with Rocky cooling off in the clubhouse, the Tigers moved 3½ games ahead of us. And the next night Rocky went the distance and hit two homers as Detroit beat us again.

We were losing games in bizarre fashion. We lost a game in Cleveland 9–7 when Jim Coates hit Woodie Held with the bases loaded and then Vic Power stole home to put the game away. To this day, Moose talks about how he hated pop-ups, and he dropped two that night in Cleveland. We lost to the Orioles when Mickey misjudged a fly ball by Jim Gentile. In Kansas City, Whitey Ford and Luis Arroyo blew a 4–1 lead in the bottom of the eighth as we lost 5–4. Lary beat us again, 4–3, as we left fourteen runners on base, and Lary himself drove in the winning run with a double.

After thirty games, our record was 16–14, five games behind Detroit. Roger was heading to the optometrist, Ralph and Johnny Sain were shuffling the pitching staff, and some reporters were writing open letters to Casey Stengel.

I sometimes wonder if Roger felt slighted early in the season. He was coming off an MVP year, but it was Mickey who was supposed to lead the team. Roger was shuttling between fifth and seventh in the order early in the year, and he might have thought he should have been third considering how he played in 1960.

All of this led up to Roger getting an eye examination on May 22.

In the middle of May, Roger was batting .210 with 4 homers. In the *Sporting News*, Joe King wrote, "Ralph Houk has to be wondering about Maris. Which Maris would he be? The MVP who showed .320 with 27 homers and 69 RBI in the first half of 1960, or the ordinary batsman who fell to .239 with 12 homers and 43 RBI in the second half of that season?"

The front office could have used a little better timing before sending Roger to the doctor, as he had had 4 homers and a .438 batting average in his last five games. When Roger went to the park after the appointment, he complained about this eyes. He started the game but lasted only an inning before an allergic reaction to some eye drops forced him out of the lineup.

"We finally get Roger hitting, and I mean hitting better than he has all year, and he shows up blind," said Houk at the time.

I asked Ralph about this later, and he said, "Roger thought he couldn't see well and wanted his eyes checked. The biggest problem wasn't his eyes, but the eye drops."

Clete Boyer said, "This may have been the start of the trouble between Roger and Ralph. Ralph acted like it was Roger's idea to go to the eye doctor. Roger didn't want to go, but Dan Topping and Roy Hamey told him to. The front office tells you to go, you go. But you'd think they would have at least told Houk. Maris was mad. The guy was in a slump for a few weeks, and they think he can't see. The Yankees sometimes acted like Roger was a machine that was never supposed to have a little breakdown."

The eye exam did little for Roger's confidence. He knew he could play, but he had also been with three teams in four years. He was the MVP, but his latest bosses had doubts about him, his eyes, or something. It was about this time of the season when Roger told a few friends, "I doubt if I'll ever hit more than twenty-five or thirty homers a year."

9

ON THE FIELD, we were struggling through the month of May, but Whitey Ford made sure we were all having a good time. Sure there was pressure—losing, the talk about Houk versus Stengel, Roger's eye examination, and Mickey finishing the month in a week-long slump. But then there was Whitey, winning games, telling us everything was going to be all right, and making life interesting in the bull pen.

"One day Whitey said we should play golf," said Bill Stafford. "We had just been issued brand-new, all-white uniforms. Whitey and I took some bats and balls down to the bull pen, where under the right-field bleachers there was an area with a lot of black dirt. We dug holes around pillars and made a nine-hole golf course. While the game was going on, Whitey and I played golf for a dollar a hole by putting a baseball with a bat. After the game, everyone wondered what we had been doing, because our faces, hands, and uniforms were black. I guess that's what happens when you get down on your hands and knees to line up a putt."

Stafford was one of Whitey's favorite targets.

"Whitey knew I hated anything that crawled," said Stafford. "We were in the bull pen, and Ralph Houk called for me to warm up. I picked up a ball and glove and walked to the bull pen mound. Then I just stopped, froze. There was this thing on the mound that looked like a little dinosaur. It stuck its tongue out at me, and I wasn't about to get near it. All the while I was supposed to be warming up, I was pinned to the bull pen wall by this dinosaur thing. I never threw a pitch before Ralph waved me into the game. I ended up getting knocked all over the park because Whitey decided to bring out his son's pet iguana."

In 1959–60, the front office and Casey weren't laughing with Whitey. Instead, they were thinking of trading him and worried about his arm.

"I saw the doctor's report," Casey said during his retirement in 1961, when Whitey was healthy and winning again. "They were noted doctors and they said Whitey had neuritis. He said his elbow had a tinge. The front office [George Weiss] wanted to unload him, maybe for Al Kaline."

What Whitey actually had was a pulled tendon in his shoulder, and compounding it was a case of gout that set in. From 1957–60, Whitey won 11, 14, 16, and 12 games. Stengel was starting him about once a week, and there were rumors of Whitey being traded to the Tigers for Kaline, Whitey to San Francisco for John Antonelli, and Whitey to St. Louis for Larry Jackson and Hal Smith.

"I think the old Yankee regime thought Whitey was on his way out," said Johnny Sain. "Whitey was thirty-two, he had won only 12 games, and there were a lot of doubts about him. When Ralph became manager and Roy Hamey was named general manager, the opinion about Whitey changed. Ralph and I sat down and tried to figure out how to get the most out of him. That's when I suggested that Whitey start every fourth day. Casey always used him every fifth day. They were afraid to pitch Whitey much because he was small [5 foot 9, 160 pounds], and the little left-hander wasn't supposed to be able to stand all that work. But what does size have to do with a guy's arm?"

Ralph Houk said, "Whitey had never won twenty games for the Yankees, and there was only one reason why it didn't happen: he hadn't pitched enough. Johnny Sain and I talked about using Whitey every fourth day. He was our best pitcher, so why not try to pitch him as much as possible? During the winter right after I got the job, I ran into Whitey at a basketball game at Madison Square Garden. I asked him about pitching every fourth day, and he liked the idea."

Whitey said, "The crazy thing about all this talk about me pitching every fourth day is that it is something I always wanted to do. I hated sitting on the bench between starts. Ralph said he wanted me to pitch more, and I said I was ready. It started in spring training. I pitched the same way as always—curve, fastball, and change-up. The only difference was that I did it every fourth instead of fifth day."

Johnny Sain and Ralph wanted to make some rather radical changes when it came to handling the pitchers.

"Whitey set the tone," said Sain. "On the first day of spring training, I wanted the pitchers to throw five minutes on the side and five minutes of batting practice. That's more throwing than most pitcher are accustomed to so early. After three days, it was ten minutes on the field and ten more minutes on the side. Actually, this was a program I had used, but only on myself. Whitey was our guinea pig. The idea was to strengthen a pitcher's arm, and I've always believed that to strengthen any muscle, you exercise it. The best exercise for a pitcher is throwing, and it worked great for Whitey. The other pitchers saw Whitey doing all this throwing, and they followed because he was Whitey Ford. Something else that helped was Whitey's attitude. He'd see me saying something to a pitcher, and a few days later, Whitey would talk to the guy and tell him the same thing. Whitey reinforced a lot of what I was trying to do."

Johnny also taught Whitey a new pitch.

"We were in the bull pen one day, and I was telling Whitey about how a quicker curve might help him," said Sain. "We always tossed ideas back and forth, because you never know when you might hit upon something that could help. One idea can change a man's life, and I've seen it happen. Whitey had a good, deceptive fastball. His overhand curve was outstanding, but it had a very big break. At times, a big-breaking curve can be hard to control. That's why a harder curve, I call it a controlled curve and it breaks something like a slider, can make a difference. Whitey started to throw it, and after fifteen minutes it was like he had been throwing the pitch for his whole life. He could throw it for a strike at any point in the count. A lot of guys get behind, and they have no choice but to throw the fastball. So they come in with it and boom, game's over. When Whitey developed the controlled curve, it made all his pitches better."

This pitch, which was basically a big slider, was also a concession to age.

"I could see that my old curve was getting slower and slower," said Whitey. "I wasn't striking out hitters like I used to. Johnny never told me what to do, he just suggested things. It seemed like it took me about five minutes to learn that slider, and I'm convinced that it kept me in baseball another five years."

Whitey pitched the opener and lost 6–0 to Minnesota. He had a shutout for six innings and was knocked out after coughing up three runs in the seventh. Then he won his next six starts before getting beat 2–1 by Boston as the month of May closed.

"We took it one start at a time," said Johnny Sain. "Whitey would start, and then we'd wait three days and see if he wanted to start again. Whitey said he would. We did that again and again. By the end of the season, Whitey told me that the only way to pitch was every fourth day."

When the Yankees were 16–14, Whitey had six of those victories. Ralph Houk and Johnny Sain couldn't bear to think where they would have been without him.

On May 21, we were 18–15 and had hit 34 homers; Roger had just five homers, and Art Ditmar and Bob Turley hadn't won in 11 starts. John Blanchard, who was to become our best pinch hitter by the end of the year, was 0 for 11 coming off the bench.

Then we started to hit.

In the next 17 games, we would pile up 32 homers, including seven in one game against Boston at Fenway Park on Memorial Day. Roger had two, as did Mickey and Moose, and Yogi hit one. Final score, Yankees 12, Boston 3.

Then came the month of June.

Anyone who remembers the great Yankees teams of the 1950s and 1960s knows what the month of June means. In 1959, the Yankees were 18–12 in June. In 1960, we were 21–8. But in sixty-one, we went 22–10, and that took care of most of the boos for Ralph Houk.

In June, Whitey started eight games and won them all.

In June, Ralph took an ailing Turley out of the starting rotation and replaced him with Rollie Sheldon. Ditmar, who had started the first game of the 1960 World Series instead of Whitey, was traded to Kansas City for Bud Daley. Houk revised the rotation, featuring Whitey, Bill Stafford, Ralph Terry, Sheldon, and Daley.

In June, writers and fans started talking about Roger and/or Mickey breaking Babe Ruth's record.

In June, Roger and Big Julie Isaacson started eating breakfast together. "At the Stage Deli," said Big Julie. "Baloney and eggs, every day at the Stage for me and Roger. I used to say, 'Rog, you're going to kill this Jew.' He said he didn't care. He was hitting and as long as he was hitting, we were going to eat baloney and eggs every morning at the Stage."

In June, Joe DeMaestri couldn't get rid of his jockstrap.

"I had the thing for ten years," said DeMaestri. "It went back to when I played for the St. Louis Browns. I just had to throw it away because it was falling apart, but every time I'd dump it in the trash, the next day it would show up again in my locker. It even happened on the road. I'd throw it away, and the next day it would be back."

That kind of thing happened a lot. You'd throw away an old pair of shoes or a glove, and it would reappear in your locker. That was clubhouse man Big Pete Sheehy's idea of humor. On the road, Big Pete would call the visiting clubhouse guy and tell him to be on guard in case DeMaestri tried to get rid of his jockstrap. Finally, we would have to take things out and burn them.

But above all, June belonged to Roger.

On May 16, he had three homers and was batting .215 with 11 RBI. In his next 17 games, Roger hit .300 with 12 homers and 25 RBI. That was the same seventeen-game stretch in which we hit 32 homers. And by the beginning of July, Roger was up to 30 home runs.

In fact, July started much like June as the Yankees hammered Washington 13–4 thanks to five home runs. After the game, Ralph Houk sat in his office, shaking his head and saying, "Did you ever see power like that?"

Of course, Ralph never hit a homer in the majors, but he had seen a lot of balls go out of the park in all those years on the bench as a backup catcher and coach with New York.

The first of Roger's two homers in that game banged halfway up the right-field foul pole. He never moved from the plate until the ball came down. "It was a hot day and I figured the ball was out of the park, no matter if it was fair or foul, so why run?" Roger told reporters.

Roger ran on the next one, but he didn't have to since it landed in the upper deck in right.

Mickey tied into a pitch and for a second, it seemed as if it just might become the first fair ball ever hit out of the Stadium, but it landed about two-thirds of the way up the third deck in left. Ellie Howard crunched one into the upper deck in left, and Moose hammered one into the left-field bleachers.

We missed a sixth homer when Bob Cerv's double slammed off the 457-foot sign in left-center. Suddenly, our record was 47–27, but we still trailed Detroit by a game. At this point, Roger had 30 homers, Mickey 28. And at this point, a reporter asked Roger, "I bet you lie awake at night thinking how you're going to break Ruth's record."

Roger looked at the guy and said, "Listen, I don't give Babe Ruth a thought. Not now or ever. I don't think about the record, and I'm surprised I've got as many homers as I do."

Ralph wasn't surprised, though. "It seems like every hit Maris gets is a home run."

Houk did have a scare on July 9 when Mickey failed to hit a ball out of the park that he thought he should have then went into the dugout and hit a metal sign that he shouldn't have. According to sportswriter Dick Young, the sound of Mickey's fist smashing the sign was heard in the press box. All Houk would say was, "I'm just glad Mickey didn't break a hand." In that game, the Yankees took care of

Boston, 8–5, knocking out Ike Delock. Tracy Stallard followed and served up a homer, not to Maris, but to Mantle. And Stallard gave up another homer, again not to Maris, but to John Blanchard.

"Then came Wilbur Wood, nineteen and aging quickly," wrote Young. "All he had to face was Mantle, Maris, and Berra—and that's all he did face. Maris doubled into the right-field corner, Mantle got a hit up the middle, and Berra walked. Wood departed, wondering why they had rushed him up from a B League."

It was also the Yankees' eighth win in nine games, giving us a 52–28 record and a half-game lead over Detroit.

A day later, Moose pulled a lower back muscle during infield practice, but it didn't matter as Rollie Sheldon won his sixth straight start. Roger hit his thirty-third homer, and Young wrote, "That's 33 with the 162-game sked one game more than half over. Soon they'll start taking the boy seriously."

Yes, they were now counting. After 82 games, Ruth had 27 homers in 1927. So Roger was four ahead of that pace, and Mickey was two up.

In the *Sporting News*, Dan Daniel brought up the subject of the 154-game schedule: "Commissioner Ford Frick will soon call a conference with the Records Committee of the Baseball Writers of America. . . . The commissioner is quite aroused over the chance that the new 162-game schedule, eight more games than ever before, will produce records. . . . Suppose Roger Maris hits 61 with the help of those extra contests? Suppose after 154 games, Maris has 58 or 59 homers, then totals 61 over the rest of the season? Frick believes it would not be right to recognize the mark after 154 games. The commissioner has strong backing in this attitude. If Ruth had gone to 162 games, he would have hit seven more homers if he had continued at his current pace. In the last eight games of 1927, Babe hit seven."

Roger had a much different opinion. "How could anyone know that Ruth would have hit seven more home runs if he had played 162 games? He could have hit a couple more, or maybe none. I don't know how many he would have hit and neither does anyone else."

The Ruth-Maris debate was heating up during the last two weeks of July, just as Roger cooled off and went 0 for 19. Mickey took the home run lead, 36–35.

That was when John Blanchard stepped in.

It began on July 21, when we went into the top of the ninth down 8–6 at Fenway Park. It was one of the few times that year when Ralph batted for Clete Boyer. With the bases loaded and two outs,

John lined a four-hundred-foot homer into the right-field seats. In Fenway Park, you pretty much have to hit the ball about four hundred feet for a homer to right; there are no cheap home runs in straightaway right field.

"Mike Fornieles was pitching for the Red Sox," said John. "I hit the first pitch he threw me."

That was good, but the next day was even better. Again it was the top of the ninth. Again, we were losing. Again, John batted for Clete. Again, John put it into the right-field seats, only this time there was no one on base, and it tied the score at 9–9.

"Gene Conley, the old basketball player, was pitching," said John. "He threw me a low fastball, and I didn't exactly kill it. It wasn't a blast or anything, but it hooked around the foul pole."

We won the game, when Luis Arroyo (of all people) doubled and scored on a base hit by Bobby Richardson. Actually, Luis was a good-hitting pitcher, but he surprised most people when he did get a hit because he was not exactly built like an athlete. "They used to tell me that I would be great on 'What's My Line'," said Luis. "People would never guess I played for the Yankees."

The next night, we had a doubleheader against Chicago and won both games. Roger hit four homers and drove in eight runs. "Roger Maris is running away from Babe Ruth like a scared kid in a graveyard," wrote Dick Young. "With 40 homers, Roger is 25 games ahead of Ruth's pace. . . . Oh, Clete Boyer had two homers and now is only 80 games behind Ruth."

By the way, John Blanchard did not play in either game.

John did start against the White Sox and Ray Herbert. In the second inning, Mickey led off with a homer deep to right. Then came Blanchard, who did the same thing. In his next at bat, Herbert decked John with an inside fastball. John got up and did it again, only this time the home run was into the upper decks in left field.

"Both of those balls were hit pretty good," said John in an understatement.

That was four home runs in four straight at bats, a major-league record that had happened only 11 other times.

In the sixth inning, John stepped to the plate. Herbert was still on the mound and John crunched another one, only this time Floyd Robinson chased it down a few feet from the right-field wall. As John ran it out, he hit the first-base bag and kept going down the right-field line.

"I was trying to push it over the wall," said John. "I hit that ball awfully well, and for a second I thought I had another homer. But I got a little under it. Still, as I was running down the first-base line, I was thinking that it just might have enough to get out, especially since Floyd Robinson wasn't that tall. At first, I almost couldn't run. I was dumbfounded because it seemed like every time I made contact, the ball was going out."

That season, John won or tied 12 games for us with late-inning hits. He had 21 homers in 243 at bats, a phenomenal ratio. But everything seemed to work against John. There was no designated hitter, a role for which he would have been perfect. The catchers ahead of him were Yogi and Ellie Howard. Finally, there was no free agency, so John was tied to the Yankees.

"When I was in the minors, it was frustrating," said John. "I was signed as a third baseman and outfielder, but Bill Dickey got ahold of me in the minors and made me a catcher. That set me back, because I couldn't do anything about Ellie and Yogi. Both guys won the MVP award, and they always had big years. No matter what I did in the minors, it really didn't seem to matter because there was no room for me. It got kind of depressing. That changed when Ralph got to be the manager, because he thought I could help the club. Until 1961, I never batted a hundred times in any season. By the time Ralph got the job I was twenty-eight, and I was just happy to be in New York. I wanted to play, but I was content to be with the club. For me, it was enough just to be there. Ralph always made me feel that what I was doing, no matter if I was playing or not, that I was still an important part of the team."

In the first week of August, the Yankees lost Roger for a game and Ralph for five.

A headline in the *Sporting News* said: "Injury Hoodoo Hits Maris for the Third Straight Season."

All of this was a colorful way of saying Roger missed a game with a pulled left hamstring. He probably played a couple of times when he should have rested the leg. Certainly, Roger was limping. But he went out there, as he always did whenever it was humanly possible.

But the story went on and on, mentioning Roger's appendicitis attack in '59, his rib injury in '60, and his other health problems early in his career. However, the story was really about Roger not hitting a home run for six games, which meant Ruth was gaining on him.

Roger was concerned about his leg because he wanted to play, but wasn't concerned about Ruth: "I don't figure to break the record, but I think Mickey might."

Meanwhile, Ralph was suspended for bumping umpire Ed Hurley. We were in the process of losing a doubleheader to Baltimore, which did nothing to help Ralph's mood. In the second game, we were losing 2–1 in the bottom of the ninth but had the bases loaded with no outs. Then Clete Boyer ran the count full, but took a third strike on a pitch Clete and Ralph both thought was out of the strike zone. Hector Lopez finished off the rally by grounding into a double play. Ralph roared out of the dugout, waving his arms. Several Yankee players and a couple of umpires held Ralph away from Hurley, but in his report to the American League office Hurley said he was bumped. That led to a five-game suspension.

"The only reason I waited until after the game to go out there is that if you're on the field to protest a ball-strike call, it's an automatic ejection," Ralph told reporters. "We were battling our brains out, and if a guy can't see any better than that, then he shouldn't be an umpire."

With Frank Crosetti managing the team and Ralph watching the games on television in the player's lounge of the Yankee clubhouse, we went 4–1. We took a doubleheader from Kansas City, the only negative note in those games being that Whitey failed to win his twentieth. He was 19–2 and left with the score 5–5 after eight innings, but Kansas City made two errors in the bottom of the ninth, and the win went to Luis Arroyo. In the second game, Mickey hit his fortieth homer, and we won easily.

Game 3 of Houk's suspension was a loss to the A's. The next night, we beat Minnesota 8–5 as John Blanchard did it again—a three-run homer in the bottom of the tenth. John was the hero, but most of the headlines that day went to Roger, who hit his first homer in ten games. This was one of those times when Roger told the reporters to go talk to someone else, and that a good place to start might be Blanchard since all he did was win the game.

In the last game of Houk's suspension, Crosetti had to juggle the pitching as Rollie Sheldon had a sore elbow. Jim Coates became the emergency starter, and he threw a 2–1 complete-game win against the Twins. The score was 1–1 in the bottom of the eighth when Roger led off with a single up the middle and Mantle followed with a triple off the left-field fence to win the game.

Ralph returned for an August 6 doubleheader. He saw Whitey pitch 10 innings, allowing 6 runs, but he didn't get his twentieth win or his third loss. John Blanchard tied the game in the bottom of the tenth with yet another pinch homer, and Yogi's single in the bottom of the fifteenth won it. After that marathon, there was another game to play. Sheldon said his elbow was feeling better, and he proved it by going nine innings and beating the Twins, 4–3. Mickey had 3 home runs in the doubleheader, giving him and Roger 43 each, which put them 19 games ahead of Ruth's pace.

We were in the midst of an amazing streak, winning with Roger limping, winning with Ralph sometimes in the dugout and sometimes not, winning with Ralph Terry and Rollie Sheldon missing starts with minor arm problems, and Jim Coates rushing into duty both times and throwing complete games. Even though Whitey had a few problems getting number twenty, we won with Luis Arroyo in relief and John Blanchard coming off the bench with pinch-hit homers.

In his next start, Whitey beat the Angels for his twentieth.

"Now my life has changed," said Whitey. "When you win eighteen or nineteen on this team, no one notices. Now, it's 'Whitey, look here for a picture.' Then there's a flash. Then it's 'Whitey, look over here for another picture.' Winning twenty is getting me a sore neck."

Then we did something new—we won a game when Roger bunted.

The score was 1–1 in the bottom of the sixth inning with Ken McBride pitching for the Angels.

"Roger walked over to me and said, 'Ralph, what do you think about me bunting for a hit,' " said Houk. "I told him it was a great idea."

As happened so often in clutch situations, Bobby Richardson started us off. He doubled and moved to third with two outs. Then Roger dropped a superb bunt down the third-base line, beating it out and scoring Bobby with what turned out to be the decisive run.

"After the game, all the reporters wanted to know how Roger could bunt when he was in the middle of the home run race," said Houk. "I reminded them of something Roger never forgot—we were also in the middle of a pennant race, and that was more important."

We had won seven in a row and took a train from New York to Washington to open a four-game series.

"Even though Roger had won that game with a bunt, he was in a little slump, and he never did hit well in Washington," said hitting coach Wally Moses. "I ran into Roger in the men's room on the train, and we started talking about hitting. I know it's hard to believe, but we spent four hours in the men's room talking hitting. Roger was worried about losing his confidence and didn't want to fall off down the stretch like he had in 1960. He also had a mental block about the Washington ballpark. He kept telling me that he couldn't hit there.

When Roger stopped hitting it was because he would start swinging like Mickey, in other words swinging too hard. Mickey's swing was long; Roger's was short and compact."

Wally Moses was always underrated as a hitting coach, and in 1961 he did some nice work, primarily with Ellie Howard, Clete Boyer, and Bobby Richardson. But he also did something for Roger during that train ride, because Roger hit two homers in four games against the Senators. Mickey and Roger ended that trip to Washington with 45 homers each. But Roger hit three more in the next two games, all off left-handers, to take a 48–45 lead. That gave him 7 homers in 6 games following his talk with Wally Moses.

The month of August ended with Whitey at 22–3. Bill Stafford and Ralph Terry each had 11 wins, Ellie Howard was hitting .349, and we just finished a tremendous three months—22–10 in June, 20–9 in July, and 22–9 in August. Yet, we could not shake Detroit, who was only 1½ games behind.

But as September began, Roger had 51 homers and Mickey had 48, and that was all the writers and fans wanted to talk about.

10

COMMISSIONER FORD FRICK gave everyone plenty to talk about when he ruled that Ruth's record must be broken in 154 games, which was the standard baseball schedule until the American League expanded by two teams in 1961. To balance the schedule, eight games had to be added, bringing the season total to 162.

That was the problem, according to Frick and other fans of Ruth. Make no mistake; Frick was a Ruth fan. He also happened to have been one of Babe Ruth's ghost writers.

Anyway, on July 18, Frick said, "A player who may hit more than 60 home runs during his team's first 154 games would be recognized as having established a new record. However, if the player does not hit more than 60 until after his club has played 154 games, there would have to be some distinctive mark in the record book to show that Babe Ruth's record was set under the 154-game schedule, and that the other total was compiled while the 162-game schedule was in effect."

Interestingly, there is no mention of the asterisk, which is what most people assume stands next to Roger's record. It was sportswriter Dick Young who started the asterisk discussion. During Frick's press conference, Young asked if the "distinctive mark" would be like an asterisk. Ford just said it would be a "distinctive mark," which could have been an asterisk or just about anything else.

Here is what *The Book of Baseball Records* actually says about the home run record:

> 61 Roger E. Maris, AL:NY, 1961 (162 G/S)
> 60 George H. Ruth, AL:NY, 1927

So there is no asterisk, but there is a mention of the 162-game schedule. And even that is a fallacy if you check the record.

The 1961 Yankees actually had 163 games entered into the record book. One was a seven-inning game that was suspended after the score was tied. Nonetheless, all the individual statistics from that game count. And Ruth's 1927 Yankees didn't play 154; they played 155, for the same reason.

But Frick's ruling raised some other problems. To take one possibility, what if Roger had hit 61 homers in 154 games, and Mickey had 58? Then in the last eight games, Roger didn't hit any, but Mickey hit four. Therefore, Mickey would have been the home run champ with 62 homers, but Roger would have set the all-time record with 61. This possibility wasn't mentioned by a professor from MIT, but by Yogi Berra.

What about the other records such as hits, strikeouts, and so on? Frick only addressed the issue of home runs, and he only did that because he was pressured into it by the enormous publicity Roger and Mickey were receiving.

Ralph Houk greeted Frick's ruling this way: "I just hope both of my guys do it."

Roger said, "If Mickey gets 60 homers in 155 games, do you think they won't allow it? If they keep it out, you'll hear some real bitching then."

Dick Young wrote that Ruth set his record in 155 games, not 154. He also said, "I think they [Mickey and Roger] should get 155 games to break the record. There would be just as much sense as permitting a man to run 95 yards to break a record in the 100-yard dash. . . . The man who hits 61 homers in the 156th game won't break the record. It's as simple as that."

American League President Joe Cronin said, "A season is a season, regardless of the number of games."

Mickey told the *Sporting News*, "I think Frick is right. Ruth set the record in 154 games and you should beat it in the same number of games. If I should break it in 155 games, I wouldn't want it."

Al Kaline said, "Whoever hits 61 is entitled to the record, no matter how many games it takes. It was the owner and leagues who told us how many games we have to play, not the players."

The *Sporting News* conducted a poll of the Baseball Writers of America, and Frick's decision was supported by a two-to-one margin. Some writers who backed Frick thought he made a critical error by not saying something about the record before the 162-game season began. A majority said there should be two sets of records, one for 154 games and the other for 162 games. In the *Philadelphia Daily News*, Larry Merchant wrote, "Frick is out of order. . . . He tries to change tides. He cannot. . . . What is a record? It is a recording of an achievement. No amount of doctoring by asterisks, question marks or exclamation points will alter the fact that when Ruth's record of 60 home runs is broken, it is broken."

This led to a discussion of Ruth versus The Modern Player.

In 1927, balls that bounced into the stands were counted as home runs. But the *Sporting News* checked with a few veteran New York writers who covered Ruth in 1927, and they said all of Ruth's homers went into the seats on a fly.

Of course, it was Ruth who changed the complexion of the game. His 60 homers were not only a record, but more than any other American League *team* hit in 1927. He also was under no heat to hit 60, or even 50 for that matter, since he already held every home run record. Lou Gehrig was tremendous in 1927, but 47 homers really didn't push Ruth. But Babe did swing for the fences, especially in September, when he hit 17 homers.

"It was well past Labor Day before anyone suspected that a new record was in the making," wrote Fred Lieb, who covered the 1927 Yankees. "We were all satisfied that Ruth's record of 59 he hit in 1921 would stand. . . . Most of us gave considerably more attention to Gehrig's chances of driving in 200 runs. The *New York World*'s Arthur Mann would openly cheer for Lou with cries of 'Get those runs across, Lou.' In the home-run contest between Lou and Babe, Mann and I were for Lou. Ruth probably had more writers rooting for him, led by Ford Frick, then Babe's ghost writer, Bill Slocum and Dan Daniel. . . . In September, Lou tailed off as he worried about an illness to his mother. He finished with 175 RBI. . . . Meanwhile, Babe hit 20 homers in his last 32 games to get the record."

On and on it went.

Some charged that Roger and Mickey were helped by expansion, which brought twenty new pitchers into the American League. In response, the *Sporting News* ran a story under the headline: "Bambino Had His Share of Patsy Chuckers in '27."

Ruth hit seven of his home runs off rookie pitchers, six served up by Tony Welzer and Slim Harriss. They pitched for the Red Sox, who were 51–103 in 1927. "The idea was that there wasn't any law against palookas in '27, and if the M-boys are drawing some, so did the Babe," wrote Joe King.

The next great debate centered on the baseball: live or dead?

"Hold it in your hand and you can feel its heart beating," said Dizzy Dean.

The folks who made the baseball disagreed in a *Sporting News* story: "Bunnies in Balls? Nonsense, Says Spalding Prexy." According to Spalding President Edwin L. Parker, "the built-in characteristics of the ball haven't changed in 35 years."

In the great rabbit hunt, *The New York Times* ignored the word of both Dizzy Dean and Mr. Edwin L. Parker. Instead, they hired Foster D. Snell, Inc., a firm of consulting chemists and engineers, to run tests on seven balls manufactured between 1927 and 1961. The balls were subjected to "surgical dissection and batterings by an explosive-driven Remington Arms Ram." They were checked also for "deformation measurements with a venier caliper."

For three pages, the *Times* ran charts and data. There were headings such as "Impact vs. Travel," "Rotational Stability," "Rebound Coefficient," and "Compressibility." They tested how far the balls went when they were hit on the seams and how far they went when they were hit on the league president's signature.

Yes, the *Times* spared no expense or space.

And what was the conclusion?

A hint was in the headline: "Is the '61 Ball Livelier Than the Ruthian Variety? Maybe Yes and Maybe No."

The scientists said, "The 1961 ball is slightly larger, slightly lighter, and slightly livelier than the 1927 ball." But they went on for three pages to say that it was not all that much larger, lighter or livelier. The report added, "The only valid conclusion which can be drawn from the data herein presented is that there are differences in the construction of the balls between 1927 and 1961. The effect of these differences cannot be estimated in the absence of the quantity of test samples."

And that is what *The New York Times* got for its money.

It should be no surpise that venerable Dan Daniel jumped into the middle of the fray and said, "As a ball gets older, it gets deader. The horsehide loses its life, the yarn goes stale and the rubber core fails to respond the way it did when it left the Spalding hopper at Chicopee Falls, Mass. Believe me, gentlemen, it's not the ball."

So what is it, Dan?

Why, the bat, of course, said Dan.

And back to the laboratory went *The New York Times*.

"It takes two to tango," said the *Times*. "It also takes a bat as well as a ball to bring a home run."

We would read this stuff in the clubhouse and laugh. Here they were acting as if they just discovered the wheel because they found out you needed a bat as well as a ball to hit a home run.

This latest report said, "Today's players are taking heavier swings with lighter bats at more or less the same old ball." Ruth used a forty-two-ounce bat, while Mickey and Roger's bats were thirty-three ounces, said the *Times*. An executive from Hillerich and Bradsby, which produced bats, told the *Times* that he "had an order slip from Ruth for a 52-ounce bat, but I don't think he ever used it. Our records show he favored a 42-ounce bat and never used anything lighter than 38 ounces."

It was not surprising that Dan Daniel was in the middle of the light-versus-heavy-bat debate, since he started it.

"The ball has not been changed, but it still has a bunch of jackrabbit in it and cutting it open will lead to daffy conclusions," wrote Daniel. "The strike zone has been lowered off the shoulders. The bat is much lighter. Now the bat weighs 34 ounces, maybe 32 in hot weather. It is highly maneuverable. The free swingers get under the ball and sent it far, and still farther."

We all wondered how a bat lost two ounces in hot weather, but that was a mystery Dan was not about to reveal. It also was something that the *Times* decided not to pursue with Foster D. Snell, Inc.

Roger made the strongest point when he said, "The weight of the bat isn't important, it's how you swing it."

And Mickey put it in perspective when he said. "Maybe the players now are livelier."

It only took a few moments to realize that it didn't matter how many balls were cut open or shot out of motor guns. Nor did it matter how many bats were weighed or sawed in half.

The issue wasn't the equipment, it was the players. And it was an ageless question—were the older players better than the current ones? Toss in the element of the Ruth legend, and people can go on writing and talking about it forever . . . as they have.

Jimmy Dykes reflected the attitude of many people when he said, "Maris is a fine player, but I can't imagine him riding down Broadway in low-slung convertible wearing a coonskin cap."

The point was that Ruth didn't just hit home runs, he almost invented them. He certainly created the image of a home run hitter.

The New York Times's Arthur Daley wrote, "Maris and Mantle are shy, introverted business men. The Babe was a boisterous, big-hearted child of nature who exuded color out of every pore. He was a legend come to life, Paul Bunyan in the flesh. . . . He once earned $40,000 on a post-season vaudeville tour. His expenses for the tour amounted to $50,000. If that isn't good finances, it's at least good Babe Ruth. No one but Babe would have dared to point to the bleachers where he would then hit a home run off Charlie Root in the 1932 World Series."

Mrs. Babe Ruth was regularly interviewed, and she usually said, "I don't want the record broken. It's the one my husband loved best. Maris and Mantle are two nice boys, but my husband wanted to be the home run king forever."

Veteran sportswriter Jimmy Powers was appalled, not by the bats, balls, or even the home runs, but by the fact that no one in baseball history had hit fifty homers without also hitting .300 until Roger.

"The caliber of play has deteriorated so badly that anything is possible," wrote Powers. "We can leave out the simple matter of park dimensions, the velocity of the ball, the uses of chemicals and abrasives. We can simply refer to the little matter of catching a baseball. Some modern players can't catch an ordinary pop fly."

No matter what Powers said, the fans loved home runs.

Gay Talese, who went on to become a noted author, was working for the *Times* in 1961. He was sent to the Stadium to write a sidebar on the question: Do you want someone to break Ruth's record?

It wasn't a survey that would qualify as a Gallup Poll, but Talese did talk to fifty fans, thirty-nine of whom said they were rooting for Mantle and/or Maris to pass Ruth. "Of the 11 who were for Ruth, most were elderly," wrote Talese. "Most of the fans wanted Mantle to do it."

Several newspapers ran contests asking readers to predict who would hit more home runs, Roger or Mickey. One of the winners was Woody Woodward, the former Cincinnati shortstop and now vice president and general manager of the Yankees.

"When I was a freshman baseball player at Florida State, I entered the *Miami News* contest," said Woodward. "I filled out the ballot and said I thought Roger would hit 61 and Mickey 54. You also had to give a reason for your answer, and I said it was because Roger was a left-handed hitter best suited for Yankee Stadium. I got fifty dollars."

Home runs seemed to be on everyone's mind. *Newsweek* called 1961 "the year everyone hits home runs." Roger and Mickey posed together so often for pictures that Mickey said, "I'm beginning to feel like a Siamese twin."

Before the season began, Billy Martin said that Mickey would break the record because of the twenty new pitchers and a strong lineup around him.

"I went hunting with Mickey in the winter and he was in the best shape of his career," said Billy. "I know this guy. With the extra pitchers and the extra games, he can do it. I've never seen him so anxious to have a big year."

Casey Stengel said Roger and Mickey were both capable of doing it.

Joe DiMaggio said, "I think Mickey has the best shot at doing it because he is a switch-hitter. Roger admits he has had some trouble with left-handed pitchers. I'll say this, these guys are making the most spectacular bid we've ever had at the record. I try to catch every game they play, at least on television if I can't get to the Stadium."

As September began, Ralph Kiner said, "Pitchers are going to stop Maris and I'll tell you how—they'll walk him. . . . When a fellow is on a streak like that, why take a chance on pitching to him? I'd walk him even if Mickey Mantle is the next hitter."

Rocky Colavito said, "Several guys in our league are capable of beating the record, but I don't think anyone will do it. Switching from day to night ball and back again is rough. Ruth never had to do that."

The New York Times got back into the act again, this time not with Foster D. Snell, Inc., but with Casey—not Stengel, but Casey the Computer. Robert Teague wrote, "A baseball expert who never has watched a game or read a box score was confronted with one of the year's pressing questions: Will Roger Maris or Mickey Mantle break Babe Ruth's record? In the twinkling of an electronic eye, it was Roger, yes; Mickey, no. Furthermore, he expects Maris to hit No. 61 in the 154th game of the season."

Casey the Computer worked for IBM and said Roger's chances were 55 out of 100 compared to only 2 out of 100 for Mickey. Casey "has eight heads, five of which are six feet high. They look like a battery of blue and gray plastic jukeboxes and they hum like airconditioners. . . . Casey was born at the cost of $950,000 and his rent at 1401 Church Street is $9,000 a month. . . . Did Casey know if the Yankees would win the pennant? No, like most fans, he never heard of the pennant race."

Well, for the three summer months, we had played .720 baseball and set one home run record after another. When the New York fans weren't talking about Roger, Mickey, and Ruth, they were wondering who might play in the World Series. The press was pretty much in the same state of mind. They all seemed to ask how a team so good could not win the pennant.

We had a much different opinion, maybe because we watched the standings and scoreboard every day. All we knew was that when we won, so did Detroit. No matter how many home runs we hit or how many games Ford Frick said a player needed in which to break Ruth's record, we never forgot that it all would be futile if we didn't win the American League pennant. If Casey the Computer couldn't figure that out, that was too bad.

Detroit was coming to the Stadium for Labor Day weekend, and we had to win. That's all there was to it. The Tigers were 1½ games back and had won 11 of their last 14 games. They had a terrific lineup that included Norm Cash, Al Kaline, Billy Bruton, Rocky Colavito, and Dick McAuliffe. With Frank Lary and Don Mossi, the Tigers had two pitchers who had been very rough on us.

We talked a lot about winning the first game, because we felt it would set the tone for the three-game series. Whitey was pitching, and if we got beat with Whitey on the mound, there could be trouble. And there was, even before the game started.

"It was early in September, and Roger and I were hanging around at the apartment in Queens," said Bob Cerv. "I looked at Roger and asked, 'Where did you get those white spots?'

"Roger said, 'What white spots?'

"I said, 'Let's go look in the mirror.' Roger and I went into the bathroom, and he looked in the mirror. He had a skin rash, and there was a spot on the back of his head where his hair had fallen out. Roger went to see a doctor, and the guy told him to stay out of pressure situations. Now there was a helluva piece of advice for Roger Maris on the first of September in 1961. I blamed it on the reporters and all their damn questions. They were enough to make anyone's hair fall out."

Meanwhile, on the day before the Tiger series, Luis Arroyo was opening his mail. He received a letter saying, "I don't like the Puerto Ricans, and I plan to shoot you if you pitch this weekend."

Luis was worried.

"I kept thinking that some guy was going to shoot me just as I jumped over the bull pen fence to come into the game. I took the letter to Ralph. He looked at it and said, 'Don't worry. I'll handle this.'

"I said, 'Ralph, I need some protection or something.'

"Ralph said, 'Just relax.'

"Ralph called the front office, who said there would be some extra police in the stands to make sure that nothing happened. I knew there was a big crowd, and I wondered how they could watch everybody, but I wasn't going to ask out."

There were 65,566 fans at the Stadium to see Whitey face Mossi with the temperature in the middle nineties. We couldn't do much with Mossi, and Whitey had to leave the game in the fifth inning, not because of anything the Tigers did, but due to a pulled muscle in his right hip. Ralph brought Bud Daley out of the bull pen, and Bud did exactly what he had done so often in sixty-one—he bought us some time. For seven innings, we couldn't touch Mossi, but Whitey and Daley were shutting down the Tigers. And then came one of the pivotal plays of the season. In the top of the eighth, Daley walked Bruton, and Kaline put a line drive into the left-field corner. Yogi played it off the wall, barely taking a step and throwing from his ear, just like the catcher he was. Yogi's peg was perfect, and it caught Kaline at second base to cut the heart out of that rally. Daley got Cash to pop out and end the inning.

"I just caught it off the wall and threw it to Bobby at second base," Yogi told me twenty-five years later. "That's all there was to it."

That may be, but it was the play that changed the game.

Luis took over for Daley in the top of the ninth.

"Ralph flipped me the ball and said, 'Luis, you better get them out or *I'll* kill you.' I know Ralph was trying to make a joke, but I was very scared. I was just glad to get them out and get into the dugout."

We went to the bottom of the ninth and still hadn't scored. Mossi got Roger on a soft fly ball to right, and Mickey took a third strike. It looked as if we were going to extra innings. But Mossi's first pitch to Ellie Howard became a single to left field. On Mossi's next pitch, Yogi slapped a base hit to right field, sending Ellie to third. Two pitches, two hits, and the dugout was alive. The Tiger bull pen also happened to be dead, because until the last ten seconds Mossi had been superb.

Moose came to the plate. He was 0 for 3 against Mossi, whose slow stuff had Moose frustrated. Moose took the first two pitches and ran the count to one and one. Then he rammed a grounder between the shortstop and third baseman, scoring Ellie with the winning run. Moose was so excited that he gave a huge hug to first-base coach Wally Moses.

"Frank Crosetti was the one who helped me," said Moose. "He said he could read Mossi's pitches from the third-base coach's box. Cro' whistled for a breaking ball. I kept telling myself to keep my weight back, then I got just enough bat on it to get it through the infield."

The first game was really crucial. We won with Whitey getting hurt, and we won with Mossi at his best. We won because guys like Moose, Yogi, Ellie, and Bud Daley did the little things that went unnoticed by the press and public but helped us win the pennant.

"Years later, I managed Al Kaline, and he started talking about how Yogi threw him out at second," said Ralph. "Al said that one play may have changed the season, and he could be right."

Ralph Terry started the second game for us.

"I loved to pitch in a big series like that," said Ralph. "To be on the mound when there is a lot on the line, a pitcher has to love that. As I warmed up, I was already thinking about a sweep. Considering how we had won that first game, anything seemed possible. So what did I do? I went out there in the first inning, gave up a base hit to Kaline, and then Colavito put one in the bleachers. It's 2–0, and we haven't even gotten to bat."

It was hot that afternoon, a game-time temperature of ninety-six, and there was a crowd of 50,261. Finally, New York was seriously caught up in the spirit of the race and wanted us to win the pennant. Of course, the fans also wanted to see Roger and Mickey hit home runs. On this day, they got to see both.

After Colavito's homer, Detroit would not score again off Ralph.

Meanwhile, we went to work against Frank Lary, whose career record was 26–9 against New York. After six innings, it was a 2–2 game because Roger hammered one off Lary into the right-field seats. It stayed 2–2 until the bottom of the eighth inning.

Luis Arroyo had taken over for Ralph with two outs in the bottom of the seventh. "I felt a little better the second day,"said Luis. "Nothing had happened in the first game. I had detectives following me off the field. I was still a little worried, but not so much."

Luis led off the eighth with a base hit. Bobby followed with a single to right, Luis waddled around second, and, in the words of Dan Daniel, "threw his round body into third and was safe." Bobby took second on the play. I got a single through the drawn-in infield, scoring Luis and Bobby. That was it for Lary, who was replaced by Hank Aguirre. Roger said hello to Hank with another homer, and that was the game.

But we were a little worried in the clubhouse about Mickey. In the sixth inning, Mickey pulled a muscle in his left forearm while trying to check his swing. He then hit a roller to second base and was booed because the fans thought he didn't run the ball out.

"I wanted to take Mickey out right after he hurt himself," said

Houk. "But he convinced me to let him stay in the game for his defense. He said he would bunt for the rest of the season, if that's what it took."

After the second game, Roger had 53 homers and was eight games ahead of Ruth's pace. But the New York press was writing off Mickey, figuring he would be out for at least a week because of the arm injury.

Asked what he planned to do without Mickey for the last game of the Detroit series, Ralph shook his head and said, "Right now, I just don't know."

Twenty-four hours later, Mickey had an answer for Houk.

"Play me," said Mickey.

"What about your arm?" asked Ralph.

"I'm all right," said Mickey, who then went out and proved it.

It was another sweltering day, temperature in the middle nineties and the humidity seemed about the same. The Tigers took a 1–0 lead off Bill Stafford in the first inning when Norm Cash homered to right, but Mickey came right back in the bottom of the first with a two-run homer that went about four hundred feet to right. Mickey was hurting, but he didn't have to worry about bunting for the rest of the year.

Stafford was great for seven innings, and we had a 4–2 lead. But Bill had to leave in the top of the eighth when the heat made him sick to his stomach. As he had in the first two games, Ralph handed the ball to Luis Arroyo. Only this time, Luis wasn't sharp. Detroit scored a run in the eighth and two more in the top of the ninth to take a 5–4 lead.

As the game went on, Mickey's arm seemed to get worse. He iced it between innings, but here he was leading off the bottom of the ninth. Forty-one-year-old Gerry Staley was on the mound for the Tigers. His first pitch to Mickey was a ball, but the next one again went four hundred feet into the right-field bleachers, making the score 5–5. Yogi followed with a single, and that was it for Staley. Ron Kline was the next Detroit pitcher, and Ralph decided to let Arroyo hit. Luis moved Yogi to second base with a sacrifice bunt. An intentional walk to Moose and a fly out by Clete Boyer meant there were two outs and two on with Ellie Howard at bat. Kline's first pitch was a strike, but then Ellie lashed a line drive into the left-field seats, and we won again, this time 8–5.

"These were the three most exciting games of my life," said Houk. "Everything happened in these games."

After the game, Mickey was still icing his forearm.

"It was strange," he said. "When I took my normal, hard swing,

I missed. Both times I hit the ball out, I took nice, easy cuts, just trying to make contact."

Houk said, "Mickey is an amazing player. He was worse off than any of us thought, but he was not about to say anything. I'll say this, for a guy who was really hurting, he had a helluva day."

The sweep put us 4½ games ahead of the Tigers, and the writers figured that was the end of the pennant race. Once again, all the attention was on Roger and Mickey, Roger with 53 homers , Mickey with 50. Every time they stepped on the field, even just to take batting practice, they got great ovations. When the game was over, the security guards ran onto the field with ropes, creating a path so Mickey and Roger could make their way from the outfield to the dugout without being mobbed. I've never seen anything like that before or since.

Actually, the writers were right. The race was over, but it was impossible for us to know it. Washington came to the Stadium for a four-game Series, opening with a twi-nighter, and Mickey's forearm was too inflamed for him to play. Ralph improvised an outfield of Yogi in left, Roger in center, and John Blanchard in right. Think about that—two catchers in the outfield and a rightfielder in center. But we were on such a roll it made little difference. Blanchard hit a home run in the eighth inning to break a 3–3 tie and win the first game. In the second game, Bud Daley went all the way and allowed only two runs. Bob Cerv was the hero this time, snapping a 2–2 tie in the seventh with a run-scoring triple. Ellie caught both games, losing eight pounds but adding seven points to his batting average by going 4 for 7.

The New York *Daily News* ran this headline: "Maris (0-for-8), Mick Idle, But Yanks Win Pair." Those things bothered Roger more than us, because he was embarrassed by them, but how could we be jealous when Roger never asked for that kind of coverage?

In the third game of the series, Mickey hit his fifty-first homer, Ellie hit number 16, and Jim Coates pitched nine innings as we won 6–1. The impressive part of the three wins over Detroit and the next three against Washington was that Whitey Ford wasn't the winner in any of those games. Bud Daley and Jim Coates stepped into the rotation and came through. But Whitey did start the last game against Washington and threw a five-hit shutout, making his record 23–3. John Blanchard drove in two runs, Roger hit his fifty-fourth homer and suddenly we had an eight-game lead over the Tigers, who died after the Labor Day Series in New York.

We won our eighth straight as Cleveland came to the Stadium. In the first inning of that game, I tripled and Roger dropped down a bunt to score me with the first run. His next time up, Roger homered to right, and we won easily, 7–3. That gave Roger 55 homers and put him seven games ahead of Ruth's pace.

After the game, one of the big issues was why Roger bunted.

"Because I wanted to win the game and score Tony," Roger told the reporters. "I saw that Bubba Phillips was playing in at third base. But on the right side, Vic Power and Johnny Temple were real deep. All I had to do was drag the ball in their direction, and I'd beat it out. They gave it to me, so I took it."

What about the home run?

"[Dick] Stigman threw me a curveball and I hit it," said Roger.

The reporters were running out of questions and Roger was about out of answers. Dick Young wrote, "Do you have any questions you'd like to ask Roger Maris after he hits No. 56? And No. 57, and 58, and 59, and maybe even No. 60? The newsmen can use your help because they've run dry."

By September 10, Roger had 56 homers, Mickey 53, our lead over Detroit was 11½ games, and the magic number was eight. We had won twelve in a row, all at home. Wins eleven and twelve were a doubleheader sweep over Cleveland before 57,284 fans. In that doubleheader, Cleveland's Jimmy Piersall had, in the words of Dick Young, "a fist-flinging, pants-booting bout with two fans who ran on the field." There also were some bitter words between Vic Power and Jim Coates, who had dusted Power with an inside fastball.

The next day, Mickey was coming down with the flu. He told Mel Allen that he wasn't feeling well, and Allen mentioned that his doctor had a shot that could take care of everything.

Twenty-five years later, recalling "The Shot," as it became known in the papers, Mickey would just shake his head and say, "I can't believe I went to this goofball.

"It wasn't Mel's fault, and I guess it maybe wasn't the doctor's, I don't know. But I had this cold, virus, or I don't know what the hell. . . . Anyway, I felt awful. Mel said this doctor would give me a shot and knock everything out of me in a couple days. It knocked me on my butt, was what it did. The doctor hit a bone with a needle. Then my side got infected. The day after I got the shot, Merlyn was coming to New York, and I was too sick to even go to Penn Station to pick her up. I sent someone else, and when Merlyn saw me, the first thing she said was, 'Boy, do you look sick.' She called the Yankees, and then I went to the hospital. By the time I got to a room, I was dizzy and had a 104-degree temperature. They looked at my side, lanced it, and took an X ray. They said the bone was bruised and I had all sorts of problems. After my side was lanced, all this crap drained out, and it really looked like hell. So they stuck some gauze in the wound, but the stuff kept draining. Everybody figured I was bleeding to death, but it wasn't that bad."

The shot wasn't life threatening, and it wasn't about to keep us from winning a pennant. All it did was knock Mickey out of the home-run race.

11

DESPITE the abcess on his hip, Mickey tried to play. If he could walk, he wanted to keep swinging for Ruth's record. Roger was still on his feet, but the pressure was weighing him down. The rush to hit 60 homers in 154 games was frantic, chaotic, exciting, and sometimes rather silly. There were crazy questions from the press and crazy things happening in general, like a stripper who took the name Mickey Maris. Everything was happening in a mad rush, and there was always that deadline looming, and the arguments about that deadline, all courtesy of Ford Frick. And they weren't chasing just any ghost—they were after the most glamorous ghost of them all. It was like nothing else in baseball history before or since.

SEPTEMBER 13

Our game with the White Sox was rained out after three innings, meaning Roger (with 56 homers) and Mickey (with 53) still had nine games left to catch Ruth. In the stands that day were Hank Greenberg and Ralph Kiner. Former sluggers were often being inteviewed because they had made a run at Ruth's record.

Kiner said, "I think Maris is the only one with a shot at doing it in 154 games. In 162, I think Maris and Mantle will both do it. If that happens, the record will be recognized by the fans."

Greenberg said, "I hit 58 homers in 1938 and I had three games left to break the record. I felt I'd do it for sure, but I didn't hit another homer in those last 20 at bats. It was the pressure, not only on me, but on the pitchers, too. It's a feeling that time is running out and you become impatient. You get paralyzed at the plate. You are afraid to swing at a bad pitch and you end up taking good ones. Then you are disgusted and you start swinging at bad ones. . . . As for Maris and Mantle, I think both can break the record, but not in 154 games. All I know is that if either one sets the record after the deadline set by the commissioner, who will be able to deny him that honor?"

Roger said, "I know I have been swinging at bad pitches, but the most important thing to me still is winning. And I'm not even going to talk about the record!"

In the *Daily News*, Joe Trimble wrote, "Time grows short when you reach September, as the song says. Well, it's choking M&M in what is beginning to look like a fruitless pursuit of Babe Ruth's ghost. Now they have only seven games left to challenge the Bam's 60. . . . It looks like Mantle who needs to average a home run a game to do it, has thrown in the sponge."

Mickey said, "I don't see how I can get it in 154 or 162 games. I'm just too tired. If I could have done something in these two games, maybe. But now. . . ." Mickey seemed more relieved that disappointed.

Roger said, "I don't even want to talk about 60, I'll take what I can get. There was a good wind today and I couldn't even get the ball up in the air. That figures. . . . Listen, I never said I was like Ruth. I never said I was a great man. But I want to break this record."

Ralph Houk said, "I had been giving some thought to moving Roger and Mickey to the top of the lineup after we clinch the pennant to get them some more at bats, but I won't do it. I don't want to do anything that will give people a chance to call it a cheap record, so the lineup will stay the same."

SEPTEMBER 14

We finally got to play the White Sox, but we should have skipped it. Chicago took both games of the doubleheader by scores of 8–3 and 4–3, but no one was paying much attention to those results. What mattered was Roger and Mickey, and what mattered even further was that Mickey went 0 for 7, and remained stuck on 53 homers.

"If I had hit a couple out, I thought I might have a chance to get the record," said Mickey, "But after this . . . well, they just stopped me cold. I didn't hit a ball decently all day. I don't have any sting in my swing."

Roger had three hits, but in the homer mania of those last few weeks, these hits didn't count because they were singles. So two more games passed with Roger still at 56.

SEPTEMBER 15

It was another day, another doubleheader, and another two games in which Mickey and Roger didn't hit a home run, making the countdown five until 154 games. But it also was a day when Whitey Ford won his twenty-fourth game and we set a season record when Yogi, Moose, and Clete Boyer hit home runs, giving us 223, breaking the record of 221 held by the 1956 Reds. Moose hit No. 222 off Don Mossi to put us in the record books as 46,267 watched in Detroit.

By now, the focus was all on Roger. Even though Mickey was still playing, anyone could see that his health had cost him a chance at the record.

This was a night when the writers made a major issue out of Roger's only real indiscretion of the year when it came to handling the press. Before the game, Roger did his usually long round of interviews, saying that "I can't believe Mickey has conceded. He is too good and too much of a competitor to really mean what he said." Roger also said, "I may not break the record in the next couple days, but I'm going to keep thinking I can do it until I've exhausted every chance."

After the game it was different. "Maris Sulks in Trainer's Room As Futile Night Changes Mood," according to the headline in *The New York Times*.

The *Times*'s Louis Effrat wrote, "How does Maris feel? Well, he didn't say. In fact, Maris wouldn't say anything . . . Maris has always made himself available for questioning. Often, it has been diffcult to get him to stop talking. But here it was different. . . . A club spokesman [Bob Fishel] said that Roger told him that he was going to stay in the trainer's quarters after the game until the questioners left. According to the spokesman Maris's reason was that he was 'being ripped by writers in every city.' "

Joe Trimble wrote, "If there is a slight sound of triumphant laughter from above, Babe's ghost is chortling . . . Maris secured himself in the trainer's quarters of Tiger Stadium . . . looking like a culprit trying to hide."

The writers went to Houk and demanded that he get Roger out of the trainer's room.

Ralph told me, "I recall that day distinctly. Roger was in there talking to his brother Rudy, who had driven in from North Dakota for the game. He hadn't seen Rudy in a while, and everything was starting to get to Roger. He had been so patient with the press, and I didn't see any reason to force him to talk. One writer even asked me how come Rudy could go in the trainer's room and the writers couldn't. I told the guy that I'll run my clubhouse the way I see fit. If Roger had a hundred brothers, then they all couldn't go in. But he had only one. If he wanted to talk to Rudy, then Roger could talk to Rudy."

Ralph told the press that night, "I'll give you the whole story. He didn't hit a home run. He did hit one single, broke one bat, and cussed out one fan who deserved it."

After the press had left, Roger said to Mickey, "These guys are driving me crazy."

Mickey nodded sympathetically and said, "I know, Rog, but you just gotta do it. You gotta deal with these guys."

SEPTEMBER 16

You could see that Mickey's hip was killing him, but he was still out there. In the first inning, it seemed that Mickey had hit one into the right-field seats at Tiger Stadium, but Al Kaline made a leaping catch and brought the ball back into the park. Two innings later, Roger hit one to right where he knew Kaline couldn't get to it—it banged against the roof over four hundred feet from the plate. The Tigers won 10–4, but that hardly mattered. After the game, the issue was Roger's fifty-seventh homer, his first in eight games. Then there was Kaline, who picked up the home run ball that bounced back on the field. Kaline tossed the ball into the Yankee dugout so Roger could keep it.

At this point, the writers were looking for the slightest hint of controversy.

"Don't you think it was a nice gesture for Kaline to get the ball for you?" asked a writer.

"I appreciate it," said Roger. "But I guess anyone would have done it."

Roger's tone of voice was pleasant, and all he meant was that he would have done it, too. But the next day, some writers characterized Roger as "ungrateful." It also was mentioned that Roger's embargo of the press lasted exactly one day.

"57th Homer Gets Ace Talking Again, But Not Effusively . . . Abusive Crowd, Bad Press Embitter Yankee Slugger."

Those were the headlines in the *Times*.

Roger said, "I didn't talk because a fan was all over me in Detroit. The guy was really foul. I was sore and I've popped off about fans before and got in trouble. I didn't want to do it again. I needed time to cool off."

September 17

This was the day Roger hit the home run I remember the best, No. 58 off of Terry Fox after the Canadian geese had flown overhead. Roger hit it in the twelfth inning, giving us a 6–4 win over the Tigers before 44,219 fans at Tiger Stadium. Mickey was still playing, still hurting, and still having problems at the plate.

Roger said, "When I stepped on home plate, I knew I had hit 58. Now that it is after the game, I realize only Babe Ruth has hit more homers than me. That means an awful lot. It's something to think about."

September 18

We had no game this day, and Roger still had three games to hit three home runs to set the record. But we would be playing in Baltimore, where he hadn't homered all year, except for the one he lost in a game that was rained out in July.

Joe Trimble wrote, "Babe Ruth's ghost, Ford Frick's edict, and the hard-to-scale walls of Memorial Stadium are all closing in on Roger Maris. . . . This was a day of rest—if a man with so much at stake and so pummeled by pressure can rest."

The New York Times filled its off-day space by asking members of the Yankees for the details of their first major-league home run.

Roger remembered everything about his—the second day of the 1957 season when he was with Cleveland, a grand slam in Detroit—but he couldn't remember the pitcher. It was Jack Crimian.

Mickey remembered his first—it was in 1951 off Chicago's Randy Gumpert. But Mickey couldn't remember his last, which was ten games ago.

Frank Crosetti said his was in 1932, off Washington's Lloyd Brown.

Then they asked Ralph Houk.

"Me?" shrugged Ralph. "I never hit one."

SEPTEMBER 19

We had a doubleheader at Memorial Stadium, the second game being a makeup for that July rainout when Roger and Mickey both lost home runs.

Mickey didn't expect to play this night. His side was just too sore as his infection had led to a 104-degree fever. He came up once as a pinch hitter and struck out.

"Before the game, Roger came into the office to see me," said Ralph Houk. "He said he was tired, worn down, and really didn't want to play. I kept thinking that there was a big crowd, and all the fans wanted to see Roger. And Roger had come so far and gotten so close to the record, that it would have been a real shame if he took a day off at this point. Roger was almost in tears. He was just sick of everything. Finally, I said, 'Why don't you just start the game, and we'll see how things go. If it gets bad, we'll take you out.' That's what we did, but Roger never came out."

We clinched a tie for the pennant by splitting a doubleheader in front of 31,317 fans, who were on Roger's side. When he walked in the first inning, they booed Baltimore pitcher Steve Barber. Roger was greeted with a warm ovation in all nine of his trips to the plate.

Virtually ignored was the fact that Bud Daley was the winning pitcher in the second game, throwing a five-hitter and striking out nine. Moose hit his twenty-seventh homer and drove in two runs in the 3–1 win.

But the real point was Maris, and, according to Dick Young, "Here in the monumental town where Babe Ruth was born, the chauvinist wind tonight whipped up to a proud fury to protect Babe's homer record. The misty advance gusts of Hurricane Esther blew hard from right and into the face of Roger Maris, leaving him homerless in nine at bats."

Baltimore's pitchers could not have been worse for Roger. Barber, a left-hander, stopped us 1–0 in the opener, beating Whitey Ford. There is only one thing Roger hated worse than left-handed pitchers, and that was knuckleball pitchers. Baltimore had two, and they both worked in the second game, Hal Brown going the first eight innings and Hoyt Wilhelm working the ninth. Roger hit nothing especially hard or far, as he had but a single to show for the night.

Roger said, "As far as Mr. Frick is concerned, I have only one game left to break the record. As far as I'm concerned, I have nine games left."

The reporters persisted, wanting to know if Roger could break the record the next day.

"You'd almost have to be Houdini to do it," said Roger.

SEPTEMBER 20

On the night before the 154th game, Roger had to get away.

"I had played with Roger in Kansas City," said Whitey Herzog. "He and I were still good friends, even though we had both been traded a couple times since our days with the A's. I was with the Orioles when Roger came to town, and he told me that he couldn't handle it anymore. The press was driving him crazy, and he couldn't walk across the hotel lobby without being mobbed. During those two days in Baltimore, Roger stayed with me and my wife. My house was quiet, and no one would find him there. My wife cooked him a nice dinner and he relaxed."

But Roger did find time to visit Frank Sliwka, whose father was in the Washington Senators' minor-league system. Twice, Roger stopped at Johns Hopkins Hospital to see Sliwka, who died a week after we left Baltimore.

"Seeing that kid dying really shook me up," said Roger.

"When we drove to the game that day, Roger was pretty quiet," said Herzog. "You could tell he was nervous. When we got out of the car at the park, I said, 'Rog, I hope you hit three home runs and we win 4–3.' Roger smiled and nodded."

It is interesting that only 21,032 fans showed up at Memorial Stadium, which was ten thousand fewer than were at the double-header the day before. Milt Pappas started for Baltimore, and he was the kind of pitcher Roger liked—a right-hander with a good fastball.

Before the game, Roger did a lot of pacing and smoking.

"I knew if I sat down in front of my locker for long, my stomach would end up tied in a hundred knots," Roger told reporters. "I kept picking up things and looking at them. I wanted to keep my hands busy."

Roger loved batting practice, but on this day there was none, as it rained before the game. A couple of times, Roger walked out of the clubhouse, down the runway, and into the dugout just to look around, to do something, anything but sit.

It was a damp, chilly day, but the weather cleared off enough so that the game could start on time.

"I was the starting pitcher, but while I was warming up, about all I could think about was Roger," said Ralph Terry. "I noticed that the wind was blowing in, which was absolutely the worst thing that could happen to Roger. We had already clinched a tie for the pennant, and we had a big lead on Detroit, so the only guy under the gun was Roger."

As usual, Roger was hitting third. But it wasn't Mickey behind him. Instead, Yogi Berra was batting cleanup as Mickey rested his hip.

"That's it, I'm through," Mickey told Roger before the game. "We're all behind you."

When Roger came to the plate in the first inning, all of us were on the top step of the dugout. I looked over at the Baltimore dugout, and those guys were standing up, too. I know I was cheering for Roger, and so were the other guys in our dugout.

"Roger really stepped into one," said Ralph Terry. "He nailed it, but right into the teeth of that wind in right. On a normal day, it's outta there."

Instead, Earl Robinson backed up near the warning track and caught the ball. Roger had hit it hard, but not quite high or far enough.

"I was hoping it was gone," said Roger. "But I felt good just hitting one that hard. I kept thinking that I had three more at bats, so maybe . . ."

"It was a strange feeling seeing Robinson catch that ball," said Herzog. "Roger was on the other team, and I wanted to win. But I hated the thought of Roger gettling saddled with that asterisk. That just wasn't right."

In his second at bat, Roger ran the count to two balls and one strike.

"I could hear the guys in the dugout yelling for me," said Roger. "When I hit it off Pappas, I knew it was out, wind or no wind. It was a low fastball. I hit it square, but I got under it enough so I knew it was gone."

The ball easily carried into the right-field bleachers, about 380 feet from the plate.

"As I went around the bases, I was thinking, that's 59," said Roger. "I had two, maybe even three more shots at it."

Roger's next at bat was in the fourth inning. Dick Hall had replaced

Pappas, and Roger had trouble with Hall's herky-jerky windup. He struck out on a high fastball.

"That pitch wasn't close to being a strike," said Roger. "I never should have swung."

It was Roger against Hall again in the seventh.

"That was when I thought he did it," said Herzog. "Roger stepped into a pitch, and I knew he had enough distance. I just didn't know if it would stay fair."

It didn't, as the ball hooked into the right-field seats about ten feet foul.

"From the second I hit it, I knew it didn't have a chance," said Roger. "But on the next pitch, that's when I thought I did it."

Maris got under one, but the wind really came into play—actually, keeping the ball in play—as Robinson caught it about ten feet from the wall.

Whitey Herzog said, "I could feel my heart when Roger hit that one. I was really pulling for him."

Ralph Terry said, "I saw that ball, and I was wondering if there was any way I could stop the wind."

Roger said, "The damn ball just died."

In *The New York Times*, Arthur Daley wrote, "After that fly ball, the screws were tightening on the rack that was torturing him. It was a slow torture because he had belted a beauty that was just foul."

In the ninth inning, Roger had something else to worry about. As if the wind wasn't enough, Hoyt Wilhelm had come in to pitch.

Herzog said, "I felt awful when [Baltimore manager] Luman Harris brought in Wilhelm. It just wasn't fair. The game was pretty much over [the Yankees had a 4–2 lead]. There just was no reason to use Hoyt, other than to make it tough on Roger personally. Roger had struck out against Wilhelm the night before, and he told me that he'd rather face the toughest left-hander in the league than Wilhelm."

Wilhelm not only had the greatest knuckleball in baseball history, but he had allowed only 5 home runs in 112 innings.

Joe Trimble wrote, "Willy's butterflies are tough enough to catch, much less hit. Anyway, Lum and Hoyt kept the climax honest as the new Orioles protected the record of the grand old Oriole, Ruth."

Herzog said, "They just didn't want Roger to set the record in Ruth's hometown. I'm convinced of that."

Wilhelm said, "Those games with the Yankees were like a World Series. There were reporters everywhere. It's twenty-five years later, and I still can see all the reporters and I remember that wind. Knuckleball pitchers aren't like anyone else; we want the wind blowing out, right into our faces. The pitch goes into the teeth of that wind, and the resistance makes it break more. But the wind was blowing from right, at my back. That has a tendency to flatten out a knuckleball. So Roger wasn't thrilled with the wind blowing in, and neither was I."

Wilhelm got two quick outs. In the on-deck circle, Roger took a couple of swings with a leaded bat. Then he put the leaded bat down and picked up his own bat. He reached up and touched his batting helmet, pushing it down on his head to ensure that it was on tight.

As John Steadman of the Baltimore *News American* wrote, "All season long for Maris, it had been a fight with time and the image of Babe Ruth darting around him like a kid chasing a shadow down a dimly lit street in the twilight of evening. He had been ahead of Ruth by nine, eight, seven, six, five, four, three, two, and finally one home run. But this was it. He had dropped one behind and this was his last chance to get even."

Wilhelm said, "In the seventh inning, Luman Harris called to the bull pen and told me to warm up because I was going to pitch the ninth. Right away, I knew I would face Roger. I had plenty of time to get ready, and my adrenaline was flowing as much for that game as any game I've ever pitched in. I would have liked to see Roger get the record; we had played together in Cleveland, and I thought he was a good guy. But I didn't want Roger to get it off me. No pitcher in his right mind wants to go into the record book like that. But I also didn't want to walk him. Roger deserved a shot at the record. With the wind behind me, I knew I had to throw the knuckleball harder for it to catch up with the wind and break like it should."

Roger told reporters, "When I came to bat, the catcher [Gus Triandos] said, 'Well, this is your last shot.' I told Gus, 'Don't think my collar isn't tight.' Then I stepped in."

Wilhelm: "My first pitch was a knuckleball that Roger took for a strike. The next pitch started high and outside, but began to drift toward the plate."

Roger: "I started to swing, but I couldn't stop. I didn't hit the ball, the ball hit my bat."

Wilhelm: "It trickled right back to me, and that was it."

Roger: "I just wish I had gone out with a real swing."

That ended the inning. Roger was in center field for Mickey that day, and John Blanchard was in right.

Blanchard said, "I carried Roger's glove out to him. I could see he was disappointed, so I told him how proud I was just to be on the same team with him. Roger smiled at me."

After the game, Roger was gracious as he told reporters, "Commissioner Frick makes the rules. If all I'm entitled to is an asterisk, then it will be all right with me. I'm the luckiest hitter in baseball history. If what I can do from now on doesn't count toward the official record, there's no sense yapping. I had my chance and I didn't quite make it."

The reaction of the press was almost vindictive.

Veteran sportswriter Fred Lieb wrote, "Perhaps it may sound corny, but my biggest sports thrill of 1961 was seeing Roger Maris hit a weak squib to Hoyt Wilhelm. . . . It wasn't that this writer had anything against Maris, but as one of the Old Guard who had been close to Ruth and who had sent word of the 60th homer over the AP wires, one can't be blamed for having nostalgic memories and rooting for the good old Babe."

Oliver Kuechle of *The Milwaukee Journal* wrote, "Maris's failure to break Babe Ruth's record of 60 homers in 154 games evokes no great regret here. . . . If the record is to be broken, it should be done by someone of greater baseball stature and greater color and public appeal. . . . Maris, aside from his threat on the record, is not more than a good big league ballplayer. He is colorless. He has never hit .300 in the majors. . . . He has been just average in the field and he is often surly. There just isn't anything deeply heroic about the man."

Bob Maisel wrote in the Baltimore *Sun*, "One thing is certain. No one will be able to accuse Roger Maris of not being able to stomach the tensest situations right down to the end."

Mrs. Claire Ruth told the *New York Journal American*, "That was one record I didn't want broken. I have the highest regard for Roger Maris. He is a fine hitter. But the Babe loved that record and he wanted to be known as the king of home runs forever."

Cab driver Val Bozella told *The New York Times*, "Maris had to do it in 154 games to count. Maybe Ruth would have hit 70 in 162 games. Who knows? Another thing, suppose Maris ate 20 hot dogs and drank 10 bottles of beer before a game? He wouldn't even be able to hit the ball out of the infield like the Babe did."

12

AFTER the 154th game, we finally rested. Even though the pennant had been won a few days earlier, just about everyone in the Yankee dugout was on edge as Roger went into those last games with Ford Frick's timetable growing heavier on his shoulders with each at bat.

"It's time to catch my breath for a day or two," said Roger. "But I still have eight games left."

We all needed a breather, a little time to think about the team and the pennant. We all remember Mickey and Roger having great years, but we weren't the kind of guys who studied the box scores or our own stats. I didn't know what I was hitting half the time, and that wasn't unusual in our clubhouse. There weren't any Pete Roses around who could tell you about every at bat and every hit. Individual stats just didn't mean that much, because you had so little leverage in contract talks, no matter what you had done. There were no agents, no free agency, and no arbitration.

"Getting that World Series check, that's where the money came from," said John Blanchard.

I've always thought that the pennant belonged to Ralph as much as anyone. Replacing Casey was an impossible situation. If he won the pennant, he was simply doing his job. If he didn't, he was a disappointment. About the only way some writers would have given Ralph credit for doing a good job would be if we had gone undefeated.

As Arthur Daley wrote, "If the hard-fibered Major won the pennant with the Bombers, so what? It was to be expected because of the rich inheritance Stengel had left. If Houk failed, he would have wasted bounty. It was damned if he did and damned if he didn't. . . . But now, it appears that Houk was like a rich man's son who handled his inheritance wisely. Yankee assets have flourished under the Houk stewardship."

Ralph and his coaches, especially Johnny Sain, probably won the pennant for us with their juggling of the pitching staff. They gambled on Whitey pitching every fourth day and won. They gambled on Arroyo when they traded Ryne Duren, and they won again. They lost Art Ditmar and Bob Turley, veterans who had been key members of the rotation for years, and replaced them with Bill Stafford and Rollie Sheldon, two guys who had yet to turn twenty-four. They picked up Bud Daley from Kansas City and stuck with him even after he lost his first four starts. By the end of the season, Daley won some very big games.

The regular lineup was relatively young but already tested by the pressures of a pennant race. Most of us had played together in the minors and later in a World Series. But few of the pitchers had the same experience.

"I'm still proud of how we put that staff together," said Sain. "Whitey was the only guy we knew we could count on, and even he was supposed to be finished. Ralph Terry . . . Stafford . . . Sheldon . . . none of them were established pitchers before 1961. Sheldon came out of Class D and won 11 games. Stafford missed a lot of 1960 and spring training in 1961 because he was in the military, but he won 14 for us. And Terry, some people were saying he was a .500 pitcher at best, he went 16–3, and that was with missing six weeks with a sore shoulder. Then there was Whitey, pitching more than ever before, and he went 25–4, the most games he ever won."

Ralph Terry said, "When you pitched for the Yankees, you just knew you were better than anyone else. We could have played the All-Star teams in 1961 and 1962 and man for man, we would have been a better team. There were times when I'd be in trouble on the mound and I'd stop for a minute and look around, and see guys like Richardson, Clete, Roger, Mickey, Yogi, and Ellie Howard. It just gave me confidence."

Bill Stafford said, "The infield was what was important to me. I was a sinkerball pitcher, and I knew if I kept them hitting the ball on the ground, they'd make the plays behind me. And if a runner got on, they'd turn a double play. I couldn't wait to get out there and pitch because I knew I was going to win."

Sportswriter Jim Ogle said, "It was a pleasure to watch the infield play. You couldn't get a ground ball through there. Seeing them was like looking at a work of art."

But there was more to the team than the obvious—hitting, pitching, and defense.

"That was the most selfless club I've ever managed," said Ralph Houk. "We thought about only one thing, winning the pennant. No one worried much about their batting average or how many runs they were driving in. Pitchers didn't care if they got the win, so long as we won. I could put on a hit-and-run play and the guys would do it. Late in the game, our power hitters would give themselves up by hitting the ball to the right side to move along a base runner. Or they would even bunt, as Roger and Mickey did. Everyone broke up double plays. It was very unusual, but that's how we played."

John Blanchard said, "There were no loners on the club. Everyone took care of everyone else and stuck up for each other. I think part of the reason so many guys had such good years was that all the pressure was on Roger and Mickey. With all the talk about home runs, they were under the gun, and the rest of us were free to play and not worry. It was a team with so much pride, we couldn't lose. It seemed like every day I'd tell my wife, Nancy, 'God, I'm just glad to be on the same team with these guys.' "

As I look back to the season, it seems that as much as almost anyone else, Blanchard was responsible for us winning the pennant because he hit so many late-inning home runs that would change the complexion of a game.

While most of us could savor the clinching of the pennant, Roger's ordeal continued. He still had 59 home runs, and he still wanted to hit at least 61, and there were so many people pulling for Roger stay right at 59.

There also was a ridiculous scene being played out by the fan who caught Roger's fifty-ninth home run ball in Baltimore. A thirty-two-year-old Baltimore fan thought he had more than a baseball in his hand. He acted as though it were solid gold.

After the game, the fan posed with Roger for a picture. Roger offered him two new baseballs for the fifty-ninth home-run ball. The fan shook his head.

"You gonna keep that ball?" asked Roger.

The fan nodded.

"Good luck to you, then," said Roger, who walked away from the fan.

Yankee public relations director Bob Fishel asked the fan what he wanted. First, he said two World Series tickets. Then he said four. Then he wasn't sure, and he kept hinting that the ball was very valuable.

Roger said the incident was stupid and to forget it. And that was the end of negotiations.

It was back to the field for Roger, who went five more days before hitting his sixtieth homer. By now, it was obvious that he had radically altered his short stroke and was trying to jack everything out of the park. He swung at bad pitches, hit pop-ups and grounders, and generally went through agony. On September 25, Roger told reporters, "I thought the pressure would be off me after the 154th game, but I was wrong. It's worse than ever now. The way this is going, I've got five games left, and I don't think I'll hit 60 by the end of the season."

But the next night, Roger hit No. 60 off Jack Fisher. It was the third inning, two outs, no one on base, and Roger stepped into a two-ball, two-strike pitch and lashed it into the third deck at Yankee Stadium, about six feet inside the foul line.

Joe Trimble wrote, "Roger Maris hit the Golden Gopher last night. . . . The Rajah swung at the sixth pitch thrown him by burly Jack Fisher. As the ball exploded from his bat, Maris froze at home plate, waiting to see if it would stay fair. He saw it crash against a concrete step adjacent to an unoccupied box seat. As it hit, Maris happily flung his bat away and began a jog around the bases in the majestic tread of the Babe. The 19,401 spectators were on their feet, screaming with delight . . . Maris toured the bases and loped into the Yankee dugout where every man shook his hand. . . . The crowd remained standing, applauding, and cheering . . . and wouldn't sit down until Maris came back out, cap in hand, and raised it with a happy bow to the fans."

This time, the ball wasn't an issue. It had bounced back on to the field and was retrieved by Baltimore outfielder Earl Robinson.

At the game was Mrs. Claire Ruth, who watched in tears as Roger's homer pounded the upper deck in right.

Roger told reporters, "This is easily the greatest thrill of my life. I stood and watched the ball because I wanted to make sure it stayed fair. I don't know what to say, how to tell you what I feel. I was in a fog. I don't remember what anyone said to me. All I know is that I'm happy."

In his last at bat, Roger singled in the bottom of the seventh. We had a 3–2 lead, and the fans started doing something strange. They were cheering for the Orioles. They wanted Baltimore to tie the game so Roger would get another at bat, but Rollie Sheldon retired the nine hitters he faced to earn the win.

The reaction in the rest of the country wasn't overwhelming to number 60. In *The Milwaukee Journal*, there was a headline, "60 Too Late." Underneath was an Associated Press story that began, "Roger Maris blasted his 60th homer of the season Tuesday night, but it came four official games too late to officially tie Babe Ruth's 34-year-old record in 154 games."

When Roger arrived at the park the next day, he went into Ralph Houk's office.

Mike Shannon said, "Roger told me about talking to Houk about a day off. Roger said he told Houk, 'I'm beat, I need a day off.'

"Houk said, 'You can't take a day off, you're going for the record.'

"Roger said, 'I can't stand it any more.'

"Houk said, 'Well, what should I tell the press when they see you aren't here?'

"Roger said, 'I don't care what you say. I need a day off, and I'm leaving.'

"Houk said, 'What should I say?'

"Roger said, 'I don't know. Tell them I went fishing.' "

I'm not sure what went on between Houk and Roger, but that was Mike Shannon's version. Ralph told the press, "I certainly think Roger is entitled to a day off. He's been through a pretty rough ordeal . . . Roger's exhaustion isn't physical, it's mental. He hasn't had a moment's peace in the last month. It's all new to him, he hasn't been trained for it. After he hit the 60th homer, he told me that he wanted a day off. I suggested he sleep on it. We talked about it again, and Roger still wanted to rest. He has been living in a madhouse, and I really admire the way he has handled it."

Mike Shannon said, "The crazy thing was when Roger got to the park the next day. He told me he was surprised that his missing a game was such a big deal in the press. All the reporters were waiting for him. Roger said that these were a lot of the same guys who asked him, 'How could you dare break Ruth's record?' Now these same guys wanted to know how Roger could take a day off.

"Roger said, 'I can't win for losing with you guys. First, you say I've played too many games to break the record. Then I don't play, and you ask how I could miss a game when I'm going for the record.'

"Roger said that just made him more determined to get that sixty-first homer."

The Yankees' last three games were against Boston at the Stadium. Bill Monbouquette started for the Red Sox before 21,485 fans. Roger was obviously swinging for the fences and more impatient than ever as he popped out twice. Monbouquette, who seemed almost as nervous as Roger, also walked him twice.

Boston manager Mike Higgins said, "We don't want to walk Maris. We want to give him a fair shot at the record, but we also want to get him out."

For the second game of the series, the crowd was 29,182, but only 19,061 paid, as it was a youth day. The left-field seats were empty, and right field was packed as fans hoped to catch Roger's sixty-first home run ball and earn the five-thousand-dollar reward offered by a Sacramento restaurant owner.

Facing Don Schwall, Roger walked in his first at bat as he got only one pitch near the plate, which he fouled off. In his next three at bats, he hit the ball right at second baseman Chuck Schilling.

And that was it. With one game left, Roger still had 60 home runs.

Roger was with Big Julie Isaacson on the eve of the Yankees' last game of the season.

"We were at his apartment with a strip of about a hundred World Series tickets," said Big Julie. "We had a bunch of envelopes, and we were putting tickets in them because Roger wanted to be sure that his friends got to see the Series. Now this wasn't Roger using his connections with the Yankees. Players have to buy their own World Series tickets, so Roger dug into his own pocket for this.

"He left tickets for Max and Hymie Asner, who owned the Stage Deli. He left tickets for waitresses, busboys, and cooks there. And for his barber, the guy who owned the barber shop, and about everyone else who took care of him all year.

"By the time we got done with all that, we had a quick bite to eat and that was it. The next morning, I picked up Roger at his apartment in Queens, and we had breakfast at the Stage, baloney and eggs one more time. Then it was off to the park. Roger was quiet and nervous. He didn't say much about wanting to hit that last home run, but I knew that was what was on his mind."

The weather was cool and clear at the Stadium. There were 23,154 fans, which seemed like a disappointing crowd considering it was Roger's last chance at the record. Of course, Frick's ruling had made it seem to many fans that the sixty-first homer would be anticlimatic.

Whitey Ford said, "Between the writers and Frick, they tried to make it out to be some kind of fluke, like the whole thing was phony. I remember thinking that day, even if Roger breaks it he won't get the recognition he deserves because of all the garbage that had been in the papers. The man was making history, and a lot of people wanted to turn the other way."

Once again, the right-field seats were jammed as the fans wanted a shot at catching a home-run ball worth five thousand dollars.

Like Ralph Terry, who started the 154th game, Bill Stafford had more on his mind than warming up.

"I already had 13 wins, and we had the pennant," said Stafford. "It had been a great year for me personally and the team, but the last thing that had to happen was Roger getting No. 61. That day, we were behind Roger more than ever because so much was at stake."

In the first inning, Boston's Tracy Stallard fooled Roger on a changeup, and he lifted a soft fly ball to left field. One chance lost.

It happened in the third inning. Stallard's first pitch was high, the next one in the dirt. The fans were booing, because the last thing they wanted to see was Roger walk. Both teams were on the top steps of the dugout. Then he threw a fastball that was out over the plate and just about at the knees.

Frank Crosetti: "When a guy on your team is going for a record, you get so into it and you find yourself pulling so hard for him, it is as if you were the guy going for the record. For me, it was like that during Joe DiMaggio's 56-game hitting streak, and when Roger hit 61."

John Blanchard: "When he came to bat, I was praying for Roger to hit one. Roger was so nervous and shook up that I prayed for God to somehow step in there and calm Roger down."

Stallard: "When Roger made contact, I knew he hit the hell out of it, but I didn't think it was going out. I turned around and saw the thing going up and up."

Ralph Terry: "When Roger hit it, I knew it was gone. It had the sound, that special crack, of a home run."

Stafford: "I was at the end of the dugout when Roger hit it. I knew he got good wood on the ball, but I couldn't see where it went because there were so many guys excited, standing up in front of me. I pushed my way through a couple players and ran on the field to see where the ball would land."

Whitey Ford: "Except for Stafford, about the whole pitching staff was in the bull pen. We all wanted a crack at catching the ball and getting the five thousand dollars."

Bud Daley: "We had been in the bull pen like that for a couple days, wearing our gloves and on our feet when Roger came up. When he finally did it, we scrambled all over the place to try and catch it, but the ball carried over our heads and into the seats."

Bob Turley: "I was one of the guys in the bull pen, and the ball landed about fifteen feet to my left and into the seats. There was a guy who had taken off his coat and was holding it above his head.

The ball landed right in that coat, but there was a guy standing in the row behind him, that was Sal Durante, and he took the ball right out of that other guy's coat."

Bob Hale: "That's exactly what happened. Even though I was an outfielder, not a pitcher, I was in the bull pen because I spent a lot of time helping out as bull pen catcher. I saw that kid Durante pick the ball right out of the other guy's coat."

Mickey Mantle: "I watched that home run from a hospital bed because of the virus. I got goosebumps when he hit it. If they had high-fives in those days, the guys in the dugout would have all busted their hands."

Bob Turley: "After Roger hit it, all of us in the bull pen got so excited that we started running to the dugout, which meant we had to go through all these narrow passageways in the bowels of the Stadium. I was running so fast that I didn't see a concrete beam, and I banged my forehead right into it. It knocked me on my butt and I thought I had fractured my skull. It knocked the wind out of me."

Roger trotted briskly around the bases, his head down. As he crossed third, something strange happened. Instead of slapping Roger on the back, as he did when most of us hit a home run, Frank Crosetti shook his hand. The only other time Crosetti shook someone's hand was when Mickey hit his five hundredth career homer.

Crosetti said, "If I had shaken hands with everyone who hit a home run for the Yankees while I was the third-base coach, I wouldn't have a hand left. In my day, we didn't go in for all that handshaking and glamour stuff. But when Roger hit No. 61, I shook his hand, I slapped his back, and then I followed him right down the third-base line, touching home plate right behind him. I felt like I had hit that home run, too."

As Roger went down the third-base line, a fan had come out of the stands, and Roger shook his hand, too.

Clete Boyer: "When Roger played, guys never came out of the dugout after a homer to wave at the fans. You hit a home run, went around the bases, keeping your head down and your cap on. That was how it was done. I understand that Ruth would go around the bases, waving his cap to the crowd, turning a home run into a show. As for Roger, he was never one to respond to the cheers. He didn't go in for grand gestures and all that crap."

Hector Lopez: "Roger was in the dugout, and the fans were screaming and pounding their feet. They wanted Roger to come out. Roger seemed sort of in a daze, but he didn't want to leave the dugout.

Finally, me, Moose Skowron, and Joe DeMaestri pushed him on to the field."

Moose: "I got chills just listening to the crowd. It was kind of funny. When we shoved Roger out of the dugout, for a second he didn't know what to do. We were yelling at him to tip his cap, and that's what he did."

When Roger came back into the dugout, there was a quiet, almost eerie silence. We saw Roger sit down, leaning his head back against the dugout wall. We didn't mean to stare or make him feel uncomfortable, but what he had done was so amazing that we all couldn't do anything but watch him. Then we heard Roger let go with a huge sigh. It was as if all the pressure he had been carrying around with him for months was finally off. I know a lot of the other guys felt the same way.

Joe DeMaestri: "We were so happy for Roger, but there was also a sense of relief. I had a feeling that Roger thought it was about time that he hit that last home run. It was like he said, 'I hit it, and now it's over. Thank God.' "

Jack Reed: "I played center that day for Mickey. When we came out for the top of the fourth inning, the fans were still cheering for Roger. I remember standing on the field, staring at Roger, almost in awe. He had just done the greatest thing ever in baseball, and there I was playing next to him, and making it even more amazing was that I was standing in Mickey Mantle's spot. This was my greatest thrill in baseball. I tell people I had the best seat in the house when Roger broke the record."

Roger's homer turned out to be the only run of the game, as Stafford combined with Hal Reniff and Luis Arroyo to throw a shutout.

After the game, the issue was the ball.

Big Julie Isaacson said "I went up to that Durante kid, and I offered him five thousand dollars right on the spot for the ball. I wanted to make sure Roger got the ball. I was writing a check, and Roger grabbed it out of my hand, ripping it up. 'Nobody should pay five grand for a baseball,' Roger told me."

Bob Hale said, "Sal Durante was a good kid. He wanted to just give the ball to Roger. He wasn't out for anything, like some of the other fans."

Joe Trimble wrote, "Sal Durante, a teenager from Coney Island who has a schnoz like the real Durante, but otherwise resembles Billy Martin, was the lucky lad who caught the ball. . . . A truck driver, Durante offered the ball to Maris, 'because it's his.' Maris, a man who thinks everything in life has to be earned and that anyone who works for something should be paid, said, 'You make whatever you can off the ball.' "

Durante bought box seats for three Yankees games that week, dreaming that he would be in the right spot when Roger connected. He told reporters, "It was a million-to-one shot. I think I'll use the money to pay off some debts, get married, and go on a honeymoon."

The five thousand dollars was offered by Sam Gordon, who owned Sam's Ranch Wagon restaurant in Sacramento.

Roger told reporters, "Now what do you think of this kid? He's got bills. He's gonna get married and he wants to give me the ball. That goes to show you that there are still some good people left in the world."

In the Boston dressing room, Tracy Stallard was mobbed by reporters, asking how it felt to be the next Tom Zachary, who was the pitcher who threw No. 60 to Ruth in 1927.

Stallard said, "I don't feel badly at all. Why should I? The guy got to a bunch of other pitchers for 60 homers before he got to me. I started against him three times, and this was the only homer he hit off me. . . . Look, I was just trying to get him out, like everyone else. I got behind two balls in the count and I didn't want to walk him. I came in with a fastball and that was it."

Roger said, "Stallard is a rookie, but he was man enough to pitch to me. He tried to get me out and I tried to hit it out."

Stallard said, "I'm not going to lose any sleep over this. I'd rather have given up the homer than walked him."

Roger said, "No one knows how tired I am. I'm happy I got past 60, but I'm so tired."

Big Julie said, "I got to know Tracy after he threw the homer to Roger. During the 1961 World Series, I didn't get to the games in Cincinnati. We watched them from my hotel suite, Tracy and I, and we sat around talking about that home run. Tracy kept saying he didn't groove that pitch. 'Julie,' he said, 'I didn't throw it up there say, here it is, hit it. I came in with a good fastball.' Tracy and I talked and talked, and I remember that he drank up all the whiskey I had in the room."

After the game, the dressing room was its usual mess with all the reporters talking to Roger.

Big Julie said, "I never saw so many writers covering a story. Roger had more guys after him than the president. Pat Maris and I waited almost five hours after the game while Roger gave out interviews. Finally, I went into the dressing room and a reporter walked right in after me. The reporter spotted Roger and asked, 'Hey, Rog, what did you hit?'

"Now, Roger had answered that question about a million times. So Roger said, 'A baseball. Yeah, I hit a baseball.' "

"Roger got rid of that guy, then he and Pat and me and my wife, Selma, went to eat at the Spindle Top on Forty-Seventh. Across the street was a Catholic church, they call it the actor's church because it caters to the theater people. That had an evening Mass and Pat and Roger said they wanted to go. Selma and I waited at the Spindle Top, and five minutes later, Roger and Pat were back. I asked Roger what happened. He said the priest spotted him and starting talking about Roger. Roger didn't want all that attention so he left."

Immediately after the season, Roger's record remained questioned. In *The New York Times*, Arthur Daley wrote, "This is a time for appraisal of values. . . . Maris wasn't the only homer-hitter in the big leagues, he was just part of an epidemic, a contagion that reached its most virulent form in the American League. The Americans produced a record 1,534 homers to go fantastically beyond their previous high of 1,091. . . . Know how many the two leagues pounded out in 1927? It was a ridiculously low total of 922. . . . The Babe alone hit more homers than any other team."

But more than twenty-five years later Roger's record comes into better focus. It is true that 1961 was the first year of expansion, which partially explained the increase in power. But the American League has gone from ten to fourteen teams since 1961, and no one has made a serious run at 61 homers. In the National League, there are twelve teams instead of eight, but again no challengers to Roger.

Roger did play 10 more games than Ruth, but he came to bat only 6 more times—684 plate appearances to 678. Of Roger's 61 homers 31 came on the road and 30 at Yankee Stadium, meaning he did more than hit the ball into the short right-field porch.

That season, many of the Yankees did better away from home. Of Mickey's 54 homers, 30 were on the road. Moose, who spent much of his career watching his 430-foot smashes being caught in New York, had 21 of his 28 homers on the road. In fact, only one-third of Moose's career homers with the Yankees were hit in New York. Ellie Howard hit 21 homers, 10 at home. In 1961, only Yogi Berra and John Blanchard had more home runs at home than on the road.

In addition to his 61 homers, Roger drove in 142 runs, scored 132 runs, and walked 94 times. The walks are a tribute to Mickey's presence behind him in the lineup. Mickey had 54 homers, 128 RBI, and 126 walks.

I've thought a lot about Roger's record, and I don't think he could have done it anywhere else but in New York. The more attention he received from the fans and media, the more stubborn he became. Not only was Roger determined to pass Ruth, he was going to prove himself to all the doubters. He did it with an incredible single-mindedness and sense of purpose. It was as if he had a vendetta against those who said he couldn't do it. He wasn't malicious, he just wasn't going to let anyone beat him down.

That year, Roger had supreme confidence in himself. It was as if he were saying, "The only person who can beat me is me." He refused to be distracted and turned all that pressure in one direction—beating the record. Being in New York, the media capital of the world, brought out the best in Roger that season. The more obstacles placed in front of him, the better he played. That is why Roger's feeling of relief was followed almost immediately by one of vindication. He had defeated everyone who was pulling against him and showed his strength at the same time.

13

I WAS in the trainer's room the day before the World Series opened when they tried to fill the hole in Mickey Mantle's leg. Mickey was still trying to figure out how a flu virus had become an abscessed hip. The first game was with Cincinnati at Yankee Stadium. Mickey was about twelve hours out of Lenox Hill Hospital when he slowly put on his uniform and went out on the field. He walked around with a limp. He tried to run once, but his abscessed hip was too painful.

"I had that bug for two weeks, then my hip got infected from the shot," said Mickey. "It couldn't have happened at a worse time with the Series starting."

Mickey was especially discouraged because he had been hurt during the World Series before. In 1951, he tore up the cartilage in his right knee in the second game with the New York Giants. In 1955, a thigh injury kept him out of four of the seven games against the Brooklyn Dodgers. In 1957, Milwaukee Braves second baseman Red Schoendienst fell on Mickey's shoulder during the fourth game, and for the rest of the Series Mickey could only pinch-run.

Mickey told reporters, "I'm weak, I'm in pain, and I can barely walk. I'm so sore."

Then Mickey went into the trainer's room. Our two trainers, Gus Mauch and Joe Soares, along with Dr. Sidney Gaynor, had Mickey down on the table. Dr. Gaynor started to unwrap Mickey, and the hole in Mickey's side was about the size of a silver dollar. Dr. Gaynor started pulling out the gauze, and he kept pulling and pulling. There seemed to be yards of it, and it was soaked with pus and blood. Moose Skowron and I were in there, and it got so bad that we had to leave the room or else we were going to get sick. It hurt just to see Mickey, so I knew his side was killing him. Ralph Houk was also in there, and he knew Mickey couldn't play.

For the benefit of the writers, Ralph prepared two batting orders, one with Mickey and one without. If Mickey didn't play, Roger would move from right to center field and Hector Lopez would play right.

Mickey tried it again on the opening day of the Series. During batting practice, Mickey was in the cage for five minutes before he could hit the ball out of the infield. When he did, it ended up in the left-field bullpen, but Mickey was still limping, and Ralph Houk wouldn't let him play.

Houk was also not about to fall into the trap that snared Casey Stengel during the 1960 World Series. There would be nothing tricky. Whitey was our star, and he started the first game. In the World Series, Ralph knew that you don't save the best for last. The Reds used lefty Jim O'Toole. Cincinnati's lineup didn't match ours, but few in the history of baseball have. The Reds were strong, however, with Vada Pinson, Frank Robinson, Gordy Coleman, Gene Freese, and Wally Post.

As it turned out, it didn't matter that Mickey missed the first game. It sounds so simple—Moose and Ellie Howard hit homers, and Whitey threw a shutout. Two–nothing, and that was it. Whitey gave up a single to Eddie Kasko in the first, a base hit to Wally Post in the fifth, and Frank Robinson walked on a dubious call of a check swing on a three-ball, two-strike pitch. The Reds never got a runner as far as second base. Nor did they hit the ball to the warning track.

But the Reds did give Clete Boyer a workout at third base.

"Clete always made great plays," said Whitey. "But no third baseman ever played better than Clete did in the 1961 Series."

Dick Young wrote, "Clete Boyer, the vacuum cleaner who looks like a man, got the raves in the Cincy clubhouse. The Reds politely praised Whitey Ford's two-hitter, but they thought Boyer fielded a no-hitter."

Clete made several nice plays, but two stood out. In the second inning, he flung his body toward the third-base line and speared Gene Freese's smash on the short hop. Still on his knees and in foul territory, Clete threw across his body to Moose at first and got Freese by a couple of steps. Six innings later, Clete made the same play on Dick Gernert, only this time Clete dove to his left instead of right, but still made the long throw from his knees.

Gernert said, "The guy is a switch-diver. I was sure my hit was through the hole. He threw the ball from his knees, I couldn't believe it, and he got me at first easy."

Vada Pinson said, "Clete Boyer gets more on the ball from his knees than a lot of third baseman do while standing up."

Jim O'Toole said, "I think Clete is better than his brother, and I always thought Ken Boyer was the best third baseman."

Clete said, "I had a game where it seemed like I could reach everything hit to me. When I think about Gernert's ball, I still don't know how I got it. I mean, I don't know how I got a glove on it, and I don't know how I got the throw over to first base. All I know is that if it were in a movie, there might have to be a hundred takes and I still couldn't do it again."

Like the rest of us, Clete loved playing behind Whitey. He said, "When Whitey pitched, we knew we'd win the first game of any series, I don't care if you're talking about a weekend in Baltimore or the first game against the Reds. Whitey was a great pitcher, but it was more than that. Having him on the mound gave us such a feeling of confidence. He would pitch, we would win, and that was how it would be. He had a way of starting winning streaks and stopping losing streaks. There's about one pitcher out of ten who is an athlete, and Whitey was in that 10 percent. That's why he was willing to try pickoff plays. He would pick runners off third base, and I don't know of any other left-handed pitchers who regularly did that. Most of the other guys were chicken, afraid to throw the ball away and let the runner score. But Whitey never hesitated.

"It's that confidence I keep talking about. Not just in himself, but in his teammates. In 1964, I was having a lousy year at the plate and Yogi was the manager. Yogi wanted Phil Linz to take my job. Phil was an all-right player, but he couldn't carry my glove. I mean, he couldn't touch me in the field. I was pretty low and not playing that much. One day, Whitey came up to me and said, 'Clete, I want you out there when I pitch, and I'm going to tell people.' That's what he did, and he had been saying things like that for years. So when it's mentioned that I made great plays behind Whitey in that 1961 Series, I feel good not just for me, but because I did it with Whitey on the mound."

The opening game was one of our best defensive efforts of the season. In addition to making a couple of super plays at second base, Bobby Richardson had three hits in the opener. But Roger came to bat four times and didn't hit the ball out of the infield.

In the second game, we had one of the few defensive collapses of the season. Clete, Yogi Berra, and Luis Arroyo all made errors. Roger got a late start on a fly ball to short center that fell for a hit. With Eddie Kasko on first base and Elio Chacon on third, a short passed ball rolled about ten feet from Ellie, who picked it up and started to throw to second base in an effort to get Kasko. But as Ellie cocked his arm, he forgot about Chacon, who was heading down the third-base line. Ellie stopped his throw and then tried to run and leap into Chacon, who slid safely into the plate ahead of Ellie's tag.

"We just played a bad game," said Ralph Terry, who started and lost. "You know things were going bad for us when Clete kicked a grounder."

The final score was 6–2 as Joey Jay beat us. Yogi's home run was about the extent of the good news.

We went to Crosley Field and had a workout before the third game. Mickey said that watching the first two games was hurting him more than his hip. He took batting practice, and about a hundred writers watched as Mickey hit five balls out of the park from the left side and one from the right—all this in just ten swings. The headline in the New York *Daily News* said, "Mantle Booms 6 HRs."

Before the workout, Ralph Houk said, "I doubt Mickey will play."

Afterward, Ralph said, "I'm not as doubtful as I was."

Bob Addie wrote in the *Sporting News*, "My biggest thrill of 1961 didn't come from any ballgame. . . . It was an off day in Cincinnati after Joey Jay had beaten the Yankees. The sun was shining, and the Yankees were getting their first look at Crosley Field. . . . Everyone was asking the same question, 'Would Mantle play?' When it was Mantle's turn to take batting practice, the crowd around the batting cage was ten deep. Mickey missed the first pitch. Mantle suddenly backed away from the plate. His mouth flew open, his face contorted with pain. He bent over the plate and pounded his bat for a few seconds, trying to regain his composure. The two thousand fans there for the workout sensed the drama. They were quiet. So were the players on the field. Time was suspended as if caught in a still photograph. Mickey straightened up and knocked the next pitch into the right-field seats. He hit five more homers. As he lumbered away, there was a spontaneous cheer from the fans and even some of the hardboiled reporters clapped in appreciation."

The next day, the game began after Dummy Hoy, a former Reds' outfielder who had just turned ninety-nine, threw out the first ball. Then the lineups were announced, and Mickey was in center field and batting fourth.

This was what changed the Series.

"I've always insisted that Mickey was a great, inspirational leader," said Bobby Richardson. "In the third game, Mickey didn't get a hit. He didn't make any super catches. But his presence, the fact that he was playing with that infected hip . . . it was a very emotional thing for us."

In the outfield, it was obvious that Mickey could barely run. Roger and Yogi made a point of taking every fly ball they could, keeping the pressure off Mickey's leg. At the plate, Mickey struck out twice, lifted a pop-up to short left, and hit a 350-foot fly ball to center. But as was always the case, when Mickey was in the lineup, Roger was a better hitter.

Billy Stafford started for us, and it was a typical Stafford game—he was the one guy on the staff who never had many runs to work with. After six innings, Stafford held the Reds to a run, but we hadn't scored off Bob Purkey. In fact, Purkey had used only forty-six pitches to shut us down.

After seven innings, we had finally scored an unearned run, but the Reds got another run off Stafford.

Entering the top of the eighth inning, Purkey had a 2–1 lead. Moose and Clete made outs, and Ralph looked at his bench and said something to John Blanchard.

"I spent eight innings watching Purkey," said Blanchard. "He had a pretty good knuckleball, and I really didn't want any part of that. But I noticed that he was throwing the first pitch over for a strike, and it usually wasn't a knuckleball. So I went up there thinking I was going to swing at the first pitch."

That's what Blanchard did, and it landed over the right-field wall.

"It would be great to say I was swinging for a homer," said Blanchard. "But it wouldn't be right. I was just glad he gave me a slider instead of that knuckleball, and I wanted to hit it hard."

This was Blanchard's fifth pinch-hit homer of the year, counting his four during the regular season, and it made the score 2–2.

That set up Roger as the hero in the top of the ninth. He had been hitless in his first ten Series at bats and had hit only one ball out of the infield. It was obvious that Roger's smooth, compact swing had suffered from his attempts to break the home-run record. He was swinging long and hard and not getting decent wood when he did manage to put his bat on the ball. But in the top of the ninth, with a two-ball, one-strike count, Roger lofted a fly ball to deep right that landed ten rows into the bleachers. The 380-foot homer gave us a 3–2 win.

Jack Reed took over for Mickey in center in the bottom of the ninth.

"Mickey could hardly move," said Ralph Houk. "Thinking back on it, I can't figure out how he lasted as long as he did that day."

Roger was excited after the game. A reporter asked him if he was swinging for a home run.

"You better believe it," said Roger. "All the way."

Stafford said, "We wanted that third game badly. After Joey Jay beat us in the second game, he told some writers that there were four or five teams in the National League that were as good as the Yankees. We were really tired of hearing all that stuff about the National League being superior. We had to live with it for a year after the 1960 World Series. I knew we weren't going to blow it again."

Whitey started the fourth game for us, needing to stop the Reds for two innings to break Babe Ruth's pitching (yes, pitching) record of 29 consecutive scoreless innings in the World Series. Whitey breezed past it with five scoreless innings, but he had to leave the game right after that. Jim Coates finished up, and we won easily, 7–0.

Whitey said, "I batted in the third inning and fouled a pitch off my toe. On the very next pitch, I fouled it off my toe in the exact same spot. Think about the odds of doing that. Anyway, after five innings my foot was swollen, and I was done."

It was a confident, fun clubhouse. We needed only one more victory to wrap up the Series, and we thought we'd do it in the next game.

Whitey told reporters, "Well, Babe doesn't have to worry. I'm not planning to go after his home run record. In fact, Roger can sleep easy, because I'm not after him, either."

It was rather ironic that someone was chasing Ruth, not just during the regular season, but in the World Series. And it was a pitcher, not a hitter.

"Poor Babe," said Whitey. "This has been a tough year for him."

Then Whitey held up the ball with which he set the record.

"Anybody want to make an offer for it?" asked Whitey. "Do I hear five thousand dollars?"

Mickey was again back in the lineup. He grounded out in his first at bat. But in his next time up, Mickey singled in the fourth inning. Then he tried to break up a double play.

"That was a mistake," said Whitey. "Twenty-five years later I still kid Mickey about making that slide. He was a great player, a Hall of Famer, but the dummy only knew how to slide on one side, and that was where he had hurt his hip. When I saw him hit the ground, I closed my eyes."

Mickey's slide had ripped open the abscess, and his uniform was crimson. The blood soaked through all the gauze and his pants, from his waist to his knee.

"When I saw the blood, I knew it was time to quit," said Mickey. "I thought my leg might get better if I ran on it. Well, it only got worse."

Wally Moses said, "I was in Ralph's office before that game when Mickey limped in and said he would play. I've never seen a guy with more determination."

Ralph Houk said, "I was in the trainer's room when they took the bandages off Mickey's leg. I couldn't believe how bad it looked. But Dr. Gaynor said Mickey couldn't get hurt any worse if he played. Mickey said he wanted to play, and when I heard Mickey Mantle saying he wanted to play, I wasn't about to bench him."

Mickey said, "They try to act like I did something heroic. I was just mad because I couldn't play. Besides, I knew we'd beat the Reds, with or without me."

After four games, the heart of the Cincinnati lineup—Gene Freese, Frank Robinson, and Vada Pinson—was 2 for 40, hitting .050.

For the second time in the Series, Bobby Richardson had three hits in a game. Hector Lopez, who replaced Mickey, and Clete each drove in two runs.

Ralph Houk: "This may sound strange, but I was more worried going into the fifth game than at any time during the season. I felt we had to win that game, or we could be in a lot of trouble. Mickey ripped up his leg too much, and he was finished for the year. Whitey's foot problem meant he couldn't pitch any more. Yogi dove for a ball and bruised his shoulder. He was also out. At first, winning the pennant was like getting a mountain taken off my shoulders. From that moment, they couldn't say a whole lot. But then we got up three games to one, and who wants to be known as the guy who blew that lead in the World Series? With all the guys getting hurt, I thought I had reason for real concern."

John Blanchard: "Ralph Houk was one of the big reasons we won that fifth game. He had started me in the second game against Joey Jay. It was a tough day to hit, a lot of shadows, and I stunk. I was 0 for 4, and I figured, well, so much for ever starting another game in the World Series. But we came to that fifth game, Jay was pitching again, and Ralph played me. Not only that, but he batted me cleanup. I said, 'Jeez, this guy believes in me.' "

Houk put Blanchard in right field, Lopez in left, and Roger shifted to center.

Lopez and Blanchard accounted for 11 of our 13 runs. Blanchard missed the cycle by a triple, as he had a single, double, and homer, good for 3 RBI and 3 runs scored. Lopez had 5 RBI with a homer, a triple, and a squeeze bunt. Ralph Terry started but got knocked out in the third inning. Bud Daley allowed 1 run in 6⅔ innings, and we won 13–5.

Daley: "We had a 6–0 lead after two innings, but Terry gave up three runs in the bottom of the third, and Houk went to me. I had pitched to one batter in the third game, and that was my first time in a World Series, but I wasn't a bit nervous. But when I came into the fifth game, I was absolutely shaking. I don't know how I got through the first couple of hitters, but I did. Then it sort of took off. The biggest thing about that game was our confidence. It didn't matter who was hurt, we knew we'd win. I mean, our guys had plane reservations from Cincinnati to their homes that night. They knew we weren't going back to New York for a sixth game, and after a while, I knew it, too."

Lopez: "I was just happy to get a chance. I got a triple to right field off Jay, and later I hit a homer to dead center. It was great to have a big game in the World Series, because I didn't play much in the regular season."

Blanchard: "I was at the plate five times and got on base five times. That's still a record."

Daley: "I wanted to finish that game. I won the game that clinched the pennant for us and I wanted to be on the mound when we won the World Series. Those still are two things I remember the most."

The Reds used twenty-one players, including eight pitchers. It really didn't matter.

In many ways, it was fitting that the heroes in that last game were Blanchard, Lopez, Daley, and Moose, who drove in three runs. Mickey, Whitey, and Roger meant so much to us, but it was the talent on the bench and the bull pen that made us a great team.

We won the World Series basically without Mickey, with Roger batting .105, with Yogi missing the last game, and with Whitey getting hurt and not able to finish his second start. We were also without Bob Cerv, who once hit 30 homers in a season. Cerv was also hurt.

As Yogi said, "We really did a job on those guys."

When we went to spring training, we expected to be in the World

Series. It was a natural progression. We didn't fear the Reds or anyone else, and the Series became an extension of the regular season. When there was a game we had to win, we found a way to do it no matter who was out. Today, so many teams depend on one or two guys. If they get hurt, the team folds. But we often played better for a week or so right after Mickey was injured. I don't know if it was because our depth was so great, or because we concentrated harder knowing we had to play better without Mickey. Even with Roger struggling and Mickey out, that bandbox in Cincinnati couldn't hold guys like Blanchard, Clete, Lopez, and Moose. They had been used to hitting balls over four hundred feet that were caught in Death Valley at Yankee Stadium. At Crosley Field, those balls were long gone. Lopez batted 9 times in the Series and drove in 7 runs. The Reds had only 11 RBI as a team. As usual in the clutch games, Bobby Richardson was great as he batted .391 in the Series.

Ralph Houk said, "When I think about it, the sixty-one club was the greatest team I've ever seen."

III

The Men

It's been twenty-five years since we won that last Series game in Cincinnati. An awful lot has happened to us in that time.

Back then, we were one in a long series of Yankees pennant winners. Now, people talk about that sixty-one club as the best of all of them. Back then, people made such a big deal about whether or not Roger would hit that sixty-first homer in 154 games. Today, you don't hear anyone talking about asterisks any more.

Twenty-five years is a long time. Naturally, I lost touch with some of the guys. I had talked with Clete Boyer, with Mickey Mantle, with Moose Skowron, and with some of the others over the years, but it had been some time since I had talked to guys like Rollie Sheldon, Bob Turley, or Bob Hale. I found out that most of them were as curious about each other as I was about them. When we'd talk, they wouldn't just ask how I was doing, but wanted to know if I'd talked with Billy Stafford, or Bud Daley, or Ellie Howard's widow, and what they were up to.

We weren't like the men of U.S. Steel, the way reporters like to write about us. We were a ball club, an awfully good ball club, made up of some very talented ballplayers who had a wide variety of backgrounds and interests. I'm glad I had the chance to get back in contact with everyone and to find out what happened to the guys who made sixty-one mean so much to me.

Ralph Houk

The thing I remember most about Ralph Houk was that he was usually alone. He didn't go out with his coaches or seem to have many friends. He was just there, by himself, always ready to talk or listen, but you had the feeling that you never knew exactly what he was thinking or what was inside him.

We knew that Ralph was a war hero. He walked into the army as a private and came out a major. He had been at the Battle of the Bulge and elsewhere. The rumor was that Ralph had led his squad up a hill, and they were attacked. When he looked around, everyone was dead, and some of those guys were his best friends. We thought that Ralph intentionally kept himself from getting close to anyone because of what supposedly happened on that hill. We never knew because Ralph didn't talk about it.

When I visited Ralph's home in Florida recently, one of the things I wanted to know was exactly what happened to him in World War II. I had been with him for ten years, counting his time as a coach, as a manager at Denver, and then running the Yankees. I knew he had been wounded and that there was still some shrapnel in his arm, and I knew he had earned some battlefront commissions. But that was it.

Oh, there was one other thing—anyone who knew Ralph Houk realized they knew a hero.

To my surprise, Ralph was rather open when I brought up the subject of the service.

"Let's go to my study," Ralph said.

He rummaged through his desk, and I thought he was just pulling out his medals—the Purple Heart and the Silver Star. But he put them down and instead handed me a piece of paper. The paper itself wasn't very impressive; there were no grandiose seals or anything, but this was what Ralph wanted me to see. It said the following:

To Lt. Ralph Houk, Cavalry Armored Troop B, 89th Cavalry and Reconnaissance Squadron.

For gallantry in action in connection with military operations against the enemy on 21 December 1944 in the vicinity of Waldbillig, Luxemborg, when adjacent platoon leaders were killed during an enemy attack on their positions, Lt. Houk acted as platoon leader for three platoons deliberately exposing himself to the withering fire, although the fire was so intense that his clothes were torn by enemy machine gun bullets. He calmly moved from one position to another directing his men. As the enemy continued to advance and realizing that his guns were ineffective against them, Lt. Houk secured a tank from an adjacent unit and fiercely directing its fire, he forced the enemy to withdraw from the area. With his gallant leadership, Lt. Houk was directly responsible for repelling the enemy attack, and by his courage and determination he reflected great credit upon himself and the military service.

The document was signed by U.S. Army Maj. Gen. John W. Leonard.

What Ralph did next also surprised me. He put down the document, stood up, and looked at a bookcase on the other side of the room.

"This is the only other thing I have from the war," said Ralph, picking up what seemed to be a pot on the top shelf. He handed it to me. It was his old army helmet.

"See this hole," said Ralph. "It came from a bullet. A sniper."

There was one hole in the front of the helmet, and it was about the size of a nickel. Where the bullet came out the other side, the hole was as big as a silver dollar.

"This was at Omaha Beach," Ralph said. "It really didn't get me. It was amazing. The bullet went right through the helmet without hitting me. It scratched the helmet liner, but the force of it knocked me over."

Ralph next talked about his first contact with the enemy: "We had knocked out a tank, and I was sent down there with five guys to see if everyone in the tank was dead. The six of us were in three lines. There was a small cliff near the tank, maybe fifteen feet high, and I figured it might be a good idea to climb the cliff and get a better view. As I was sneaking up, I glanced ahead and saw this guy. For a second, we both froze. Obviously, neither one of us expected to see the other. I couldn't believe it; this German was coming right at me. So I opened up on him with my BAR [Browning Automatic Rifle]. I just fired and fired, but I didn't hit the guy. He just took off. I remember it being snowy and muddy at the same time. We all wore these big boots, and we couldn't really move."

Then Ralph's voice trailed off.

I mentioned his promotions, and Ralph said, "Most of it came through attrition. The men ahead of me were eliminated, either wounded or killed. I never got to be a major until I left the Army. They advance you a rank when you get out."

More than ever, I was convinced that Ralph's military experience was a strong influence on him as a manager.

"That could be," he said. "If I did handle men correctly, I think part of the reason was being in the war. I saw men killed and came to an understanding of what it was like for a man being away from home. The army teaches you that you're the guy who has to make the decision. There is a chain of command, and the responsibility ends with the guy at the top.

"Combine being in the Army with being a backup catcher in the bull pen all those years, and I developed an idea of what I wanted to do if I ever got a chance to manage. I learned that the hardest people to handle weren't the stars, but the guys who didn't play every day. That's why I went out of my way to talk to the guys on the bench, let them know that they were important to the team. And they were, because they helped create the attitude in the clubhouse. I believe in talking to players and hearing what's on their minds, but I don't think a manager can get too close to people in baseball. You can't jump on a player if you've been out to dinner with him the night before. I did the same thing with my coaches. If I wanted to take one of them out for dinner, I took them all. That way, no one could say, 'Houk only goes out with Fred.' You can't play favorites."

When I touched base with the people associated with the team, I found that they had a wide range of opinions about Ralph.

Bill Stafford: "He was the best manager I ever had. He knew exactly when to pat me on the back or kick me in the pants. There was a game where a grounder was hit to the right side of the infield, and I forgot to cover first base. We hung on to win 2–1. After the game, Ralph came over and said how well I'd pitched and how great everything was. Then he said, 'And Bill, you gotta get to first base because if the next guy had hit a homer, we lose 3–2.' He knew how to build me up and keep my head in the game at the same time."

Rollie Sheldon: "I was really embarrassed in July when we played Detroit. Chico Fernandez stole home on me. I wasn't concentrating, and I forgot about Fernandez being on third. I was really down, but Ralph didn't say a word to me. Instead, he pitched me in the next game. He knew I felt awful, and he wanted to show his confidence in me."

Joe DeMaestri: "What I liked about Ralph was that he was a players' manager. By that, I mean that he put his best nine guys on the field and let them play. He didn't have to make a move every five minutes to show people he was the manager. And I wasn't one of the guys who played, but Ralph had a way of making me feel a part of the team just by talking to me."

Sportswriter Jim Ogle: "As a manager, Casey was a legend. Ralph was a rookie, but he walked into a situation where about everyone had a good year. None of the regular players got hurt, six guys hit over .300, and Ralph became a genius overnight."

Clete Boyer: "Ralph had to wait a long time to get the job. It's like going into a bakery, taking a number, and then sitting there until you're called. When you do get called, it's almost an honor. I think Ralph was honored to manage the 1961 team. He took over a great team. He didn't have to scream, and he didn't have to tell us what to do, because we already knew how to play. At his first meeting, Ralph said we knew how to play the game better than he did. So if we wanted to bunt, bunt. If we wanted to hit-and-run, then hit-and-run. While he had a great team, it was to his credit that he didn't mess it up."

Bud Daley: "After I was traded to New York, I lost my first four games. I was feeling terrible. It was after the fourth loss that Ralph came up to me in the clubhouse. I said, 'Ralph, maybe you ought to put me in the bull pen.' Ralph said, 'Oh, we won't do that. The law of averages says you're gonna win pretty soon.' No one I ever played for was as positive as Ralph."

Jack Reed: "In 1960, I played the outfield at Richmond, and I was in big trouble. I was known for my speed and throwing, and I came up with a sore arm. I was surprised when the Yankees invited me to spring training in 1961, because even I wasn't sure if I could throw. When I arrived at the Soreno Hotel, I ran into Ralph in the lobby. He shook my hand and said, 'I want to tell you something. If your arm is sound, I'll take you with me to New York so you can go in for Mantle in the late innings. We want to rest Mickey's legs.' I reported to camp the next day and I got number 15 instead of the usual 115 I'd gotten in the past. I knew I was in the plans if my arm came around, and it did."

John Blanchard: "Casey was afraid to lose a game with a young player. He thought the press would climb all over him, and he didn't want that to happen. Ralph didn't worry about what the writers or fans would say. He just did what he thought was right."

Mickey Mantle: "Ralph told me, 'You're the leader of the club, and you ought to start acting like it.' Ralph wanted me to think I was even a better player than I was. He wanted me to be more aggressive and he actually said, 'As Mantle goes, so goes the Yankees.' I used to strike out, whack the watercooler, and then walk all the way out to center field looking like I just died. Ralph wanted me to cut that crap out."

Ralph also was very aware of the beating Clete's ego took in the 1960 World Series. Eighth was probably the best spot for Clete in the lineup, considering the speed we had at the top and the power in the middle. But early in the year, Ralph used Clete leading off. It was to let him know that the manager had confidence in him. Casey had Clete looking over his shoulder before he went up to hit. By batting Clete first and seldom taking him out for a pinch hitter, Houk removed that anxiety. Once Clete saw that Ralph believed in him, he went back to the eighth spot and had a nice year. It might have seemed strange for Clete Boyer to lead off, but none of us questioned Ralph. He was the Major, a guy we knew and trusted. We figured Ralph had a good reason for whatever he did.

We backed Ralph because we knew he was behind us. If we lost a tough game, Ralph would take the heat instead of blaming someone in the clubhouse. In 1961, seven of the eight starting players had at least five hundred at bats. Ralph did believe in making decisions about players and living with them. Nevertheless, he was most effective with the guys on the bench.

"Those are the players you have to worry about," said Ralph. "I learned a lesson in 1947 when I was a part-time catcher. I used to play against left-handers, and I was hitting pretty well. Bucky Harris was the manager, and one day he stopped using me against lefties. He never said a word why, and I was afraid to ask. In those days, if a bench player opened his mouth, there was a good chance he'd end up in Podunk. That's why I made a point of talking with the reserves. In fact, a couple times I had starters ask me if I was mad at them. I asked why, and they said I hardly spoke to them. I thought if you were playing and doing well, you were happy. But it's the guys on the bench who can sink a ball club or win a pennant. My job was to make them feel a part of the team and keep them ready for the times when they had to play."

Early in the season, Ralph was booed. We didn't move into first place until June, and the pennant race was tight until early September. A lot of fans and writers wanted Casey back.

"I used to wonder how Ralph could keep it all inside," said John Blanchard. "You knew his stomach was churning. He had to be nervous. He was human, wasn't he? But it seemed that Ralph never changed."

"It really wasn't that bad," said Ralph. "I knew we would win. I just knew it because of the players. I had more problems with the writers than anything else. Some of them simply resented the fact

The Major, Ralph Houk, and the city of Saint Petersburg welcomed the Yankees back to spring training for the start of the 1961 season.

Above: The core of the '61 club gathered for photo day during spring training *(from the left):* Moose Skowron, Bobby Richardson, Mickey Mantle, Ellie Howard, Yogi Berra, John Blanchard, and Clete Boyer. *Below:* The extended Yankee family enjoys a day in the sun in Florida.

Above: Pitching coach Johnny Sain imparts his wisdom to three young hopefuls: Bob Meyer, Rollie Sheldon, and Howard Kitt. *Below:* Houk, at home in either uniform: as new manager of the Yankees or back in his days in the Marines.

Above left: Mickey Mantle shows his awesome power from the left side of the plate. *Above right:* Roger Maris watches his 60th homer clear the fence. *Below:* A rare quiet moment for Roger and Mickey in the spring of '61.

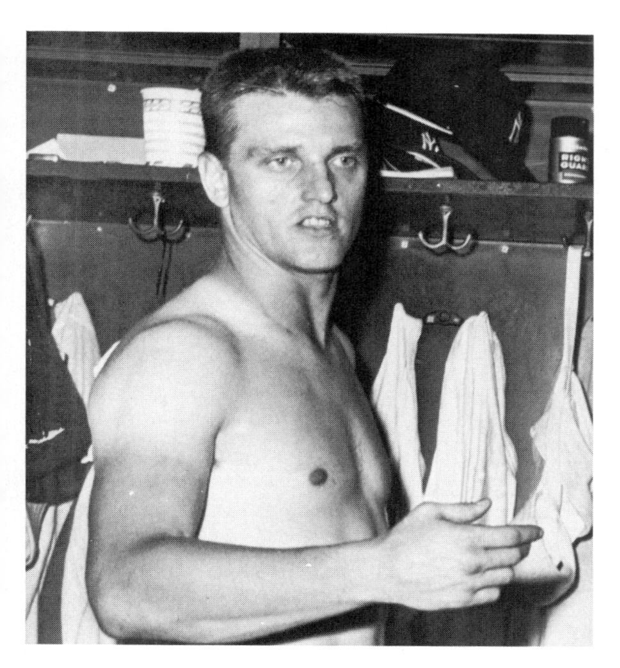

Maris faces reporters in Fenway Park after again failing to connect for No. 60 in the last week of the season.

How Mickey and Roger managed to smile through so many photos together in '61 is a complete mystery; they couldn't turn around without being asked to pose for one.

Yankee Stadium erupts as Maris drives No. 60 into the night.

Moose Skowron, Whitey Ford, and Ellie Howard in the locker room after winning the first game of the '61 Series; Whitey pitched a two-hit shutout, and Moose and Ellie each homered.

Mantle grimaces in pain as he tries to swing during Game 4 of the Series. His abscessed hip, a result of "The Shot," kept him out of all but two games. *Below:* Whitey Ford delivers the first pitch of Game 4, in which he broke Babe Ruth's other record, for consecutive World Series shutout innings.

Bud Daley accepts congratulations from John Blanchard after recording the final out of the Series.

Left to right: Roger Maris, John Blanchard, Ellie Howard, Ralph Houk, Ralph Terry, and Yogi Berra celebrate in the locker room.

The catching corps: John Blanchard *(left)*, who would have started anywhere else, and the two men who blocked his path: Yogi and Ellie *(below)*.

Right: Bob Turley, the man who threw fast and could think even faster. *Below:* Ralph Terry conducts a clinic for a group of aspiring pitchers in Fort Lauderdale.

Above: Houk helps Rollie Sheldon listen to the watch he was awarded as the outstanding rookie of the spring. *Right:* Luis Arroyo rests on the bench in the bull pen, waiting for the call in the late innings to come and seal another Yankee win.

Opposite above: The infield, in its usual alignment *(left to right)*: Clete Boyer, Tony Kubek, Bobby Richardson, and Moose Skowron. *Left:* Skowron where he was most at home: with a bat in his hands. *Above:* A young shortstop named Kubek.

Opposite below: Bobby Richardson takes his cuts in the batting cage. *Above:* Clete Boyer makes the play the '61 Reds are still talking about, diving to his right and throwing from his knees.

Right: Bob Hale, our class clown who grew up to be a high school principal.
Below: Ellie Howard and Bill Stafford in the Yankee locker room at Comiskey Park.

Whitey Ford—"The Chairman of the Board"—one of the greatest, if not the greatest, money pitcher ever.

When the chase was finally over: Roger with Sal Durante, the kid who caught the 61st home-run ball.

that I was there. You know how some of those guys were, they always knew more than we did. Casey would talk to those guys all day long, and he'd eventually let something slip about a player and they'd have a story."

Ralph did learn a few things from Casey.

"I could never talk like Casey, but I used some of his methods with the press. If you made a decision during a game and afterwards it didn't look very good, you'd better have some reason, even if it's a lie. They don't know if it's a white lie. There was a time when Casey used Ellie Howard as a pinch hitter in Yankee Stadium against a good curveball pitcher. On the surface, it seemed like the worst thing you could do. Ellie was a right-handed hitter who liked fastballs. Also, Yankee Stadium was a terrible place for a right-handed hitter. I was on the bench that day, and I'm sure that Casey wanted to send someone else up there, but he called for Ellie. When Ellie got to home plate, Casey realized he'd made a mistake, but it was too late. He'd wanted a left-handed hitter. But Ellie got a hit, and we won the game. When the writers asked Casey why he used Ellie, he said, 'You guys probably don't know what a great record Ellie has against so-and-so.' Actually, Ellie never got a hit off the guy, but Casey always had an answer ready. And if a writer said, 'Casey, Ellie didn't have a hit off that guy,' Casey would say something like, 'But I remember Ellie hitting the ball hard off him.' He always had an answer, and I tried to do the same."

Ralph didn't quite equal Casey in terms of longevity—Casey managed for twenty-five years compared to twenty for Ralph—but some of the lessons he learned from Casey, combined with winning three pennants in his first three seasons, helped Ralph to last a long time.

The irony is that Ralph never won a pennant after those first three years with the Yankees. He managed a lot of very weak clubs, especially the Yankees of the late 1960s and early 1970s and the Detroit Tigers of the middle 1970s. Ralph's final record was 1619–1531, for a .514 winning percentage.

Ralph can make one claim that even eluded Casey, though—he was never fired. He left the Yankees on his own in 1973 and moved on to Detroit. After the 1978 season, Ralph retired for the first time. He had taken over the Tigers in 1974, and they had a 72–90 record in his first season. They were 86–76 in Ralph's last year.

But he couldn't stay away. "Tony, I got bored. How much golf can you play? That's why I took the Boston job in 1981."

Houk managed the Red Sox until 1984, and this time it seems he has retired for good. Ralph lives in Coral Gables, where he has found that you can play a lot of golf and spend plenty of time fishing without going crazy, assuming you really are ready to call it quits.

Bob Turley

Bob Turley was at his best whenever the attendance at the fourth World Series game was announced. We would be sitting in the dugout and word would come over the public address system that there were something like 47,388 fans in the park. We would all turn to Bob, and it would only take a few seconds for him to say, "Well, guys, our take is $7,528.36 a man."

He was never wrong. I mean, Bob would get our World Series share not just right, but right to the last penny.

Bob had been an exceptional pitcher for us. He was a guy who threw hard and then threw even harder when he got in trouble. Sometimes the ball went over the plate, and sometimes it didn't. That's how it is when your nickname is Bullet Bob. It wasn't until Whitey Ford taught Bob a curveball that he became something special. In 1958, Bob won 21 games because the hitters couldn't believe he had a breaking pitch. They would just stand there, staring and waiting for his fastball.

By 1961, Bob's real role was not on the mound, but in the dugout. He had a bad arm that would eventually need surgery, but his mind was astounding. Bob would sit on the bench, watch a pitcher throw for an inning, and then say, "I can call this guy's pitches."

And he could.

It didn't matter if the pitcher threw hard or relied on slow stuff. Give Bob two innings, and he would predict about 140 out of 150 pitches.

"Mickey Mantle said I called about 25 percent of his home runs," said Bob. "During most of the game, I'd sit in the bull pen. But when it was Mickey's turn to hit, I'd run down to the dugout, and we'd go to work."

I can still hear Bob's shrill, penetrating whistle.

"That's how Mickey and I communicated," he said. "My whistle was the kind that could penetrate the loudest crowd noise. Mickey and I would always start by assuming the pitcher would throw a curve. If I didn't whistle, Mickey knew it was a breaking pitch. If I did, he got set for a fastball. If I missed a signal, Mickey would touch his cap, and I'd know. If he couldn't hear me, Mickey would touch his stomach."

Bob was able to determine what a pitcher would throw the same way he could break down our World Series shares—fast and accurately. His mind was always churning. He couldn't just sit on the bench and wisecrack his way through a game like Whitey Ford.

"It started when I was with the St. Louis Browns," said Bob. "That was 1951 and 1952, and you couldn't imagine how bad those teams were. I was a starting pitcher, which meant I had four days on the bench between starts. Well, there is nothing duller than sitting there day after day and watching us get beat, so I had to come up with something to keep my head in the game.

"Early in my career, I saw someone stealing pitches. It intrigued me. I liked the challenge, and I started doing it. After a while, it got to the point where I could do it left and right. Soon, I started betting guys on the bench and winning regularly by calling pitches. When I was traded to New York, Casey Stengel watched me in the dugout. The Browns or Baltimore never used me to call pitches, but Casey did. He hooked me up with Mickey and a few of the other hitters.

"During some games, I'd go into the television room and have them put the camera tight on the pitcher so I could get a good look at his motion. Sometimes, you could tell what was coming by the way a guy held his glove or gripped the ball. There were always little clues."

Why was this more effective with Mantle than other hitters?

"Some guys don't like to know what is coming," said Bob. "With others, you tell them here comes a curve, and they would swing at it, even if the pitch bounced five feet in front of the plate. Poor Moose [Skowron] was like that. After a while, Ralph Houk told me not to call any pitches for Moose because he'd swing at everything.

"Roger Maris only wanted pitches from a few guys who gave him a tough time. Mickey was the one who really liked to know what was coming. He'd tell me to guess, even if I wasn't sure. Mickey once said, 'Bob, you know more about pitching than I do, so tell me what you think is coming, and you'll still be right at least 70 percent of the time.' After a while, I'd tell Mickey what to look for in a pitcher's motion, and he was able to call his own pitches. He had great vision."

If for no other reason than his ability to call pitches, I knew that Bob was a smart guy. He used to work crossword puzzles and while the rest of us were reading the *Sporting News*, he'd be sitting there with his head buried in *The Wall Street Journal*.

That's why I say that I had no worries that Bob would end up in the Salvation Army soup line after he quit baseball, but I was stunned when I found out the following:

He has a home and two acres on the Gulf of Mexico in Marco Island, Florida.

He has his own yacht, complete with a captain.

He has his own jet, complete with a pilot.

He also has a home in Atlanta, complete with servants.

Then Bob told me this: "You know, Tony, the most I ever made as a player was $35,000 a year. Now, I make more than that in a day."

I believe it.

Bob isn't the kind of guy who starts talking about a roll of quarters and makes it sound like a million bucks. The words come from his mouth matter-of-factly as if he were telling you what was on his grocery list. So when Bob says, "We've been very fortunate, we have all the niceties of life," I believe him.

All I know is that he isn't doing too bad for a guy who never went to college and whose father was a meat-packer.

"This is part of the story I tell," said Turley. "Basically, what I've made I've made on my own. What I've learned about business has been self-taught or from courses I took while working."

And how did Bob make all this money?

"Good investments," he said.

Great sounds more like it.

It is a complicated story, one of a guy who started small and ended up big, of a guy who bought low and sold high.

Since he retired from baseball in 1965, Bob has owned and/or run the following businesses: a bowling alley, a restaurant, a night club, a furniture company, a stockbrokerage firm, and an oil company.

"I've probably been in at least thirty different companies," he said. "I'd get involved with a business that was struggling, build it up, and sell out. Then I'd move to something else that was in the same position. I've been able to do it in most areas of business."

But it is the A. L. Williams Insurance Company that pays for the plane, the boat, and the home on the shore.

"Last year we did about $55 billion in business," said Turley. "We do more business than Prudential and Metropolitan Life combined, and I have sixteen thousand people working for me."

It was almost as if Bob were speaking another language. I'm not much on corporate dealings. I'm in television, but I don't even have an agent. But Bob and I do have one thing in common—our time with the Yankees later helped our careers.

"The toughest thing in business is getting important people to listen to your ideas," said Bob. "When you're a former player, especially a former Yankee, that will usually get you through the door. Then it is up to you to know your product. It's funny. You need tremendous confidence to make it as a player. You have to believe that no one can beat you. It's the same thing in business. In all the ventures I've been in, I'd buy a business that was in trouble because I believed I could turn it around. There are certain elements that must be present to make a business a success, but you have to trust yourself to know that you can get into this thing and in two years turn it around so you can sell it for a profit."

And what does Bob remember about the Yankees?

"That part of my life is like a dream. I almost think it never happened because I'm so deeply involved with what I'm doing now. But sometimes, I remember a game, one of those in the World Series or an important one for the pennant race, as if it had just ended five minutes ago. A lot of different games go through my mind. That's when I know I was there, and I really treasure those times."

Clete Boyer

"Did I ever tell you about me and Roger on the golf course?" asked Clete Boyer.

We were in a restaurant near Clete's home in Largo, Florida. Clete was one of the first players I sought out because he is a good friend. And in many ways, to know Roger Maris was to know Clete

Boyer. For five years, they roomed together with the Yankees, and they stayed in touch after Roger retired in 1968 to run his beer distributorship. While Roger remained out of baseball's mainstream, Clete stayed in the game as a coach with Atlanta and later Oakland. I was surprised to find out that Clete and Roger had thought about being together in baseball once more.

"The last time I saw Roger was in May of 1985," said Clete. "I was coaching with the A's, and I got a couple days off to visit him. I could tell that Roger was near the end, and I told the front office I had to see Roger. If they didn't like it, I didn't give a damn. The guy had cancer, and believe me, I knew what that meant. I went through it with my brother Ken—the treatments, the hopes that he might be getting better, and the end when you know he's not. I knew in my gut that I had better get down to Florida and talk to Roger.

"So I drove down, and the night before I was to go to Roger's house, I called. His wife [Pat] said, 'Clete, I don't know if Roger will be feeling well enough for you to come by.' I figured maybe I should just go back. But the next morning, Pat called and said, 'Roger had his first good night's sleep in three weeks. He'd love to see you.'

"I hadn't been with Roger for five months, and I was stunned by the way he looked. Roger saw my expression and said, 'If you think I look bad now, you should have seen me three months ago. I looked in the mirror, and I couldn't believe it was me I was seeing.' That was Roger, straight about everything, even what cancer was doing to his body. We spent the morning and afternoon talking, and I thought it might be best if I went. The man was sick, but Roger made me stay. Then he said, 'Let's go watch my kid play golf.'

"The next thing I know, we're out walking the course and watching Richard play. Roger was so happy just to be outside on a nice day, and he got a kick out of seeing his son hit the ball. I mean, think about how it was to be like Roger. You're sick, you're hurting, and you know you're dying of cancer. You got a great family. You got a beer business that covers eight counties and probably makes you a half-million a year. You're fifty-one, and what else could you want? But that afternoon on the golf course, Roger almost made dying of cancer beautiful because he was so content with himself. It's all strange. My brother Ken, Roger, and Ellie Howard all died at fifty-one. Ellie and Roger even died on the same date, December 14."

For eight hours, Clete and I talked. We had lunch, and they took away those plates and brought some more beer. A few hours later, it was time for dinner, so we ordered and ate again. Then we walked outside and ended up standing in the parking lot, talking some more, and much of the conversation was about Roger.

"I called Roger a couple months before he died and said I'd like to see him again," said Clete. "Roger said, 'I don't feel so good now. Tell you what, when I'm doing better I'll call you and we'll get together.' I waited a month, and Roger never called. So I started calling him, but I never could get him. I knew Roger was really sick, because when he said he'd call you back, he'd call you back. If he said he'd be some place at five o'clock, he was there at five o'clock. It turned out that they were taking him to different hospitals, one in Tennessee and another in Houston.

"In our last conversation, Roger told me that one of his biggest dreams was that I would become a big-league manager. Roger said that when he was in New York [in April 1985] to throw out the first ball, he told George Steinbrenner that he ought to hire me to manage the Yankees. He was telling all kinds of people that I ought to be a manager. See, me and Roger came from the same school. Maybe it was the old school, at least that's what guys say about us today. But what was wrong with the old school when it produced guys like Roger Maris?

"Me and Roger were a lot alike. For five years, we were roommates, and we saw each other more than we saw our wives. And if I ever got a manager's job, Roger was all set to come back and be my hitting coach. We had talked about it for years. The writers and the public, they didn't know Roger. They didn't know how much he loved the game, how much he missed baseball. Don't misunderstand. Roger was happy in Florida. He had a great family and had time to watch his kids grow up, but few people knew what he could have contributed to the game if someone had just asked him. But nobody did. And if you knew Roger Maris, you knew he was not about to go begging for a job."

I had spoken to Pat Maris on the same subject, and she said, "Roger talked about Clete being a manager all the time. Yes, I think he would have gone to work with Clete if he had gotten the Atlanta job in 1981. He loved Clete and always said Clete would be a great manager."

In the spring of 1986, Clete was out of baseball for the first time in thirty-one years. He said he was doing fine, but clearly he was suffering from a serious case of withdrawal. After he and Oakland broke off at the end of 1985, Clete wanted to coach again. He missed going to the park and seeing the guys, but he refused to make calls or write letters letting people know he was interested. Before the 1986 season, there were rumors that Phil Niekro would be the Braves' next manager, and Clete had plans to coach under Phil, but that fell through, and Phil ended up pitching for Cleveland.

Meanwhile, Clete ended up at home. His wife, Terry, owns a floral shop and is an airline stewardess. "She's very motivated, likes to work," laughed Clete.

"Roger and I looked at it the same," he said. "You go out, work hard, and people notice. Then they ask you to come work for them. Why should Roger Maris or me get on the phone and call every damn team in baseball for a job? It's not how we were raised. Okay, look at it this way. The owners, what do they know about baseball? They don't even know where to go for advice, and they get conned into doing things by guys who are supposed to be baseball men, but they don't know any more than the owners.

"Let me put it to you like this—if these guys are so smart, how come they let a guy like Roger sit down in Florida for all those years and never even asked him if he wanted to coach? Didn't they know what a strong influence he could have been on young players? Couldn't they see that a guy with Roger's desire and knowledge would love to share it? What Roger wanted was a chance to go to the park early, to be around the guys, and work with young hitters. Anyone who talked to him for more than a few minutes could figure that out.

"It still makes me so mad just to think about it. All these people thought Roger hated baseball, and what he really wanted to do was get back into baseball. Maybe Roger shouldn't have said some of the things he did after he left baseball, but he was hurt by a lot of the things that happened to him, especially in New York after 1961. So he put up this false front, this 'baseball can go screw itself' attitude. Roger was proud, hardheaded, and stubborn. When he said something, he felt determined to stick by it even if he really didn't mean it. So when some people would suggest to Roger that he contact some teams about a coaching job, he'd say he wasn't interested.

"Here is what it was. Roger didn't want to embarrass himself. He didn't want to be somebody's celebrity first-base coach. He knew what happened to Mickey Mantle when he came back to coach with the Yankees. It was a joke, and Mickey said as much. Roger didn't want any team saying it had Roger Maris as its first-base coach so it could draw a few more people. Roger didn't want to just pick up batting helmets, pat guys on the back, and tell them how many outs there were."

Obviously, Clete becoming a manager was more than Roger's dream. It was something Clete craved for a long time. In 1981, the Braves talked to him about the position, but owner Ted Turner hired Joe Torre instead. When Billy Martin left Oakland, there was some talk that Clete might take his place. After all, when Martin was the manager, it was Clete who did Oakland's pregame preparation. But it was Steve Boros, not Clete, who took over for Billy. And it was Jackie Moore, not Clete, who took over for Boros. This was hard for Clete to handle, especially since it was Clete who gave the signs at third base for two years when Moore was the manager. Jackie told Clete, "Do whatever you think is best." Clete ran the game for the A's. That's also why Roger's death was so devastating to Clete. Not only did he lose a great friend, but the two men lost their dream.

"Roger and I talked a lot about how it would be if I got to be a manager. I told him that his job would be to work with the hitters before the game, talk to them when they were in slumps or looking for help. During the game, he would stand next to me in the dugout. I'd need advice and a cool head. That was one thing; Roger knew how to handle pressure. How else would he have been able to hit the sixty-one homers when the whole world was jumping down his throat? Where Roger would have meant so much to me was after the games. We'd have a few drinks, unwind, and talk about what happened.

"Roger Maris was a student of hitting. He used to watch films of himself hit after he retired and pick out the things he did wrong. That was one thing he did regret, that baseball didn't use films as much as it does now. 'If I had seen myself bat, I could have been a .300 hitter,' Roger would tell me. 'I can see the things I did wrong, and I know I can do the same for other guys.' "

This reminded me of a conversation I had had with Whitey Herzog. Whitey told me, "Roger liked hitters and wanted to work with them. When I managed Kansas City, Charlie Lau was my hitting coach. With a number of hitters, Charlie had a lot of success, but he couldn't do anything with John Mayberry. John was our first baseman—big, strong, and lots of power. But in 1976, John had slipped from 34 to 13 home runs. In the spring of 1977, I brought Roger to spring training so he could work with John. You could see that Roger enjoyed being back. He liked to work with John around the cage, and I think Roger helped him. If nothing else, John got some of his power back and hit 23 homers."

Clete had heard the same story from Whitey Herzog.

"That's exactly what I'm talking about," said Clete. "You see, Whitey knew what Roger could do. I knew it. But how many other guys did? When I think about the people they have now as hitting coaches . . . well, it makes you wonder. I never claimed to be a great hitting coach, but I would have been known as one if I were the batting coach for George Brett or Don Mattingly. Those guys don't need coaches. And Charlie Lau? You gotta be kidding. He had one theory—ping, ping, ping. Make everybody into a singles hitter. I'm like Ted Williams. I think Charlie Lau set hitting back twenty-five years.

"Roger knew that it isn't George Brett who needs a coach, but the guy who was batting .240 and hadn't hit the ball out of the infield for a week. Those are the guys Roger would have helped. Roger was great at building up your confidence. He did it for me all the time when we played."

As a player, Clete was the best third baseman I've ever seen, bar none. Brooks Robinson was great. Graig Nettles was great. But Clete was a better defensive player. Brooks and Graig received more publicity because they were better hitters than Clete. Brooks and Nettles played deep, daring hitters to bunt on them. Clete played shallow and took away the bunt. He was also quick enough to cover the ground in both directions, and no one could dive to the right, backhand the ball, and throw from his knees like Clete. The statistics show that Clete led all third basemen in putouts, double plays, and assists from 1961 to '63, but the Gold Gloves always went to Brooks Robinson.

Frank Crosetti, who had been with the Yankees for more than forty years, told me, "Clete was as a good a third baseman as I've ever seen. He never got the publicity because he didn't hit for a lot of power or for a high average. The only difference between Brooks and Clete was that Brooks was a better hitter, not fielder."

"Clete was a much smoother fielder than Brooks," said Bill Stafford. "The play Clete made that still amazes me was on the ball hit down the line. He'd dive for it, catch it across his body, and then throw from foul territory to first base, and the guy never got off his knees. It fascinated me that anyone could do it. And Clete didn't do it once a year, he did it day after day."

"Most players have a special skill," said Clete. "Mine was that throw that Stafford talked about. After you figure out you have this talent, you get kind of cocky, and you want to do it again and again."

Clete was with the Yankees in the best and worst of times. He was there for the pennants in 1960–64, and he was there when the team hit the bottom of the standings in 1966. Meanwhile, he was stuck in Yankee Stadium and its Death Valley in left field, which killed Clete's power.

"Those last few years were tough on me and Roger," said Clete. "Tony, you had retired. Bobby Richardson had retired. Mickey and Whitey were showing their age. Moose had been traded. Roger had the hand injury. A lot of the guys who had made us a great team were gone, hurt or old. Ralph Houk came back to manage, but he had changed. He went from being a guy who I thought walked on water when he first managed [1961–63] to being the general manager. I used to think he stood up for us against the front office, but then it turned out he *was* the front office. When he came back in 1966, everything was different. To tell you the truth, I don't think he much liked me and Roger. Ralph's great club was gone. I mean, the guy had gone from a bull pen coach to a genius in one year, from 1960 to 1961. But in 1966, everything had gone to hell, and I think Ralph was looking for an excuse to dump me and Roger.

"And there were incidents. In the spring of 1965, Joe DiMaggio, Hal Reniff, Roger, and myself were having dinner at this nice place on the ocean. We were sitting near the door. A guy was leading his girlfriend out the door, and she spotted Joe D. and Roger. She asked them for an autograph, and as she walked away, Reniff made a crack about her. The guy came over and asked us to apologize to his girlfriend, and Reniff insulted the guy. Back and forth it went. You know how it is after you've been playing golf all day and have had a few drinks.

"Finally, the guy leads his girlfriend out of the place, but then he comes back and starts in on me. He thought I said something about his girlfriend. We go outside and keep arguing. The guy wants to fight, and we get into a scuffle. I hit him and knocked out two of his teeth. Roger and Reniff had gone outside with me. Joe D. was the smart one; he cleared out and left by another door.

"Anyway, the guy goes to the hospital, and they take some pictures. His lips were gorgeous, all puffed out. First, the cops arrested Roger because the guy didn't know what or who hit him. So they arrested me. Eventually, I go to court, and it turns out there are about thirty thousand people who saw the fight. It only lasted about thirty seconds, and the only guys there were Roger and Reniff. It ended up costing me five grand. But the kicker was that the guy was a male model. For two years, I had to listen to guys ragging me because I hit a male model.

"Like I said, all these things added up. At the end of the 1966 season, the Yankees decided to clean house. Roger goes to St. Louis for Charley Smith, and I get traded to Atlanta for Bill Robinson. It didn't matter that I was the only guy left who could play the infield or that Roger was still a good player. If they had any real brains, they could have packaged us together and gotten something good for us. But that's the kind of moves they were making back then."

When Clete went to Atlanta, those fly balls to left that were caught in New York went out of Fulton County Stadium as Clete had 26 homers and 96 RBI in 1967. He played with the Braves through 1971 when he was called in by Commissioner Bowie Kuhn for supposedly betting on football pools. Clete said that a lot of guys did it and that there were pools in every clubhouse, but the commissioner wanted to make an example out of Clete. Basically, he was blackballed. No one would touch him, and Clete ended up playing in Japan and eventually returned to the States as a coach.

"I'd still like to coach, but it would have to be under the right circumstances," said Clete. "The attitude in baseball that bothers me is that there are players earning five hundred thousand dollars who don't know how to put on their jocks. You have to tell them when to bunt, when to run, when to wipe their nose, and when to have a drink. Some of these players are babies, and about 30 percent of them don't care about winning; all they want is a spot on the roster. And there are too many managers and coaches who only care about keeping their jobs. I look at a lot of the guys managing today, and it seems like they're all cut from the same mold. There is so much politics involved. I mean, who says you have to have been a lousy player to be a good manager? Why didn't someone ever talk to Mickey Mantle about managing?

"When you're a dedicated coach who has been in the game for thirty-one years, it's hard to answer to an owner or someone in the front office who doesn't have a clue about what is going on. I know I can be a good manager, but I guess I never played the right games. When Billy Martin gets another job, I'll go to work for him. Billy understands what I do for a team, and he knows I can run a team. He appreciates what I do, and that's what a coach needs."

Yogi Berra

One spring morning, I found Yogi Berra feeding baseballs into a pitching machine. We were in Kissimmee, Florida, and Yogi looked like a Hawaiian pineapple on legs thanks to the Houston Astros uniform he was wearing.

Yogi spotted me and gruffly asked, "What are you doing here?"

That's a typical Yogi greeting.

We were standing on the mound behind the pitching machine, and I started to tell him about this book.

"So you're the guy writing the book," he said. "I heard somebody was writing a book. They want me to write one, too, but I don't know if I should."

We talked for about a half hour as Yogi dropped balls into the pitching machine. The Houston pitchers were practicing their bunting, and periodically they would yell at Yogi to quit talking to me and put balls in the machine. It was just like when Yogi caught. He drove the batters insane with his constant chatter, and then he would toss pebbles into their shoes.

Finally, I convinced him to get off the mound and talk about 1961 for a while.

"Can't do it right now," he said.

"Why?" I asked.

"Gotta shave."

"For what? This isn't TV. I just need you to talk into this tape recorder for a few minutes."

"Gotta look good for that, too," he said.

I thought Yogi might have been kidding. Yes, he really said things like "no one goes there anymore, it's too crowded." But Yogi also didn't say a lot of the words sportswriters have put in his mouth.

In this instance, all I know is that Yogi showered and shaved before he sat down to talk.

I only had to be around Yogi for a few minutes to be reminded that he remains one of the most popular men in sports. Old guys and young kids recognize him instantly, even in a Houston uniform. And they all want his autograph, even though his latest job is as a low-profile coach to help out first-year Astros manager Hal Lanier.

The fact is that people just like Yogi. I don't know if it's because of his nickname, his looks, or because of the things he says. For whatever reason, most people seem to think Yogi is kind of a cute character despite the fact that he usually isn't glib.

In the outfield, Yogi wasn't pretty, but he had an accurate arm, and he reached more balls than you'd imagine. I don't know how he did it, but Yogi just got there in time to make the play. He was a great clutch hitter and a smart catcher. Basically, Yogi played like a guy who had tremendous insight into the game.

The New York press always took care of Yogi. He could be curt and sometimes surly in his answers, but the writers never slashed away at him. That certainly wasn't the case with some other guys who weren't sophisticated. A young Mickey Mantle and Roger Maris come to mind.

I really think Yogi's looks were his shield. I mean, how could anyone write or say anything nasty about Yogi Berra?

Before the 1961 World Series, Dan Daniel wrote this in the *Sporting News:* "Here we have the most sociable, best-liked player in the American League. Most of Yogi's popularity stems from his genuine, down-to-earth quality as a man. Some of it comes from his being of Italian descent."

That's the effect Yogi has on people. Other guys who were Italian had to fight all the tired Mafia clichés, but with Yogi it became an asset, at least according to Dan Daniel.

And Daniel also had this to say: "The greatest move Berra ever made was to marry Carmen Short, who was a waitress in a St. Louis restaurant when he met her. Carmen is beautiful. Carmen is sympathetic, the ideal ballplayer's wife. Carmen is the financial genius of the family. . . . Berra is a very wealthy man."

Mickey Mantle and a lot of the other guys always thought Yogi was, let us say, passionately frugal. When you were in a restaurant with Yogi, he never showed very quick hands when a waiter dropped the bill on the table.

As Casey Stengel once said, "Yogi looks like he can't run, but when they bunt the ball in front of the plate he jumps out at it like he just spotted a silver dollar on the ground."

Before games, we had to autograph about ten dozen baseballs, and we could never figure where they all went. Then we started hearing Yogi stories, about how he had traded an autographed ball for a meal at this restaurant or how had swapped a couple balls for a suit at that department store. In 1961, autographed Yankee baseballs were precious, and Yogi operated on an Indian barter system.

When it came to money, Yogi never missed a trick.

Now, he is easily a millionaire, and he probably got there on his Yoo-Hoo stock alone. Yogi didn't become president of Yoo-Hoo by attending Harvard Business School, but he could have taught the professors in Cambridge a few things.

For instance, he had almost the entire 1961 Yankee team wearing Yoo-Hoo T-shirts under their uniforms. After a game, Mickey or Whitey would take off his jersey, revealing the Yoo-Hoo T-Shirt. Then a photographer would take a picture, and on the front page of the next day's sports section would be Mickey Mantle or Whitey Ford in a Yoo-Hoo T-shirt. Yogi also had several of us take publicity photos in the Yoo-Hoo shirts.

Can you imagine how much that publicity would cost Yoo-Hoo today? Yogi got it for the price of a few T-shirts.

But none of us thought much of it. One day, Yogi walked into the dressing room with his Yoo-Hoo T-shirts and passed them out. We all said, "Thanks, Yogi," and wore them. When Yogi gave you something, you took it.

Whitey and Mickey did get a measure of playful revenge late in the 1961 season. Yogi had his locker next to Whitey's, and Yogi didn't like to buy things like deodorant. And being near Whitey, he saw no reason to do it. He just took Whitey's can, rolled it under his arms a few times, and put it back in Whitey's locker. One day, Whitey and Mickey took Whitey's deodorant can and put some pine tar in it. After the game, Yogi took his usual shower, dried off, and grabbed Whitey's deodorant and rolled it on. When Yogi put down his arms, it was as though he was in a straitjacket. His arms were sealed to his sides. When Yogi tried to move his arms, it was extremely painful because he ended up tearing the hair under his armpits. Poor Yogi ended up in the trainer's room, and I think Gus Mauch had to cut away the hair under his arms before he was free.

If nothing else, that got Yogi buying deodorant.

That was one of the few times Yogi ever got the worst of anything. He has cashed twenty-one World Series checks and was always paid well by the Yankees because he knew how to negotiate.

While the rest of us would talk about our contracts in the winter, Yogi would seek out Dan Topping and Del Webb at the team party. Usually, this was right after the World Series, and Yogi figured that the owners were never going to be any happier than they were at that moment. He would talk money with these guys right at the party, often working out a deal before they had a chance to consult with the team's lawyers and accountants. By using this tactic, and you've got to realize that it is very hard to say no to someone who looks and acts like Yogi, he usually got one of the biggest raises on the team.

Yogi dumb? Dumb like a fox is more like it.

Casey Stengel summed up Yogi like this: "He watches all the sports and knows about them all. If he turned on the television and saw roller skating, Yogi would watch it and pretty soon he would know what makes the skates roll."

In the Houston camp, Phil Garner told me, "Yogi says some strange things, but they are only strange in the way he says them. If you take the time to listen for a few moments, you know that Yogi is a very astute guy."

On that spring day when Yogi and I talked in Kissimmee, he was sixty-one years old and looked and acted about the same as ever. That amazed me, considering that Yogi had just gone through the meat-grinder of managing the Yankees. The only reason he had come back to manage was that the one thing in baseball he never did was manage a World Series winner. I remember running into Yogi late in 1984. We were in the lobby of a Toronto hotel, and Yogi was convinced that George Steinbrenner was going to fire him the next day. Yogi said that when it happened, he was going to let loose, tell all, and go down with guns blazing.

But George brought Yogi back to manage again in 1985—and fired him after sixteen games. And Yogi never said anything. I'm sure he was deeply hurt and probably still is, but you'd never know it by his words or actions.

Yogi had been through this before with the Yankees in 1964, being fired even though his team won 99 games and made it to the World Series. After that season I called him, and Carmen said he was crushed and in tears. When Yogi got on the line, you could tell he had been crying. But Yogi never knocked anyone, not even the people who knocked him.

That afternoon in Kissimmee, Yogi was his usual self. "No use talking about all that bad stuff," he said. "I got a good job now. I'm happy."

Yogi's neighbor in New Jersey is Dr. John McMullen, owner of the Houston Astros, and the families are close friends, especially their wives. So it didn't take much for Dr. McMullen to convince Yogi to join the Astros.

"I'm not in it for the money," said Yogi. "I got enough. But I was lost without having a uniform on. Now, I don't have to worry about that."

And Yogi walked away in that distinctive waddle of his. The uniform may say Astros, but it was still the big leagues. There will always be a place in the big leagues for Yogi Berra.

Rollie Sheldon

One day he was a guy who came out of the University of Connecticut, and the next day he was on the Yankees. That's what I remember about Rollie Sheldon.

Keep in mind that I made a habit of paying attention to who was playing where. It was part business, part curiosity. I read the daily sports pages and the *Sporting News*. I knew who was playing well on other clubs, and who the prospects were in the Yankee farm system.

When Rollie Sheldon showed up at spring training in 1961, it was no surprise that I had never seen him before. But I had never even heard of the guy. It was as though he were the pitcher from nowhere. The New York press was certainly caught up in the Sheldon mystique. Joe Trimble of the *Daily News* called Rollie "the Rookie from Class D," which sounds like the title of a juvenile-fiction book.

Yes, Rollie was a character John R. Tunis would have loved. But it was another sportswriter, Dan Daniel, who wrote, "Sheldon came into the Yankee farm system from the University of Connecticut, where he was better known in basketball than baseball. The Ucons had a dozen pitchers and he was rated no better than No. 4. Rollie is the quietest Yankee. Reticent, now and then smiling, he is all pitching business."

Twenty-five years later, I still didn't know much about Rollie. And most of the players I talked with didn't have many memories of him, either.

Bob Turley: "He was our Connecticut Yankee. He was kind of stiff-walking and pitched with a stiff overhand delivery. He was a nice, pleasant guy. He didn't say much. He had a couple of okay years, and then I lost track of him."

Bobby Richardson: "About all I remember about Rollie is that he lied about his age."

Johnny Sain: "Rollie was mature for his age, but of course it turned out he was older than we thought. He wasn't afraid to throw the ball over the plate. He didn't have great stuff, but he did all right for a while."

In my scrapbook, my mother had put in an odd picture of Rollie and Ralph Houk. Rollie has his hand up and is pressing his wrist against Ralph's ear. It's hard to tell exactly what they are doing.

The cutline said, "In addition to a $25,000 bonus, Roland Sheldon has a new wristwatch before pitching a single inning for the Yankees. He was awarded the gold engraved wristwatch by the New York baseball writers for being the club's outstanding rookie in spring training. Manager Ralph Houk helps Sheldon listen to it tick."

Well, that explained what was happening in the picture, but it didn't say much about Rollie.

A check of *The Baseball Encyclopedia* revealed that Rollie was in the majors from 1961 to 1966. His career record was 38–36, 11 of those wins coming in 1961.

Those were the numbers. We all know that numbers don't tell the whole story. But after looking at Sheldon's record, I realized that they probably didn't tell any of the story.

As I talked with Rollie, it wasn't just to find out about what he had done since baseball. I didn't even know much of what he did in baseball.

When we made contact, Rollie was living in Lee's Summit, Missouri, a suburb of Kansas City. He has been a claims representative for Allstate Insurance since 1969.

"You know, Tony, I saw you before you even knew I was around," he said. "After I signed with the Yankees in June of 1960, I worked out with the team in New York at the Stadium. I'm sure you didn't notice me. I was just another kid they had signed and let play catch on the field before the game."

He was right, I didn't remember.

"Anyway, I watched the game that night, and what I remember the most was Bob Shaw hanging a slider to Moose Skowron and Moose creaming it, pounding it off the scoreboard in right-center. It went right off the 407-foot sign. I had never seen a ball hit that hard, and I wondered what I was getting into."

Rollie seemed to want to talk, so I just sat back and listened. And why not? Most of what he said was new to me.

"I grew up on a farm in Woodstock, Connecticut. We raised tomatoes, about thirty-five hundred plants a year. It was truck farming, growing the tomatoes, loading them on the truck, and taking them to town to sell to the supermarkets. I spent a lot of time at my grandfather's farm, and it was there I started with baseball. Behind the barn was a wire, homemade backstop in what we called the Calf Yard. We'd get together three people, and we'd have a game. One guy would pitch, one guy would hit, and one would play the field. We made up our own ground rules and played games that way.

"In high school, I played baseball but never really pitched. I was an infielder. After I got out of high school, I went into the Air Force because I hadn't prepared for college, and a lot of guys from my town were signing up. I had never traveled, so it seemed like something to try. I wasn't sure what I wanted to do with my life. About the last thing on my mind was pro baseball. Anyway, it was in the Air Force that I first pitched. Even then, I was mostly an infielder until my last year. I was stationed in West Germany, and our team got a new coach. This master sergeant thought I had a good arm, so he put me on the mound and told me to throw as hard as I could."

It didn't sound like the start of a guy who would be pitching for the Yankees three years later.

"After I got out of the Air Force, I went to Texas A&M on a basketball scholarship. I was six foot four, which was good size in those days. I had played with a lieutenant who later became the freshman basketball coach at Texas A&M. He gave me a scholarship. After a semester, I got homesick and enrolled at Connecticut. That's where I started playing baseball.

"But I still didn't think about pro baseball until after my second year in school. We had just lost a game to Boston College and had been knocked out of the NCAA playoffs in the spring of 1960. The next morning, a Yankee scout named Harry Hesse was at my door. This was my first hint that scouts had a serious interest in me.

"Harry and I sat in the living room and talked contract. Harry called Bill Skiff, who worked in the Yankee front office, and got approval to give me a twenty-thousand-dollar bonus. Then he opened his briefcase and said, 'Since you're only twenty years old, you'll need to get your parents to sign this permission slip.' Being twenty was news to me, since I was twenty-three. At the time, my parents were in the kitchen sipping coffee. They had left me alone to talk with the scout.

"So I go into the kitchen and whispered, 'This Yankee scout thinks

I'm only twenty. I really want to play pro ball.' My parents understood what I was saying. If Harry Hesse wanted me to be twenty, I would be twenty."

The picture I had was wrong. Rollie's bonus was twenty thousand dollars, not twenty-five thousand dollars.

"After I worked out with the Yankees, they sent me to Auburn of the New York–Penn League and I was 15–1. It was Class D, the bottom of the ladder, and all I was hoping to do the next year was maybe get to Class A. Anyway, the winter after my year at Auburn was when I first met Ralph Houk. He was at a banquet near my hometown, and I happened to be sitting in the audience. Someone asked Ralph about my chances of making the Yankees, and I can still hear Ralph saying, 'I don't care if the guy went 15–1 in a girls' softball league, we have to take a look at him.'

"So I went to spring training full of confidence. In retrospect, Ralph probably didn't really think I had a shot to make the team. He was just saying that to be polite, but I believed I could do it. I stayed at the Soreno Hotel in Saint Petersburg. While the major leaguers had only two guys per room, I had three or four. Most were guys from Class D like myself. Some of the guys would get cut, and others would move in."

I can still see Rollie that spring training. He had a pretty good sinker, and he kept throwing ground ball after ground ball. By the end of spring training, he was still there and still throwing grounders. I think he sort of caught a lot of us by surprise.

"You know, I was never told I had made the team," said Rollie. "Normally, Big Pete Sheehy would tell you that Ralph wanted to see you in his office. That meant you were gone. Big Pete never came up to me, and pretty soon it was opening day. I was so fresh, so raw that I thought anything was possible. I believed that a pitcher from Class D could walk into training camp and make a team that had just been in the World Series. A lot of things fell into place. That spring, I developed a rather deep blister on the middle finger of my pitching hand. It went through several layers of skin. The trainer cut it open, put some black stuff on it, and a couple days later, it was completely healed. It was amazing. That blister alone could have sent me back to the minors. In spring training, rookies who get hurt aren't rookies in camp for long.

"About the biggest news for me that spring was when a couple of writers from Connecticut came to camp and figured out that I couldn't be twenty. They knew when I had graduated from high school, and they knew I was in the Air Force and had gone to college for a couple years. They confronted [Yankee public relations director] Bob Fishel about it. Bob went to me and said I didn't have to admit anything. I told Bob that I didn't care. I was just going along with what the scouts wanted. It really wasn't a big deal, and I don't think it hurt or helped me make the team.

"For me, the turning point was an exhibition game against the White Sox in Sarasota. Chicago had a good hitter, Roy Sievers, and I struck him out twice. That showed me that I belonged. I used to run to and from the mound every inning. That whole spring was like a great adventure. When the season started, Ralph used me in spots against the weaker teams like Minnesota and Washington. He knew how to break a rookie in."

At one point, Rollie won six straight games when he filled in as a starter for Ralph Terry, who had shoulder problems for about six weeks.

"I was never the same after 1961," said Rollie. "Something happened to my shoulder. I don't know when or how. But I'd be pretty strong for four or five innings, then all of a sudden it wasn't there any more. I mean, everything was just gone. Maybe it's because there are only so many pitches in an arm, or maybe it's because I didn't pitch much until I got to the majors and my arm wasn't built up enough to stand the strain. Maybe it wouldn't have happened if I had four or five years in the minors like most guys. All I know is that it was a frightening, insecure feeling."

New York traded Rollie to Kansas City in 1965. A year later, he moved on to Boston, then Cincinnati, and finally the White Sox.

"The crazy thing is that I grew to hate spring training after 1961. Perhaps part of the reason I made the Yankees in 1961 is that I was too young to know the pressure facing a guy in my position most springs. In fact, spring training is the only part of baseball I don't miss. When I think of spring training, I can still feel the fear and anxiety that comes as cutdown date draws near. I hate that. I kept playing until 1969, bouncing between the majors and Class AAA. In the minors, you think all you need is a couple good outings, and you'll be back up there. My last year, I played in all three Class AAA leagues. I had pitched as long as I could, taken about all the chances there were. Finally, I just got tired of making the rounds, so I quit.

"In the clubhouse, the guys always used to say things like, 'You'll be carrying a lunch bucket pretty soon the way you've been pitching.' But the reality of one day having to carry that lunch bucket and working nine to five is something ballplayers keep trying to put off and put off. It's going to be a tough transition, and you know it. In my case, I've been lucky to be with Allstate, a great company, ever since.

"I still wish that I could turn the clock back to 1961 and make that be the rest of my life. I think that's only natural. Someone asked me if I could have made the Yankees in 1961 if I knew all that I did by 1969. Who knows? But in that case, not knowing certainly helped me. I didn't have the feeling of always competing for a job and worrying about not getting it. In 1961, I just pitched and figured if I pitched well, it would all work out. I didn't think about roster spots, or options, or the other things that go into decisions.

"Being part of that 1961 team was like a dream. It was when everything was perfect. I still play baseball, sort of. Actually, it's overhand softball. The bases are sixty-five feet from the plate, and the mound is fifty-eight feet. You can pitch any way you want. I've developed a pretty good breaking ball, and I still have a little velocity, even though I'm almost fifty.

"I still like baseball. When the Royals are in town, I go to about one game a week. I don't stop down to see any of the guys. Usually, there is a security guard who keeps you away from the field. I'm not a pushy guy. I don't go around telling people I used to play for the 1961 Yankees. I'm just content knowing that I might have been the weakest link on the strongest club ever assembled."

Luis Arroyo

Some guys were never meant to be a Yankee. There was Tex Clevenger, who had a vicious sinker and slider. You'd watch him throw on the sidelines and in batting practice and you'd figure this guy was one of the better pitchers in the league. But when Ralph put Tex on the mound, something happened to him. For whatever reason, he lost his stuff somewhere between the bull pen and the mound; it's like he just couldn't adjust to being in New York and having to win.

Then there was Johnny Keane, a fine man and an excellent manager in St. Louis. He came to New York and was so in awe of the Yankees that he couldn't make a move.

I never thought about what it meant to be a Yankee. I just was one from the time I signed with them at seventeen. Of course I loved being a Yankee and playing with all that talent, but it was a fact of life. It was only when a player came to us from another organization that we'd see that some of them were overawed while others thrived.

Luis Arroyo was born to be a Yankee. He certainly had the nervous system for it, as Luis was known to sleep in the bull pen during the first few innings.

Luis wore Panama hats and smoked fat cigars. He started pitching in 1948 and had been with fifteen different teams when he came to New York in the middle of the 1960 season. You could see he was thrilled to be there. He had taken his knocks, and most people didn't think he could help us. But fact is that the 1961 Yankees would not have been a great team without Luis in the bull pen.

Casey Stengel called him Yo-Yo, because the old man couldn't pronounce his name. And Yo-Yo he became. Besides, he kind of looked like one. When he climbed over the bull pen gate and onto the field, the Yankee Stadium fans would chant LOO-EEE. He'd walk to the mound with a chaw of tobacco in his left cheek, his cap tilted slightly to the right, his glove hand pounding against his side with every step, and his stomach jiggling as it hung generously over his belt.

That was Luis Arroyo in 1961. He was thirty-five, his hair sprinkled with grey, and his left arm turned so far inward that it seemed ready to fall off if he threw one more screwball. But 1961 was the season of seasons for Luis, his first and last great year. Luis now lives quietly on the same farm where he was born, in Penuelas, Puerto Rico. It's about twenty acres featuring horses, cows, and tropical fruit, including mangoes.

"I scout for the Yankees down here, so that keeps me active in baseball," he said. "Sometimes I run into somebody and they ask, 'Weren't you the same Arroyo who had that great year in 1961?' I like it when they recognize me. People who don't remember me are surprised when they find out I pitched for the Yankees. I guess I don't look like a Yankee. I never did. Dan Topping called me the bartender because he said that's what I looked like. All I know is when I walked up to the New York dressing room for the first time, they wouldn't let me in. The guard didn't believe I was a player until he called someone in the front office to check with them. I was five foot eight and over two hundred pounds, and it wasn't exactly all muscle. Everybody else was six foot, six foot two, and about two hundred pounds with lots of muscles. My locker was next to Whitey Ford's. I tell you the truth, there were days I'd walk into the room and see Whitey's name plate and then my name plate, and I'd ask myself, 'Luis, what are you doing here?' "

In 1961, he was 15–5 with 29 saves and a 2.19 ERA. He even hit .280. Luis's record for his other seven big-league seasons was 25–27 with 15 saves and a 4.43 ERA.

"The Yankees found me in 1960," said Luis. "I was pitching for Jersey City in the International League. It was a Cincinnati farm club. The year before, the Jersey City team had been the Havana Sugar Canes, but the franchise had to be moved when Castro took over in Cuba. That was a break, because being in Jersey City made it easier for the Yankees to come down to scout us. But for a long time, it was pretty bad for me. In 1959, I even quit the team for two weeks. I was thinking about it again in 1960. I was thirty-four and not going anywhere. Then the Yankees bought my contract. I don't know if it was because I always pitched good against their Richmond farm club. Or it might have been because some of the front office guys went to see their prospects at Richmond and saw me pitch and noticed I had come up with a screwball. Also, Ryne Duren was having trouble in the bull pen, so they needed somebody.

"All I know is that the Yankees pulled me out of Jersey City, and believe me, I never thought I'd see New York. I reported to them on June 24, 1960. Roy Hamey was the general manager, and he told me, 'Luis, you're already on a major-league salary in New Jersey, and we can't pay you any more than that.' I didn't care. I signed for the same ten thousand dollars I made in New Jersey."

Luis was 5–1 with five saves and a 2.89 ERA in 1960. After that season, Stengel said, "Imagine finding a guy as good as him lying around dead somewhere?"

"The first time I saw Luis pitch was in 1950," said Whitey Ford. "What I remembered was that he was maybe the only pitcher I had seen who was smaller than me. He was a fastball and curveball pitcher. When he showed up in New York with that screwball, I couldn't believe it."

Whitey won 24 games in 1961, and Luis saved 15 of them.

"I never realized I was having that good of a year until near the end of the season," said Luis. "I started quick, saving games the first few times I pitched. Then it would happen over and over. If we had a lead, I'd come in and get a couple guys out, and the game would be over. Or if the score was tied, I hold them for a inning and then Roger or Mickey would hit a homer, and I'd get the win. I started throwing the screwball in 1958, but it wasn't until Johnny Sain started working with me that I was really good. He showed me three different kinds of screwballs.

"There was so much that I loved about 1961. At the start of the game, I'd go down to the bull pen, and sometimes I'd take a nap through the first five innings. Then Jim Hegan, the bull pen coach, he'd come by and tap me on the shoulder and say, 'Luis, it's time.' I knew then it was a close game and I got myself ready.

"You know, Whitey was always so good to me. He'd pitch seven innings and then say, 'Okay, Luis, take it from here' when he handed me the ball. When a great pitcher like Whitey had confidence in me, it made me pitch even better. When they had Whitey Ford Day, they had me pop out of a big roll of Life Savers because I had saved so many of Whitey's games. When Whitey received the Cy Young Award at the New York baseball writers banquet, Whitey said he had a nine-minute speech. He was going to talk for the first seven minutes and let me do the last two. And that's what he did."

Luis had a couple of things working for him. The first was being a left-handed screwball pitcher. The natural inclination of most managers is to stack their lineup with right-handed hitters against lefties. That's what they did when Whitey pitched. But Luis's screwball made him far more effective against right-handed hitters because it broke away from them like a right-hander's curveball. Luis had more problems against left-handed hitters, but few managers would send up a lefty to bat for a right-handed hitter when Luis pitched. The park also helped Luis. He gave up a lot of long fly balls that Mickey chased down deep in center or left-center field.

"The only thing I feel bad about is what happened after 1961," said Luis. "Roy Hamey begged me not to play winter ball in Puerto Rico. I told Hamey that I had been pitching winter and summer all my life, and I never had a sore arm.

"Hamey said, 'No way, Luis. We don't want you to throw too much and hurt your arm.'

"I said, 'If I don't pitch, I'll get hurt.'

"Hamey says, 'How much will you make for pitching winter ball?'

"I said, 'Eight thousand dollars.'

"Hamey said, 'I don't want you pitching in the winter.' Then he took out his checkbook and wrote me a check for eight thousand dollars. 'Take this and go home.'

"Ralph Houk was in the meeting, and I remember him standing up for me, saying I needed to pitch to stay in shape, which was true. But Hamey, he just wouldn't change his mind. That winter, I was real lazy. I ate a lot, drank more than I should have, and I got fatter. When I reported to spring training in 1962, I started to throw, and I could tell my arm wasn't the same.

"We opened the 1962 season in Detroit. It was so damn cold, I'll never forget it. I don't know how anyone is supposed to pitch in that weather. I went into the game, and I knew I did something to my arm. That night, I woke up at three in the morning, my arm was killing me. I couldn't lift it. They sent me home to New York where some doctors told me to rest it. But I was never the same. After 1963, I was finished. I know part of it was the screwball, all that twisting made my elbow hurt, and that's why I didn't last very long.

"After I left the Yankees, I was a manager and general manager in the Mexican League for ten years before I went into scouting. I did pitch long enough to get my pension, which was my main goal when I got to New York. I have one son who is a dentist, and another is an architect. I still have my scrapbooks from 1961, and sometimes I take them out and just look at the stories. It makes me feel good to know I was there."

Bobby Richardson

At Roger Maris's funeral, there was a line in front of Bobby Richardson.

"I heard Bobby's eulogy for Roger, and there were tears in my eyes," said Moose Skowron. "I told my wife that I wanted Bobby to talk at my funeral, and I'm going to book him right now."

But when Moose reached Bobby, Mickey Mantle already had him cornered.

"I wanted Bobby for my funeral, too," said Mickey. "But Bobby said I talked about death too much, and not to worry because he was going before me, and I'd have to give his eulogy."

I've always said that the heart of the 1961 team was Bobby Richardson and Whitey Ford. Those were the guys you counted on, the guys who never were down if they had a bad day and who never pointed a finger. Bobby could go oh for a week, and you'd never know it.

"Bobby had enormous self-control," said John Blanchard. "When the rest of us would strike out, we'd break bats, throw helmets, and cuss up a storm. Mickey always gave the watercooler hell. But Bobby was the perfect gentleman. He'd come back to the dugout, put his bat in the rack calmly, and then sit down. I never knew how he did it."

I roomed with Bobby for most of my Yankee career. For that reason, I was often lumped together with him as part of the Milkshake Kids, him at second base and me at shortstop. We were good friends, but we weren't clones. We'd have dinner, then Bobby would head back to the room to study his Bible or meet with some church people, and sometimes I'd go out with Mickey and Whitey for a few hours.

Bobby didn't do much with the guys away from the field. He never said it, but I think Bobby felt a lot of the players were involved with too many worldly things. He never preached to us or judged us. What I remember most about Bobby is that he lived his life as if everyone watched it.

If we had a night game, Bobby would be up early the next morning to visit the local Baptist Church or Salvation Army. Every Sunday, he would be speaking somewhere—the Fellowship of Christian Athletes, Youth for Christ, or the Salvation Army. That was his whole life.

If you have any doubts, consider what he did with his money—he gave away most of it. He was always sending checks to some cause or buying a jeep for a missionary in Africa.

What I respected Bobby for was that he was a bootstraps Christian. By that, I mean he never blamed his failures on the Lord's will. He really believed that God helps those who help themselves.

And Bobby Richardson was determined and tough. If a pitcher knocked him down, Bobby was never afraid to head to the mound yelling. The pitcher also knew that he better not do it again, because behind Bobby was the entire Yankee team. He played hard and hurt and didn't complain. In September of 1961, he was bothered by painful boils but refused to come out of the lineup.

"Everybody respected Bobby because he was so sincere," said Blanchard. "He never forced his religion on us, but we knew what kind of man he was. I remember a game when Moose was having a tough time. The pitcher kept getting him out with slow stuff, and Moose would come back to the dugout so frustrated that he'd start cussing out the pitcher. Back and forth he'd walk, screaming at the pitcher. But when Moose passed Bobby in the dugout, he'd stop and say, 'pardon me, Bobby,' then he'd take a couple more steps and go right back to yelling. A lot of us would crack up, even Bobby."

When I heard Blanchard's story, it reminded me about the party they held in 1962 for the premiere of the movie with Mickey, Roger, and Doris Day. they had a police escort and two buses for the players, their wives and children to take them to party. In the first bus, Toots Shor stood up and told a couple of off-color jokes. Bobby made them stop the bus right in the middle of downtown traffic so he and his wife Betsy could get off. No one thought much of it. The players didn't ask what Bobby was doing; they wondered why Toots opened his mouth.

"Bobby spoiled more jokes," said John Blanchard. "You'd be telling one, and you'd just stop right in the middle if Bobby came by, you'd just change the punch line and blow the whole thing. Locker-room humor wasn't for Bobby and we knew that."

"I always appreciated the fact that my teammates accepted me," said Bobby. "We were different in some ways, but we got along."

Hector Lopez had this memory of Bobby: "He used to hold a Mass before Sunday games. I used to go just to hear him talk. Then we'd have coffee and Danish. I liked that, too."

The Yankees were not a very religious team, but we would be sitting on the bus and our batting practice pitcher, Spud Murray, would pull out his harmonica. Then Bobby would ask, "What's your favorite hymn?"

Mickey always wanted to sing "Rock of Ages," so that's what we'd do. It wasn't so much a religious thing as something the team did together. When we were through, there would be wisecracks.

"Hey, Mickey," someone would say, "what's your religion?"

"I'm just like Bobby," Mickey would drawl. "Southern Baptist, born again."

Yes, Bobby took religion seriously. He was the first player to hold a baseball chapel service, starting a movement that now exists in every big-league clubhouse. But he was never insulted when Mickey and the guys kidded him about being Baptist.

Mickey wasn't much on church, but Bobby did talk him into going with us when we were in downtown Minneapolis. We stopped in this Baptist church.

"Remember when Mickey walked into the church and all the commotion it caused?" asked Bobby. "The service was continually interrupted because people were coming up to Mickey with scraps of paper for him to sign."

What I remember most is the collection. Mickey dumped all kinds of bills in the basket, about fifty dollars.

When we walked out, Mickey asked Bobby, "Did I put enough in?"

Bobby said, "I saw all that money in the basket, and I wanted to grab it and stuff it back in your pocket."

Religion has remained the core of Bobby's life. He retired after the 1966 season and has coached baseball at the University of South Carolina, Carolina Coastal College, and now Liberty Baptist. He worked at the Ben Lippen School, where he and Betsy lived in a home with teenaged boys and girls. A few years ago, Bobby decided to enter politics and run for the U.S. House of Representatives from his district in Sumter, South Carolina. His campaign manager called me and asked me to support him and attend a rally. Mickey, Whitey, and a number of the other guys were coming.

The hitch was that Bobby was running as a conservative Republican, and I'm a Democrat who has supported George McGovern, Mo Udall, and people like that. I called some of my friends in the Democratic party, and they told me the man Bobby was opposing was more in line with my political beliefs. I ended up in the strange position of having to tell my old roomie that I had all the respect in the world for him, but I couldn't back him in this instance. He lost a close election.

Bobby has had several jobs since he left baseball, a surprising number, considering how stable he was. But I'm sure they don't think of what they're doing as jumping around. Both Bobby and Betsy said, "The Lord will take care of us, and whatever the Lord tells us, we'll do."

But there is a difference between the Richardsons and a few other Christians. They don't hire a public relations firm or call a press conference when they do something. They also don't live the Gospel in their spare time. It really is their lives.

Two of Bobby's sons are ministers, and his daughter married a minister. I'm like a lot of guys on the Yankees. I wish I could be more like Bobby, but I can't. But I do hope my sons grow up like him.

Johnny Sain

I met Johnny Sain in his van, which was parked about ten miles from the Atlanta Braves' spring training camp in West Palm Beach, Florida. The van was a seventeen-footer, and Sain was living in it.

When I stepped inside, Johnny said, "I want to show you something." From under the bed, he pulled out a sewing machine.

"See the curtains, made them myself," said Johnny. He also said he had taken up the cuffs on his pants.

Then there's the matter of the face-lift.

"My wife is about eighteen years younger than I am," said Johnny. "She said that one day she might want a face-lift, but she was afraid it would be too painful. I told her not to worry, I'd get one, and then she'd know. Guess what? It didn't hurt at all."

Not only is Johnny Sain the only man in the majors with a face-lift, but I don't know anyone else who has gotten a hair transplant. I do know that Johnny is seventy and he looks about fifty-five, so he must have done something right.

Johnny's travel van is his home for much of the season. It has a place to sleep, to cook, and even has a cellular telephone. It is where he lives in spring training and where he lived when he was pitching coach with Richmond. Now that he is with Atlanta, Johnny got an apartment so it would be more comfortable for his wife. It wasn't too long ago that the van was Sain's only home.

"I got divorced in 1972," said Johnny. "I walked into the courtroom, stood up, and said, 'I'm willing to sign over everything to her.' That's what I did. I lost the farm, the Chevrolet dealership, everything. I was fifty-five and had nothing but my baseball pension. So you better believe I had to learn how to take care of myself. But I was lucky. I found a wonderful woman to marry, and Ted Turner came along to hire me. It was Ted and the Braves who helped me put my life together."

Today, Johnny Sain is a legend. Think pitching coach, and whose name comes to mind? A strong case can be made that until Johnny Sain, a pitching coach was just another coach. There was the first-base coach, the third-base coach, the hitting coach, and pitching coach—all pretty much equal.

Since Sain, it is commonly said that the most important person a manager will hire is his pitching coach. A lot of the pitching coaches who gain notoriety become managers—George Bamberger, Roger Craig, and Ray Miller are a few examples. It used to be that a former pitcher would never become a manager because he supposedly only knew about pitching. Now, successful pitching coaches are made managers for the same reasons that once excluded them—because they know so much about pitching.

Johnny Sain is well aware of the changes because he has a sense of baseball history and how people fit into the scheme. And that's because Johnny Sain is so much a part of that history.

In Johnny Sain, we are talking about the guy who threw the first pitch to Jackie Robinson and the last pitch to Babe Ruth. In 1947, he won 21 games and hit .346. In a three-year span ending in 1948, Sain started 64 games and completed the first 63. That included a stretch in 1948 when he started nine games in twenty-nine days, won 7 and lost the other 2 by scores of 2–1 and 1–0. In eleven years, he struck out only 20 times.

He coached baseball's last thirty-game winner in Denny McLain. He coached seventeen twenty-game winners, none of whom had won twenty before Sain arrived. On and on it goes. Four of the managers he worked under became manager of the year. Ralph Houk, Mayo Smith, and Sam Mele never won pennants before Johnny got there or after he left. Johnny was the pitching coach the last time Minnesota was in the World Series. In twenty years as a coach, twelve of his teams have finished at least third, and there have been five pennant-winners.

And if that isn't enough, Johnny flies his own plane.

Johnny Sain is very good and very different. That's why he lasts three years somewhere, and then it is time to move on. It's not that Johnny is interested in managing. If anything, the last guy a manager would have to worry about taking his job was Johnny, because his tunnel vision starts and ends at the mound.

But Johnny has a tendency to take his ten pitchers and separate them from the rest of the club. Johnny's pitchers are *his* pitchers. For example, I remember times when Frank Crosetti said something about why a certain pitch was thrown in a certain situation. Johnny responded, "Listen, Cro', I don't tell your infielders where they should play, so you don't tell my guys how they should pitch."

"There was a day when I threw a sidearm curve and it hung, and the guy hit a double," said Ralph Terry. "I got into the dugout, and I was jumped on about that pitch by Yogi and some other guys. Johnny stepped right in and said, 'If you got something to say to my pitchers, you say it to me. I'll talk to my pitchers.' Believe me, a pitcher appreciates a coach who has guts enough to stand up for you like that."

Maybe a pitcher does, but a manager doesn't always. Johnny Sain's ten pitchers were sacred, and if anyone criticized them, it was war. It is inevitable that pitchers will be criticized, so there will be conflict.

"Johnny was a master psychologist," said Ralph Terry. "A lot of players not only don't relate to their coaches, they don't even pay them the slightest bit of attention. If a guy was having a problem, Johnny would go to that guy's friend and say something like, 'I'm a little worried about Fred.' Then, since you were the guy's friend, you'd say you were worried, too. Then Johnny would say, 'You know, he might be all right if he would throw a little more over the top.' Then Johnny would walk away, and you'd tell your friend what Johnny had said about throwing over the top. Johnny took time to know who his pitchers' friends were and what his pitchers were interested in. That helped him become a better communicator."

Some of Johnny's ideas were also unique, like his personality. Take his theory about treating arm injuries.

"When I pitched for the Yankees and hurt my shoulder, I took radiation treatments," he said. "I did this on my own. When I told the Yankee team doctor how the X-ray treatments helped me, he got mad. I said that I didn't care if he liked it or not, it helped me, and it might help someone else. I believe that Ed Lopat and Allie Reynolds had those treatments. Whitey Ford had those treatments. I believe that radation treatments might have won a few pennants for the Yankees. In 1961, Bill Stafford, Terry, and Ford all took the treatments, and within two weeks, they all were back pitching. The last time I was in New York, I asked Ford and Lopat if they had any side effects, and they said they didn't. I know I didn't. You can't get radiation treatment today because it is illegal, but I believe it does less damage to the body than cortisone. I know if I had a sore arm, I'd find a way to get radiation treatments."

Then there is Johnny Sain and the spinner.

"I used to watch Ralph Terry always holding a baseball, spinning it in his hand," he said. "The most important aspect of pitching is getting the ball to move, and it moves because of the spin. I was trying to think of something that would help pitchers understand the value of spin. I was in a hotel room, and I had an apple in my hand, spinning it as if it were a baseball. Then I went to the television, broke off the aerial, and stuck it through the center of the apple, creating an axis. It made it easier to see the spin of the ball. Later, I got a ball, drilled a hole through the middle, and put a spike through the hole. I patented the thing, and we've sold about seven thousand. I never made any real money on it, but it is interesting."

Then there is Johnny Sain on running.

"Most guys want their pitchers to run as if they were training for a track meet," he said. "You don't run the ball up to the plate, you throw it. I believe you exercise, but you exercise your arm first. I like a lot of throwing between starts. It's not that I'm against running, it's just that my priority is throwing. I like my pitchers to run, but not as much as most coaches. Look, I used to believe in running. I thought you had to run until you fell over. But I found out that you could be the greatest runner with the most endurance and still be a lousy pitcher."

The debate on Sain could last an eternity, but he is the first guy I'd hire if I ever managed. He never imposes his will on a pitcher. He takes what a guy has to work with and makes the most of it.

"Johnny looks at a guy who won six games the year before and wonders what he can do to help the guy win ten," said Ralph Terry. "It might mean teaching the guy an extra pitch. Or it could be just changing his thinking around. But he never tried to make a fastball pitcher into a guy who throws junk."

It has been said that Johnny Sain is in love with the breaking ball. A strong case can be made that Sain is the reason more off-speed pitches are used in the American League than the National League.

"If anyone keeps their eyes open and thinks for a minute, they will realize that most pitchers don't throw ninety miles per hour," said Johnny. "So they need to change speeds and make the ball move. Show me a guy who can throw a curve over at any point in the count, and I'll show you a good pitcher. It's just common sense. The more pitches you can throw over the plate at any point in the count, the more unpredictable you can be, and the better pitcher you will become. You can't teach a guy to throw ninety miles per hour, but you can teach him a change-up or a quick curve."

When Ralph Houk was a bull pen catcher and Johnny a reliever with the Yankees, they had conversations like those during games. They both had plenty of time since Ralph never played and Johnny was at the end of his career.

"From all those long talks in the bull pen, I found out that Johnny and I had the same outlook on pitching," said Ralph Houk. "Just listening to him, I knew I wanted him as my pitching coach."

"Casey Stengel used to say that I'd make a good pitching coach," said Johnny. "In 1959, Harry Craft was managing Kansas City, and he hired me. That year, the A's traded Roger Maris, Ralph Terry, and Hector Lopez to the Yankees and didn't get much in return. Here we were supposedly trying to build a winner, and we were trading away our best players. Parke Carroll was the general manager, and I told him that it seemed to me that he wasn't trying to put together a good organization, so I quit. In 1960, I stayed home in Havana, Arkansas, and ran my Chevrolet dealership. At the end of that season, Ralph Houk called me and said, 'Something big is gonna happen, really big. I'm going to take over for Casey, and I want you to be my pitching coach. Don't say a word because no one knows.' A few weeks later, it happened, and I went to New York for an interview.

"One of the owners, Del Webb, takes me into his office and leaves Ralph sitting in the hallway. We talk for ninety minutes about my theories of pitching, things like how I like guys to start every fourth day and how important it is to change speeds. Webb said, 'These are the kind of things I've wanted done around here for years.' So I know I'm in good shape.

"Next, I go to talk with Roy Hamey about my contract. Hamey said, 'Johnny, we won't have any trouble. We know what you made in Kansas City and we'll take it from there.'

"I said, 'That's fine with me.'

"Hamey said, 'We know they paid you $12,500 in Kansas City. We'll give you $16,000.'

"I said, 'Mr. Hamey, money isn't important to me. If I can do the job, I know you'll pay.'

"Hamey said, 'Well, Crosetti is getting eighteen thousand dollars, and he's been with us for a long time. I don't want to give you more than Cro', so let's make it seventeen thousand dollars.'

"I said, 'Mr. Hamey, money really isn't that important. I know if I do a good job, you'll take care of me.' So we settled on seventeen thousand dollars."

And in 1961, Johnny Sain did a very good job. That winter, the Yankees lost Eli Grba and Bobby Shantz in the expansion draft. Bob Turley had a bad arm, Art Ditmar was getting old, Ryne Duren was having drinking problems, Ralph Terry had to recover from throwing that home run ball to Mazeroski in the World Series, and Whitey Ford had won only 12 games and had some arm trouble.

Johnny and Ralph Houk completely overhauled the pitching staff. They took Rollie Sheldon from Class D and got 11 wins out of him. They turned Luis Arroyo into the best reliever in the league. Bill Stafford won 14 games as a rookie, Terry went from 10 to 16 wins, and Ford, starting every fourth day for the first time in his career, also won twenty for the first time, as he was 25–4. This was a story that was lost in all the homers hit by Roger and Mickey.

"Let's face it, if we don't get the pitching, we don't win," said Johnny. "Everyone knew that. So I figured I did pretty well in 1961, but after the season, I got a contract in the mail for eighteen thousand dollars. I sent it back with a note saying, 'Mr. Hamey, evidently you don't remember our conversation from last year, so it would be best for you to tell me how I can bow out of the Yankee picture.'

"Hamey called me right away and asked me how much I wanted. I didn't say anything, and he raised his offer to nineteen thousand dollars.

"I said, 'Mr. Hamey, I understood that you would take care of me if I did a good job.'

"Hamey said, 'How much do you want? Twenty thousand dollars? Twenty-one thousand dollars? You can talk to me.'

"I said, 'I just don't know, Mr. Hamey.'

"Hamey said, 'How about twenty-two thousand dollars? Listen, I can't go higher than $22,500.'

I said, 'Did you say $22,500?' and Hamey said he did. I said, 'Send me a check for twenty-five hundred dollars now and a contract for twenty thousand dollars.' I wanted to keep my contract at twenty thousand dollars so that the Yankees wouldn't wake up one day, look at my contract, and decide that Johnny Sain was making too much money."

In the three years that Johnny Sain was the Yankee pitching coach, New York won three pennants, two World Series, averaged 103 wins, and had the second-best earned-run average in the league each season.

When Ralph Houk became general manager in 1964 and Yogi was named manager, that was the end of Johnny.

"In the three years I was under Ralph Houk, we had the greatest organization maybe in baseball history. We had a great manager, great coaches, great players, a great farm system, and a great front office. If it sounds like everything was great, that's because it was. There were times in the 1963 season when I'd see Yogi and Crosetti whispering in the runway, and it was only later that I realized Cro was teaching Yogi how to manage.

"But the first real tipoff I had that Ralph wasn't going to manage was after the third game of the 1963 World Series. We had lost the first three games to the Dodgers, and he just wasn't as fired up as a manager would be in that spot. Before the fourth game, Ralph gave a strange speech saying things like, 'No matter what happens, I'm proud of you guys. I want you to walk out of here with your heads held high, and I want to thank you for all you've done for me.' That's the kind of thing you say after the World Series is lost, not after three games.

"The thing was that Ralph didn't level with me. Ralph and I were as close as two friends could be. He talked to me about his family problems, about buying a house, and everything else. But he never said a word that he was going upstairs to be the general manager. It gnawed at me that these guys refused to tell me what was going on. I would have done all I could to help Yogi, but they left me out.

"After the season, I went home to Arkansas, and I got a call from Yogi asking if I would be his pitching coach. At first, I said I would. But then I got to thinking about how they never leveled with me. That really hurt. So I asked the Yankees for a two-year contract and a twenty-five-hundred-dollar raise. I knew they'd never go for it, and they didn't. At that point, I just wanted out because I could see how they wrecked a great organization."

There has always been a team with a job for Johnny Sain, and there have always been pitchers Sain could help. The only time Jim Bouton, Mudcat Grant, Earl Wilson, Denny McLain, Wilbur Wood, Stan Bahnsen, and Jim Kaat were twenty-game winners was when they pitched for Johnny Sain.

By 1977, Johnny had landed in the Braves organization, where he lasted longer than anywhere else—seven years at Class AAA Richmond.

"I loved the seven years at Richmond, and I'm excited that I'm with Atlanta now," said Johnny Sain. "It doesn't matter so much where I work so long as I have pitchers to work with."

Bill Stafford

Every team has one pitcher like Bill Stafford. He is the guy who gives up two runs in nine innings and doesn't get a win. He is the guy who leaves with a 2–1 lead after eight, and the reliever doesn't get the save.

"Some guys get a lot of runs to work with and some don't," said Stafford. "It just seemed like I was one of the guys who didn't."

Bill threw pretty hard and had an outstanding sinker. His pitches were heavy, much like those of Mike Garcia and Mel Stottlemyre. When you hit Bill's sinker, it felt as if the ball had been soaked in water for about a month.

"I was lucky," he said. "Before I got hurt, I could throw about any pitch over and at any point in the count, and usually keep it low."

The control came from his father. Actually, the backstop his father built in the backyard of their home in Athens, New York.

"My dad redid the whole backyard," said Bill. "We had a big screen backstop with two layers of canvas hanging behind the plate. One layer had holes, so I could aim for spots. The other was just a big hunk of canvas that the balls would hit when they went through the holes. I'd take a dozen balls out to the mound and throw at the holes in the canvas. They'd hit the canvas and drop straight down. Then I'd pick them all up and do it again. People used to wonder why I threw so many strikes. The reason was I practiced."

In 1961, Bill was twenty-two and went 14–9 with a 2.68 earned run average.

"I could have won twenty games that year, easy," said Bill. "Six of my nine losses were by one run. Luis Arroyo had a great year, but I left games with leads six times, and Arroyo didn't hold them. I went through a stretch of three starts where I threw a two-hitter and lost,

1–0; I left a game after nine innings with the score 0–0; and another after ten innings when it was 0–0."

It was strange year for Bill. One of his best performances was a 1–0 win over Boston. That also was the game Roger Maris hit his sixty-first homer, so few people noticed.

"I could have won the ERA title," said Bill. "But on the last day of the season, Dick Donovan needed two innings in order to have pitched enough to qualify. He started the game, went two scoreless innings, and then left with the title."

Rollie Sheldon and Bill were the two young pitchers who stepped in when when Art Ditmar and Bob Turley struggled and lost their spots in the rotation.

"I had spent six months in the military," said Bill. "I didn't get to spring training until there was about ten days left. So I began the year in the bull pen, pitching myself into shape. I didn't get any starts until the middle of May."

Making starters out of Sheldon and Stafford was one of Ralph Houk's moves that turned around the season. Ralph was willing to give the young guys a chance. The Yankees knew Bill would become a fine pitcher, although they probably didn't think it would happen quite that fast.

"In high school, I was a shortstop until one of our pitchers got hurt," said Bill. "Then I went 5 innings in an emergency and struck out 15. A little later, I pitched a 17-inning game and struck out 31. In my senior year, I pitched 7 games—5 no-hitters and 2 one-hitters. On the night I graduated from high school, I had scouts from fifteen of the sixteen teams at my house. I was ready to sign with the Dodgers. They offered me four thousand dollars, which was the highest amount you could pay without placing a player immediately on a big-league roster. I told Al Campanis that I'd sign with Brooklyn if he threw in a pair of spikes, but he said that would put him over the four-thousand-dollar limit. The Yankees made me the same offer, but they threw in the spikes, so I went with them."

We used to kid Bill about the way he walked. It was sort of a swaybacked gait, his back very stiff.

"That's because I hurt my back in my second year of pro ball. I was with Binghamton, New York, and we stayed in private homes. It was in July, and we were leaving for a bus trip at 8:00 in the morning. I came down the spiral stairs with my suitcase. My heel hit the edge of the stairs, making me slip, and the suitcase went flying up. I should have just let the stupid thing go. Instead, I just hung on to the suitcase, and I ripped up the muscles in my back. That year, I pitched a couple games wearing a brace that went from my shoulders to my waist. I couldn't bend over. It was kind of weird. Every time I pitched even with the Yankees, my back would go out a little, and one leg would actually get about an inch longer than the other. The trainer would have to pop it back in."

Bill was 14–9 again in 1962. That made his big-league record 31–19, and he hadn't turned twenty-four.

"After the 1962 season, I was disgusted with myself because I was losing so many close games. I felt I should have won twenty games in 1961 and 1962. I told myself that there was no way in hell I wasn't going to win twenty in 1963. So I rested for about ten days after the World Series and then I worked out harder than ever before. I did a lot of exercises, running, throwing, and playing racquetball. When I went to spring training in 1963, I was in the best shape of my life. I pitched about forty innings, which was unheard of in Florida, and I didn't give up a run in my last eighteen innings. I ran my butt off down there because I wanted to be in the best shape of my life.

"We opened the season in Kansas City, and the temperature was in the high twenties. No matter what I did, I couldn't work up a sweat. I wore an electrically heated jacket between innings, I did everything I could to stay warm. I had a 2–0 shutout going in the bottom of the seventh. There were two outs and no one on and I had a one-ball, two-strike count on Billy Bryant. Ellie Howard called for a slider, but I shook him off. I wanted to blow Bryant away with a fastball. I reached back and let loose, and I felt something snap in my shoulder, it was like someone broke a twig. Right then, I knew I had hurt my arm bad. But I was too damn stubborn. I just kept pitching, making it worse. I was never the same after that."

Billy was 4–8 in 1963. After that 31–19 beginning, he was 12–21 for the rest of his career and retired in 1967.

"I tried everything. I took radiation treatments to break up the calcium. I went to see a doctor, who wanted to operate. He said he was going to cut through a bunch of muscles, but there was only a fifty-fifty chance that I might ever use my arm again. Back then, they didn't even tell pitchers to ice their arms, because they didn't know that the arm bleeds internally after you pitch. Looking back, I realize that I had a rotator-cuff injury, but they didn't have a name for it twenty years ago. It was frustrating because I was only twenty-three. I mean, if I had been with the Yankees for ten or fifteen years, I might have been able to learn to pitch differently. But I'd see guys out there winning with worse stuff than I had, and it got to me. I wanted to cut loose, to show everyone how I used to be able to throw, but I couldn't because of my shoulder. It got me down, and I hung on, hoping my arm would get better. By the time I was twenty-eight, I knew I was finished."

Bill managed a chain of seven health clubs for a time. He later was a vice president for Wendy's Hamburgers. Now, he lives in Canton, Michigan, and is a sales representative for Mike Schecter Associates.

"We have the rights to use all major-league baseball premiums on glass, paper, or plastic. If you see a picture of a ballplayer on a cup at McDonald's or somewhere, it comes from our company."

Ralph Terry

Ralph Terry always had a baseball in his hands. There wasn't anything unusual about a pitcher sitting in front of his locker with a baseball in his hands, rubbing it, spinning it, just sort of getting the feel of the baseball. What made Ralph different was that he sometimes talked to it.

On the day he would pitch, Ralph would sit back in his locker, and remember that our lockers were those five-by-five cubicles. He'd flip a baseball up and down and say, "Curveball to Al Kaline."

Or: "Kaline, first pitch up, then slider low and away."

With his wrist, he would pretend to be throwing a slider.

Sometimes he'd hold the ball in his hand and look at it. Then he'd bounce the ball off the floor, catch it, jiggle it in his hand and say something like, "Now why can't I throw you where I want to?"

"I roomed with Ralph, and he didn't talk to the baseball," laughed Bob Turley. "Well, he really didn't do it that much. I mean, it was just sometimes."

As for his wardrobe, Ralph didn't exactly get it out of *Gentleman's Quarterly*. If *Mother Jones* had been around then, that's where you'd have found Ralph's outfit—jeans, a nondescript shirt, no socks, and loafers. On the road, he wore the same sport coat day after day.

"Ralph Terry was the first Mark Fidrych," said Johnny Sain. "He was a deep thinker, and a lot of people didn't understand him. And because he was so intelligent, a few guys were uneasy around Ralph. A smart guy can make you nervous, but I loved Ralph because he always was thinking."

"During the game, it was like Ralph was in another world," said Moose Skowron. "I'd go to the mound, and he'd have his back to the plate, and he'd be staring at the flags or something. I don't know what he was thinking about out there, but he didn't hear half the things I'd tell him."

I know exactly what Moose is talking about. Ralph would be staring at the flag with this glazed look. I'd go to the mound and say something like, "Ralph, you with us?" Finally, Ralph would nod, and I knew he was okay.

Ralph was so deliberate because he had to think everything through. He wouldn't throw a pitch unless he was absolutely sure it was what he wanted to throw. He had a tremendous feel for pitching and was always thinking a couple of batters ahead.

"He was like Thomas Edison," said Yogi Berra. "He always wanted to throw something different. He just should have went with his best pitches."

Maybe Ralph did take side trips to other planets, or maybe he just liked to look at the flags, but he was 16–3 in 1961, and he missed six weeks with a sore shoulder. The next year, he had 23 victories, and no right-handed Yankees pitcher has won more games in a single season since 1928. From 1960–64, his record was 66–38.

And I'll tell you something else about Ralph Terry. I once bought a very small piece of an oil well in which he owned an interest, and the thing paid off. Ralph Terry is no one's fool.

"I've done all right for a guy born in a log cabin," said Ralph, who was actually born in a town called Big Cabin, Oklahoma. "Ours really wasn't that big. I don't remember too much about it because I was only there for the first few years of my life. But we're talking about getting water from a well, and an outhouse. This was eastern Oklahoma, which isn't that far from Arkansas, so we're talking about the backwoods."

Ralph was signed by the same scout who discovered Mickey Mantle, Tom Greenwade.

"I was seventeen and had never been much of anywhere," said Ralph. "Greenwade pulls up in front of my house in a big black Cadillac and says to me, 'Son, how would you like to play in the biggest city in the world?' He talked about how the big three—Raschi, Reynolds, and Lopat—were getting old. 'In two or three years, you'll be ready, and that will be just the right time.' All I wanted to know was, where did I sign?"

Ralph came up with the Yankees in 1956. He was traded to Kansas City in 1957, and then he came back to the Yankees in a 1959 deal. Casey Stengel thought Terry experimented too much, and it wasn't until Ralph Houk became the manager and Johnny Sain was named pitching coach that Ralph started to win big.

Early in his career, Ralph was a power pitcher. Later, he relied more on finesse. He kept the ball around the plate and changed speeds. He was able to adjust because he was such a bright man.

But even Ralph couldn't handle Gabe Paul.

"I was traded to Cleveland before the 1965 season," said Ralph. "Yogi was the manager, and he didn't think much of me. Also, the Yankees needed a relief pitcher, so they got Pedro Ramos for the stretch drive in 1964 in exchange for the good old player to be named later. Well, you're talking to the player to be named later. After the 1964 season, the Yankees gave Cleveland a list of five names from which Gabe Paul could pick one.

"The crazy thing was that I pitched great at the end of 1964. In late August, Whitey pulled a hip muscle, and I stepped in and threw two shutouts. We had a two-week trip where I had three wins and two saves. Right before the World Series is when I found out I was on the list of guys who might go to Cleveland. So I go to see Houk, who was the GM at the time, and say, 'I understand you traded me.' I was pretty disgusted. I think they would have liked me to say I had a sore arm so Cleveland would pick someone else, but I was too stubborn to lie.

"And that's how I ended up with the Cleveland Indians in 1965."

That's also where Ralph ran into trouble.

"I made thirty-eight thousand dollars with the Yankees in 1964. When I went in to talk contract with Gabe Paul, he said he'd give me thirty thousand dollars.

"I said, 'Listen, Gabe, I've been in the league for six years. I've had a lot of good seasons to build up this salary. You were the guy who traded for me, remember?'

"Gabe said, 'I don't want to feel like I got a lemon or a pig in a poke.'

"I said, 'What the hell does that mean?'

"Anyway, I finally signed a performance contract, which was illegal in those days. We agreed that I'd get thirty thousand dollars if I won ten games and fifteen hundred dollars a win after that. Basically, I had to win fifteen to break even. So I said, 'Gabe, your best pitcher won twelve games last season. If I win fifteen, I should do better than break even.' We talked some more and the guy conned me. I agreed to the deal after he promised me that I'd get every opportunity to pitch.

"By the All-Star break, I was 9–3. Suddenly, I'm out of the rotation. Birdie Tebbetts was the manager, and I asked him why I wasn't pitching. Birdie said, 'We're falling out of the race and I want to check out some of the young pitchers for next year.'

"I said, 'Hey, I've got to win fifteen games to get my money back.'

"Birdie said, 'I don't know anything about that. I'm the manager, and I'll pitch who I want.'

"That's when I knew I'd been had. I didn't pitch for two weeks and then got a start against Minnesota, beating them 2–1. That made me 10–3. I sit for a week and then get a start in the second game of a doubleheader against the Angels. I beat them, too, and I'm 11–3. Then I don't get another start for six weeks.

"I went to see Gabe and asked, 'What's going on around here?'

"Gabe said, 'What do you want?'

"I said, 'Do you think you got a lemon or a pig in a poke?'

"Gabe said, 'You're doing a fine job. You're pitching great.'

"I said, 'Gabe, I don't think I'm in the plans. Birdie is using the young guys. Let's throw the deal out and just give me the same money I made last year.'

"Gabe said, 'Don't worry about a thing. We'll straighten it out at the end of the season.'

"I had never been screwed by a GM like this before, so I lapped up what Gabe said and figured he'd eventually take care of me. Meanwhile, I still don't pitch. We're down ten runs in some games and I don't even warm up. Since I don't have a sore arm, they can't put me on the disabled list. I got beat in my last three starts, but two of the games were scores of 1–0 and 3–2. So I ended the year with 11 wins, meaning I got my thirty-thousand-dollar base and a fifteen-hundred-dollar bonus.

"At the end of the season, I go to talk to Gabe, and I can see that he is surprised that I'm in his office.

"Gabe said, 'I've been in baseball for forty years, and a deal is a deal.'

"I said, 'Gabe, you just lost a pitcher.'

"Gabe said, 'You'll never make this kind of money on the outside.'

"I said, 'Screw you and screw Cleveland.'

"That winter, Gabe traded me to Kansas City, but I had lost my heart for the game. Maybe I was too idealistic, but I couldn't believe what Cleveland did to me just to save a few bucks. After that, I mentally divorced myself from baseball. A few years ago, I saw Gabe at an old-timers' game. I introduced him to some friends by saying, 'This is Gabe Paul, the man who got me out of baseball.' Gabe gave me a funny-looking grin, but that's how I felt.

"It took a lot to sour me on baseball because I loved it. It was something to watch Mantle and Maris hit all those homers. I liked the idea of taking the mound and thinking, 'This is a big game. We gotta have this one.' Then I loved to get the newspaper the next day and read how I had won.

"But I didn't have the transition problems a lot of players experience when they quit. I had been in the oil business since 1961. I took my five-thousand-dollar World Series share and bought into a well in Barber County, Kansas. As time went on, I moved from just investing to actually putting together the deals.

"Then there's golf. I really like it, and I play a lot. I had a couple of friends who shared that passion. We pooled our resources in the middle 1960s and bought an estate in Mendham, New Jersey. It was two hundred acres with a forty-three-room English Tudor mansion and horse stables. We designed the course, and it became the Roxiticus Country Club. After I was released by the Mets in 1967, I went to work there as the pro."

Ralph has since moved to Larned, Kansas.

"I'm still in the oil business, and I play a lot of golf, even some tournaments on the senior tour. One nice thing about golf—you are in complete control. No one can stop you from playing because they want to put a few pennies in the bank."

And there is something else Ralph has to like about golf—no one thinks you're strange if you talk to the ball.

Bud Daley

There is a picture of Bud Daley sitting on a sofa, his feet propped up on his suitcase. He is wearing a plaid sport coat, a thin tie, a white shirt, and a straw hat. He has a Mona Lisa smile, the kind of look that says "I'm blowin' this burg and headin' to the big town."

The picture is labeled "Adios Boys," and it was taken by a wire service photographer on June 14, 1961.

"You better believe I remember that picture," said Daley. "It was at the Minneapolis Hilton, the day I was traded from Kansas City to the Yankees. We had just gotten back to the hotel, and my phone rang. One of the guys on the A's said he had picked up his phone and the wires must have gotten crossed. Anyway, the guy said he heard Charlie Finley and Roy Hamey making a deal that would send me to New York. I didn't even wait for the official word. I packed my bag and went straight to the lobby. I wanted to be there so I could get out as fast as I could when Finley told me about the deal. That's how it felt to go from a last-place club to the Yankees."

It had been at least twenty years since I saw Bud Daley. Most of my teammates had stayed in the public eye, either remaining in the mainstream of baseball as coaches or managers or celebrities such as Mickey Mantle and Whitey Ford. There is always someone offering you a nice job if you're Whitey Ford or Mickey Mantle, but if you're Bud Daley, it's a different story.

Bud was like a lot of the pitchers with the Yankees in the late 1950s and early 1960s—they were effective but were hidden behind Roger, Mickey, Whitey, and the other stars.

Now, they are lost in many of our memories. When I spoke with my old roommate, Joe DeMaestri, the subject of our pitching staff came up, and Joe said, "You know, Tony, I was on a talk show the other night, and I couldn't remember any of our pitchers but Whitey and Luis Arroyo."

The Yankees continually fortified their pitching staff with guys like Bud Daley. There was Art Ditmar, Bill Stafford, and Duke Maas—we had them for a couple seasons, they might have a year in which they won fifteen games, and then they would move on. Roger, Mickey, Ellie, and Moose would hit the home runs and get their names in headlines, but it was the Bud Daleys who kept the score close.

Before I called Bud Daley, I looked through my scrapbook and searched the dusty corners of my mind. I found out that Bud had won the game that clinched the pennant for us. He was also the winning pitcher in the final game of the World Series.

Bud was a left-handed junker. He used curves, changes, a few knuckleballs. He also threw a lot of 420-foot outs in Yankee Stadium. Because he was a lefty, the other teams would load up their lineup with right-handed hitters. The hitters would almost fall down swinging at his slow stuff. They'd hit the ball a mile in the air to left field, and the park would just eat it up. Bud was 4–8 with a 5.40 ERA when we traded for him in 1961, and he went 8–9 with a 3.96 ERA for us. He did some of his best work in long relief, when he didn't get credit for a victory or a save but he held the fort long enugh for us to come back and win.

Now it was time for the road atlas. Bud lives in Lander, Wyoming, which is about 120 miles west of Casper. Lander is in the middle of Wyoming, which basically is the middle of nowhere.

"About fifty-four hundred feet up at the base of the Wind River Mountains," said Bud. "It's a town of about eighty-four hundred. Great for hunting and fishing."

Somehow, it didn't surprise me that Bud ended up in a place like Lander. He loved to fish. In spring training, he would go down to the pier in Fort Lauderdale, catch a bunch of fish, and bring them back to his hotel room, throwing them in his bathtub. Then he would talk to one of the cooks at the hotel restaurant, who would prepare the fish for some of us.

Other than spending a lot of time outside, I had no idea what Bud was doing in Lander, but I figured he was probably wearing a hat. When we acquired Bud from Kansas City, he showed up wearing a hat. I found out why when he took it off—all Bud had on top was a little peach fuzz.

Bud was best known for his right arm—it was sightly withered and turned inward as if he had been a screwball pitcher for about a million years.

"That's because I was an instrument baby," said Bud. "When the doctor took me out of my mother's womb, the instrument slipped and pinched a nerve in my right shoulder. For the first six months of my life, my arm was paralyzed. My mother continually massaged it, hoping she could somehow make it better. Eventually, it got to the point where I could move it. I never really thought much of it, because it's the only right arm I've ever had."

You'd think with his withered arm that Bud would have been a terrible hitter, but I remember him usually getting wood on the ball and sometimes slapping out a few hits. It was kind of like they way he pitched—a lot better than he looked. He never hit a home run, but his career batting average was .192.

"I never thought that my arm would keep me out of baseball," said Bud. "A Pittsburgh scout sent me to a doctor, who said that he could operate on me. There was a fifty-fifty chance I'd have a normal arm, but there also was a fifty-fifty shot I'd never be able to use it at all. I told the doctor to forget it because I was just fine."

For ten years, he was good enough, maybe smart enough is a better phrase, to pitch in the big leagues.

"I loved Bud Daley," said Johnny Sain. "I first had him in Kansas City. I was talking to those guys about switching from a five-man to a four-man starting rotation. All the other guys were grumbling, wondering if their arms would get hurt and not ready to try something simply because they hadn't tried it before. But Buddy said, 'This is great, give me the ball.' I mean, this guy had a deformed right arm, and he wasn't afraid of anything. That's why it was super when we got him in New York. His attitude fit in with the rest of the Yankees."

Bud pitched until 1965.

"I had elbow surgery for bone chips before the 1964 season," he said. "The doctor told me that he might have gotten all the chips; then again, maybe not. No matter what happened, they would be back a year later. Well, by the middle of 1964, I knew they hadn't gotten them all."

Bud wasn't as lucky as a lot of us. When my career was over, I had been identified with the Yankees for a long time. Playing in New York for nine years got me through the door at NBC.

"The most money I ever made was twenty-four thousand dollars in 1962," said Bud. "The thing was that I never thought about what I'd do after baseball, didn't even talk about it with my wife. I guess I just thought I could go on and on, despite having the arm trouble. My wife saw me pitch once in 1964, and she begged me to quit. She said that she could hear me groan after every pitch, and she was sitting in the stands. She hated to see me hurt so much."

Bud was raised in Orange County, and that is where he returned after the 1964 season.

"I knew a guy who was an insurance salesman, and he said he could get me a job in that business. I did that for six months, just long enough to know that I wanted to sell anything but insurance.

Next was a job as a salesman for a packaging company. For ten years, I sold boxes in the Long Beach area. One day I came to work, and I was told that the company was having financial problems. The plant manager, myself, and some others were being laid off.

"I was in a pretty tough spot. That's when I thought of Lander. My stepfather's brother had started an organization called The National Outdoor Leadership School in Lander where they taught kids to survive in the wilderness. We had visited them up there and loved it. So I told Dorothy, my wife, to put the house on the market, and we were going to Wyoming. It was amazing. The sign went up in front of the house at 11:00 A.M., and by 5:00 P.M. we had a buyer. We loaded up the car and drove to Lander, with no house and no job, but a few dreams."

That was in 1976. Bud approached Lander as if it were a hitter, sizing up its strengths and weaknesses and trying to figure out how he could best beat it.

"It took about six months to get to know the town. I realized that there was a need for a lawn sprinkler company, so my wife and I started our own, B&D Sprinklers. It has gone really well. The pace in Lander is a lot different than it was in L.A. You call a plumber, and he says he'll be right over. That could be in an hour or next week, no one rushes to do anything. All in due time, you know how it is.

"There is one other lawn sprinkler company, but he has the same wait-till-tomorrow approach as a lot of people up here. Me, when they call and want something done, I'm right there as fast as possible. I think that's why our business has been a success. The good service almost shocks some people to death. Our season is about seven months, and I go seven days a week. As for the other five months, we shovel snow."

Bud and Dorothy have been married for thirty-four years and have four children. They live on a hill overlooking Lander. Out his back window he can see thirteen-thousand-foot mountains and perpetually snowcapped peaks. It is hard to imagine anyone being farther away from baseball.

"I've been to only two baseball games since I quit," he said. "Both times, I ended up sitting next to guys who thought they knew everything about baseball, and they knew nothing. I mean, it drove me crazy to have to listen to guys like that. Why go to games and put yourself through something like that?

"I do admit that there are times when I sit up here, maybe I'm out in the woods or just looking out of my window at the mountains, and I'll think that I was foolish that I didn't try to pitch another year. Or sometimes, I wish I had stayed around as a pitching coach. I never had a great fastball, so I had to learn the other things—surviving on breaking stuff and my wits. I look at some of these guys who are pitching coaches now, and I wonder, what can these guys be teaching the kids? All they ever did was throw fastballs. I played with and against a lot of those guys, and I know they don't know nearly as much about pitching as I do."

"Then I think about things and realize I've done pretty well for myself. I never had the stuff of some pitchers, but I lasted ten years. After baseball, I had no skills but kept at it, rode out the hard times, and now I've got a nice business in one of the most beautiful parts of the world. I've never been the kind of guy to live in the past or tell everyone I meet that I played for the Yankees. Basically, I'm happy with what I am."

Moose Skowron

No one can forget the day his first child is born, but if you had Moose Skowron around, you would remember every detail. In 1962, Moose knew that my wife, Margaret, was due soon, and he was full of advice.

"I've got two boys," he said. "I've been through this before."

I told Moose not to worry.

"Listen, call me when Margaret starts having labor pains," he said. "I'll come over to the house, sit with you, make sure you take it easy."

Again, I told Moose not to worry.

"Promise you'll call me," he said.

When Moose gets like that, you have no choice but to promise. We were renting a house in River Edge, and Moose lived just down the road. About three in the morning, the pains began, so I called

Moose. He came over, and there wasn't much to do but wait, so we sat around playing cribbage.

About five, Margaret said, "Tony, I think it's time to get to the hospital."

Moose heard that, and he just lost it. Suddenly, he wasn't talking about all the experience he had had as a father and dealing with hospitals. Instead he went for the telephone.

"Who are you calling?" I asked.

"These guys I know in Jersey," he said.

"What guys?"

"You know, FBI guys."

"What?"

"I know these FBI guys in Jersey," he said. "I mean, these guys are great. They know exactly what to do at a time like this."

Moose had the telephone in his hand and was dialing when I stopped him. The crazy thing was that the only person in the house panicking was Moose. I finally settled Moose down and we got Margaret to the hospital, and everything went fine.

But that's just Moose. He always wants to do things for people. And he is so sincere. I don't think a more naive guy ever played in the majors. He looks like a carnival strongman, so muscular. Twenty-five years after it went out of style, Moose still has a crew cut. Underneath the muscle is a very soft guy.

Even his nickname is a bit of a misnomer.

"Everyone thinks I'm called Moose because I'm big and I played football at Purdue," he said. "But it happened when I was just a kid. My grandfather gave me a haircut and just about shaved my head. The kids in the neighborhood started calling me Mussolini, and it stuck."

In 1957, I roomed with Moose. I think we had a natural empathy for each other because we are both Polish. For us, a big night was going out with Bobby Richardson to the nearest YMCA to play Ping-Pong. Or else Moose and I would stay in the room and play Battleships, this board game. One day, Moose was very excited because there was a mirror behind where I was sitting, and Moose could look into it and see all my moves.

"That was great," said Moose. "I knocked you out of the box, game after game."

Moose got a kick out of little things like that.

As Bob Turley said, "Moose was the nicest, most gullible man I've ever met."

Maybe that's why Moose is the perfect guy for baseball fantasy camps. When I talked with him in Chicago, he had just returned home, and he was worried.

"Tony, there was this veterinarian playing second base," said Moose. "I was the second-base umpire and a ball was hit up the middle. The vet dove for it and broke his collarbone. Such a nice guy. I feel terrible for him."

Moose attends about eight fantasy camps a year, which should give him enough plate appearances for the batting title.

"I love those camps because I get to meet guys who liked and even idolized me as a player," said Moose. "The campers call me General Patton, because I make them work hard. I do the same thing to them that the Yankee coaches did to me.

"When I first came up, I wasn't much of a glove at first base. But I worked and worked. One spring, the Yankees even had me take dance classes at the Fred Astaire Studio in Saint Petersburg so I could improve my footwork. I tell the campers that story, and I think they know what I'm saying.

"These guys are all at least thirty-five, some over fifty. They are doctors, lawyers, professional men. There was this neurologist who said his lifelong fantasy was to pitch against me. I asked him what would happen if I hit a line drive back at him. I could ruin his career, you know? And the neurologist said, 'Moose, that would be my biggest thrill.' So what was I supposed to do? I went to bat, he took the mound. His first two pitches went over my head. The next one hit me in the elbow. But so what? He was a nice guy. Now he sends me Christmas cards."

What makes Moose ideal for fantasy camps is that they are so real to him.

"At one of the camps, a couple of the guys were very shy," said Moose. "They didn't say a word to no one. I worried about those guys feeling like they were left out. So I came up to them and said, 'Let's go to dinner.' While we were eating, I told them about my rookie year and how I was scared and shy. One day, Allie Reynolds and Vic Raschi came up to me and invited me to dinner. While we were in the restaurant, they said, 'Moose, when you're making the big money, you take care of the young players.' Every spring I did that.

"The campers really like to hear our war stories. They are so interested, it makes you feel good just to talk to these guys. The camps are super. They last a week. In the mornings and afternoons, the campers play games and get instructions from us. At night, we have a social hour when the guys can have drinks with us and get autographs. It ends with a game between the campers and players. You know, I'm fifty-five and I still like playing, even if it is in a fantasy camp. At least my 420-foot fly balls don't get caught like they used to in New York."

Since Moose was a right-handed hitter, the worst place he could have played was Yankee Stadium. He would hit these 420-foot shots to left field, and the park would eat them up. He'd come back to the bench, mumbling and complaining and then yelling about the park. Mickey or Whitey would say, "Moose, you know I think your top hand is flying off the bat too fast."

They would be kidding Moose, but he always took them seriously, and sometimes he would end up in a slump. He took everyone seriously. When he wasn't hitting, he'd worry and he'd listen to advice from anyone—the coaches, Mickey, the batting practice pitcher, you name it.

"I hated it when I was in a slump," said Moose. "I'd hit a ball 450 feet to center, and they would catch it. I'd hit it 400 to left, and they would catch it. After a while, I wondered what I was doing wrong. I felt like I was letting the whole team down. I took the game home with me. People would say, 'Moose, you worry too much.' But I got depressed when I wasn't doing my best. That was the thing about the Yankees. It was such a great club, twenty-five guys who always helped each other out. We'd cheer for each other, help each other when things went wrong. And if a guy didn't break up a double play, you better believe we hollered at him. I remember seeing Mickey Mantle cry after the 1960 World Series because we lost. Other guys cried after we lost games. On that team, losing was the worst feeling because it was like you let your family down."

Moose played for fourteen years and hit .282, with 211 homers. Five times he batted .300, and he was a guy with no discipline at the plate. If you think Yogi Berra was a bad-ball hitter, you should have seen Moose. You could bounce the ball up there, and he would swing at it. He just came off the bench swinging, and I don't know how many balls Moose hit that were off his ear or in the dirt. And he hit the ball so hard. Moose would nail one and the pitchers didn't have time to get out of the way. Balls would bounce off their arms and legs.

"The guys would kid me because I never knew what pitch I hit," said Moose. "Roger and Mickey would want to know what I hit out. How did I know? It was hard enough just seeing the ball and hitting it without thinking about the pitch."

Joe DeMaestri said, "Not only wasn't Moose sure what kind of pitch he hit, he didn't even know where he hit the ball. He'd jerk his head out, and his entire body would be pointed to left field. His top hand would fly off the bat, but he'd hit the ball out to right. It would be like a bullet. He swung so hard he couldn't tell you what happened because he didn't see what he was doing. Moose would have no idea what happened. He'd be running around the bases looking for the ball in left field, and here it was in right."

Moose waved his huge thirty-six-inch bat as if it were a Ping-Pong paddle. He was fearless at the plate, but not off the field. Injuries terrified him. As Jimmy Cannon wrote, "You're Bill Skowron and you never knew there were so many doctors in the world until you became a Yankee."

The July 20, 1961, *The New York Times* discussed Moose's nineteenth homer in these terms: "Skowron returned from lumber limbo wearing a Mae West corset, which pulls in the back and belly and pushes up his chest. Doesn't make him look as good as Mae, but it keeps Moose's sore muscles at bay."

Moose was so muscular that he could pull something just by taking a deep breath. He never lifted weights, but his shoulders and legs were so big that he was always tearing his muscles apart.

In 1957 when we roomed together, Moose tore a hamstring. That morning in our hotel room, Moose sat down on the toilet and couldn't get up. I had to pull him to his feet, help him get wrapped and dressed, and take him to the park. Casey Stengel saw Moose and asked how he was doing.

"You should have seen Kubek," said Moose. "He had to help me when I was in the bathroom."

Casey said, "I don't care if you can go to the bathroom, can you play?"

Things like that would always make Moose laugh. They also helped him play when he was in pain.

There was a day during the 1961 season when we were in Kansas City. Some guys were in Moose's room, and they started kidding him about being a football star at Purdue. Mickey said he could have played at Oklahoma. Roger said he had a scholarship there, too.

Next thing I remember Mickey, Roger, Moose, and Ellie Howard are playing football, tackling each other. The guys turned out the lights, and the game spilled out of Moose's room into the hallway. There was one of those old radiators in Moose's room, and he got tackled into it, banging up his leg.

John Blanchard said, "Moose loved to be at the center of the guys' jokes. He loved the attention. When I think of Moose, I remember him and Bob Cerv before games. The two of them would face each other. They would lock their hands behind each other's necks. Then it would begin, the banging of heads. They'd do it for fun, but they wouldn't stop until there were tears running down from their eyes. I know Moose and Cerv had fun doing it, but there's nothing more horrible than hearing two skulls bang together."

"I loved those Yankee teams and all the stuff we used to do," said Moose. "That's why it hurt so much when I was traded. I was having some personal problems, and it was probably best for me to leave New York and get a fresh start, but it still bothers me when I think of how I got the word I was going to Los Angeles. At 3:30 in the morning, I got a telegram that read something like, 'Your services are no longer needed.' I had been in the organization for nine years, and we had won seven pennants.

"I went to the Dodgers in 1963, and we faced the Yankees in the Word Series. The first two games were in New York. I was rooming with Frank Howard, and I was nervous as a pussycat. I couldn't sleep at all. I had a good World Series, hit .385, but I wish I had been with the Yankees. Those guys were my friends, and it really didn't mean anything that I was on the team that beat them. I just missed those guys."

Moose's top salary was thirty-seven thousand dollars in 1962. He works today in Chicago for a printing company that sells personal checks to banks.

I think Bob Turley, who has made millions in the insurance business, summed up Moose best: "He is this big kid who always enjoys things. He loves to go to banquets and pick up a couple hundred dollars as a speaker. He talks ninety miles a minute, and people just instantly like him. He also works for the state of Illinois, teaching bicycle safety in the schools. How can you not love a guy who relishes showing little kids how to ride a bike?"

Bob Hale

I never figured that our class clown would end up being the principal, but that's what happened to Bob Hale.

Imagine hearing the national anthem. Then imagine hearing Porky Pig. Then put them together and you have Bob Hale in the Yankee dugout in 1961. Twenty-five years and a Ph.D. later, Bob can still do Porky Pig, which makes him different from any principal I ever had.

Our conversation went like this: "Bob, so what are you doing these days?"

"I'm a principal." Bob said.

"A principal?"

"Roosevelt Elementary in Park Ridge, Illinois," he said.

I was quiet for a moment and then said, "No kidding."

"No kidding," he said. "I have a Ph.D. and everything."

"A Ph.D.?"

"In educational administration," he said.

"Really?"

"Really," he said.

He is a principal who plays softball with the boys, jumps rope with the girls, and sits on the swings with the first-graders.

"The biggest kick I get is when one of the little kids comes up and hugs my pants leg," he said. "You know it's sincere because little kids only do and say what they feel."

I listened to Bob talking about his life now, a life so different from the one he had at the end of the Yankee bench in 1961. As he spoke, I could still hear Bob in the corner of the dugout. The national anthem would start and so would Bob. It would end and so would Bob, with a "and that's all, folks."

"Porky Pig made me a star," said Bob. "I got to do it for Joe Garagiola on a pregame show for the NBC 'Game of the Week.' It was during an old-timers' game in Baltimore. They had Luis Aparicio, Robin Roberts, and myself give the lineups. Aparicio and Roberts had just been elected to Hall of Fame, and I was there to do Porky."

The Yankees picked up Bob from Cleveland. He was a decent pinch hitter, and the Yankees wanted another left-handed bat to come off the bench. He didn't play much, just 11 games with a .154 batting average.

"It was great getting traded to New York," said Bob. "I was with Cleveland, and we were in fifth place and had just lost three straight to Kansas City. We were flying to Los Angeles and the manager, Jimmy Dykes, stands up and says, 'Well, guys, we ain't been playing well, so tomorrow we'll have a special workout. I want de la Hoz, Dillard, and Hale and a couple other guys.' I'm thinking, hey, wait a minute. Mike de la Hoz? Don Dillard? Me? We didn't even play in the Kansas City series.

"So the next day, we go to the workout. We were supposed to take batting practice and then run for half an hour. Vic Power was just coming off the disabled list, and he had to work out, too. Vic said, 'Let me hit first.' Vic had great bat control and he hit every ball out of the park, foul. Luke Appling was our coach, and you'd have thought he had to pay for the balls, he was so mad. We had to cancel batting practice because we were out of balls. Then we were supposed to run, but since it was June and we thought we were in shape, we went straight to the showers.

"Appling screamed at us. 'This is the last day to make a trade, and some of you guys are gone.' "

"So I said, 'That's right, Luke, and I'm going to New York.' I don't know why I said that because there were no rumors or anything. I just said it. A couple hours later, it happened. It was very strange."

The Yankees bought Bob for twenty-five thousand dollars on June 28, 1961.

"I got on a red-eye flight from L.A. to New York, and I didn't sleep at all. I just kept thinking about the fact that I was going to be with the Yankees. When you play with Cleveland, you don't even dare to dream that you'll be in the World Series.

"When I get there, the Yankees were having old-timers' day. I walked into the clubhouse, and I saw Vic Raschi, Joe DiMaggio, Bill Dickey, and King Kong Keller. I mean, this was a lot different from Cleveland. I looked at all these great players and wondered, What was I doing there? Then I got a program and went around asking for autographs. It was a thrill just to be in the same room with these guys.

"According to Ralph Houk, I was on the club for one reason—to pinch hit and maybe hit a sacrifice fly off a right-handed pitcher. Basically, I ended up being the best cheerleader the Yankees ever had. I had a left-handed catcher's mitt, and I warmed up pitchers in the bull pen. I hit fungos and was always at the park whenever anyone wanted to take some extra batting practice. I wanted to make myself useful. I got to write an article for the *Long Island Daily News* titled 'How the 25th Man Views the World Series.' I was proud to be there, proud to be one of only four hundred guys who were in the majors at the time."

Without Bob, the Yankees would have hit only 239 homers that year.

"I'll say this much, when I hit my one homer, I got my picture in the papers," said Bob. "Five of us hit homers that day, and they lined us up, holding our bats out. There's the Murderer's Row—Maris, Mantle, Skowron, Blanchard, and Hale. And you know what? Bob Turley called the pitch I hit out. He whistled for a fastball, and that's what it was. Without Turley, my big-league home run total would have been cut in half."

Bob retired after the 1962 season, which he spent at Class AAA Richmond.

"It ended in late July," he said. "I was having a good year, and I went home to be with my wife for the birth of our son. When I got back to Richmond, I found out that the Yankees had farmed out Joe Pepitone. They wanted him to play first and me to sit. I begged to be sent anywhere, even to Class AA, so I could play. But the Yankees said I had to pinch-hit at Richmond. I told them to forget it. I wasn't about to die on the Richmond bench, so I got in my car and drove home to Chicago. I was twenty-nine, married with three kids, and had no real skills and one year of college."

For the next seven years, Bob went to DePaul in the morning and worked from 3:00–11:00 P.M. as a recreation center director.

"Going back to school wasn't that hard," said Bob. "I think I was respected because most of the people in my class knew I was a baseball player and now here I was, starting over. At first, I never thought about a Ph.D. I just wanted my bachelor's degree so I could teach and coach. When I quit playing, I knew that no one would give me something for nothing. It really was time to go to work.

"I was the first college graduate in my family. My father was a bookkeeper and later worked for the IRS, but he had no college. In fact, he wanted me to play pro ball. During my first year in the minors, I jumped the club and came home. I was eighteen, homesick, and I missed my girlfriend. My father gave me some very practical advice. He said, 'Why don't you marry that girl and go back to playing ball like you should?' That's exactly what I did.

"I think I'm one of those guys who has a light bulb over his head. I was always thinking, always striving. I made the most of my athletic ability, and then I did the best I could in school. I taught in elementary schools, high school, and college. I've coached baseball at all amateur levels, and I still scout for the Dodgers. After I got tired of coaching, I went into administration and was fortunate enough to become a principal.

"Okay, I was never a Roger Maris, Mickey Mantle, or Bobby Richardson. What makes me feel good is when I went to that old-timers' game in Baltimore [Baltimore *Sun*] columnist Bob Maisel wrote that I had things in the right perspective. I wasn't there looking for a job, and I wasn't there to live in the past. I showed up to see some of my friends and have a nice weekend with my wife.

"I met some of the guys, guys who hit forty homers and drove in 140 runs, and found out they were working behind the counter of a paint store or driving a truck. It wasn't easy for them. For me, the good times began in baseball but have really continued for the rest of my life.

"In my office, I've got some of my bubble gum cards that kids had bought for me at card collector shows. There also is a framed newspaper box score from the game when Roger hit his sixty-first homer. I went in to play first base for Moose in the late innings and I was 1 for 1. I was proud just to play in the same game when Roger broke the record. Park Ridge is a relatively small town, about forty thousand. I know most of the people here and they know me. It's white, middle class. We have the same values and want the same things. Like I said, people don't remember what I did in the majors. But they know I was there with the 1961 Yankees, and that makes me feel good."

John Blanchard

There were times when John Blanchard seemed afraid of everything. He worried about playing, about not playing, about being noticed by the manager, and about not being noticed.

Flying terrified him. So did Casey Stengel. So did the thought of not being in the majors for five years so he could qualify for the pension plan.

But it wasn't until he left the Yankees that he had to sing "Happy Birthday" to a mule in Kansas City. And it was later when John used to sing "Ninety-nine Bottles of Beer on the Wall' and then try to drink them all.

John was sensitive, and he took things to heart. In fact, he still does.

"Every day I think of some game situation where I screwed up," said John. "Today, I remembered the 1960 World Series. I was catching, Pittsburgh had a runner on first base, and Roberto Clemente was the hitter. Clemente popped up a bunt in front of the plate. Now, I was thinking that I'd let the ball bounce, field it, and throw to second base for the first out. Maybe Clemente wouldn't run, and we'd get a double play.

"So that's what I did, and I executed it just right. But Clemente did run, and all we got was a force-out at second base. When I went into the dugout, Frank Crosetti said I blew it. I should have caught the ball. The idea was to keep Clemente off base because he could run. That play didn't cost us the World Series or anything, but you know, Tony, I wish I had caught that pop-up. These things run through my mind all the time, and they happened more than twenty-five years ago."

Nothing came easy for John, especially traveling.

I remember a trip from Boston to Chicago. I was sitting next to Joe DeMaestri, and Blanchard was across from us. John would take sleeping pills, close his eyes, do anything to keep calm in the air. On this particular trip, we were over Lake Michigan and hit a severe storm.

The pilot came on the intercom and said, "Boys, we've been trying to fly around this storm since Boston, but it's so massive and high that we have no choice but to go into it."

Johnny Sain looked out the window and said he saw water spouts over the lake. A bolt of lightning hit one wing, and it went right through the plane. Sain said, "Don't worry, I fly my own plane. This isn't uncommon."

I looked over at Blanchard, and John was drenched with sweat. He wanted to crawl under the seat. But it was DeMaestri who cracked first. He ran up the aisle to the cockpit and told the pilot, "Captain, you've got to set this thing down."

The captain said, "How can I do that when I can't see anything? I'm just happy we're still alive."

I took another glance at Blanchard, and I think he was praying. I do know I'd never seen anyone's face that white.

In the back of the plane, Roger Maris, Jesse Gonder, and some other guys were playing cards. We went over a real bumpy spot, and Gonder threw his cards up in the air. Suddenly, he ran up the aisle and screamed, "Mr. Pilot, you gotta set this thing down, sir."

"I can't do that, we're over water," said the pilot.

"I don't care, set it down in the lake," said Gonder. "I know I can swim. If we blow up, I know I can't fly."

And that was when poor John Blanchard lost his lunch, and his breakfast and supper, too.

John laughed when I reminded him of this story, but he said, "I never liked to fly, and I don't care who knows it. I hated flying. I was scared, very scared."

He also seemed to be that way about Casey Stengel.

"Tony, if you had been cut as often as I was, you would have had problems with the old man, too," said John. "In the late 1950s, it was the same thing every spring. Here comes John Blanchard to camp. He had a good year in the minors. He was a promising prospect. I got so used to getting a ticket to the minors, they could have saved us all a lot of heartache by giving it to me on the first day. I would have gone quietly. I don't think Casey said three words to me in three years."

I recall a few instances when Casey had something to say to John.

There was a game in 1960 when Stengel got mad at Yogi Berra and threatened to take him out of the game. Casey brought John in from the bull pen and told him to get on the catcher's gear because he was going in for Yogi. It was an afternoon game, humid, with the temperature about ninety. John just sat there for seven innings, wearing all the catcher's equipment, waiting for the word from Casey that never came. At the end of the game, John's uniform was soaked with sweat, and he never even got on the field.

In another game, Casey actually let John hit. But Casey didn't like the way John swung, because when he missed he almost fell over. Casey was roaring, and the next thing we knew, he was out of the dugout and yelling in John's face. Then Casey jumped up and down and landed right on John's foot, spiking him. John could hardly stand up, and Casey had to take him out for a pinch hitter.

"All I ever wanted to do was play for the Yankees," said John. "I didn't care if I sat for a week and did nothing but warm up pitchers in the bull pen. Being there made everything worth it. Yeah, I could hit, and I had a little power. I do wish we'd had the designated hitter back then because I could have cleaned up. But I didn't think about those things. I was never one of those 'play me or trade me' guys. From the first day I stepped into that Yankee dugout, the only thing I had in mind was staying there for five years so I could get my pension, and I was scared to death that I wasn't going to make it.

"It was kind of crazy. During the winter, I'd worry about being in a car wreck or slipping on the ice, something that would break a bone or hurt my knee and end my career. Then all those years in the minors, all that time on the bench in New York would have been shot. I was a pretty good basketball player, and the Minneapolis Lakers made me an offer, but I never touched a basketball after 1951 because I thought I might get injured and that would be it. I wouldn't even shoot baskets in someone's driveway."

Listening to John, it's easy to forget that he was a fine, confident hitter. The bat was his source of strength. He was never timid at the plate. If he had been a regular, I think he could have been good for twenty-five or thirty homers a year. In 1961, he hit 21 homers as a part-time player, one every 11 at bats. He batted .305 and had a .613 slugging percentage.

From 1961 to 1963, John had 50 homers in 707 at bats. But he never had much of a chance until Ralph Houk became manager.

John did get his five years in with the Yankees.

"Then they traded me and Rollie Sheldon to Kansas City. I know being in baseball means you get traded and released, but I was shocked. I had been with the organization for fifteen years. I never wanted to play anywhere else."

Some of the players tried to console John by telling him he would be a regular with the A's. His response was to weep.

CBS owned the Yankees, and they were getting rid of everyone. They traded Roger Maris for Charley Smith. The standing joke around the league was that Art Carney and Jackie Gleason must have been making deals for the Yankees.

"The trade just sapped my competitiveness. I just lost interest. Do you know what it was like to play for Charles O. Finley? I remember this game when Fred Talbot was pitching. It was an eight o'clock game, the umpires were ready, and Fred had warmed up. I'm in the dugout with all my equipment on, and I turn to [manager] Haywood Sullivan and say we should get out there.

"Sully says, 'We've got to wait.'

"So I sit there for a few minutes and I said, 'Sully, what's going on? We've got to take the field.'

"Sully says, 'No, I've been told to wait.'

"All of a sudden, the center-field fence opens, and here comes this guy leading a donkey. He walks the donkey all the way around the warning track and down the right-field line. They come up to the mound, and this big birthday cake appears out of nowhere at home plate.

"Sully says, 'Okay, guys, everybody on the field.'

"I said, 'What's this?'

"Sully says, 'We all have to go to the mound and sing "Happy Birthday" to the mule.'

"And there you had it. A birthday cake at home plate, a mule on the mound, and twenty-five guys singing 'Happy Birthday.' I just hated being there and hated everything about it.

"We finally start playing the game, and we're leading the Red Sox 2–1 in the ninth inning. It's hotter than the devil, and Talbot has had it. We have Catfish [Hunter] warming up in the bull pen. Sully goes to the mound and waves in Catfish. But Catfish doesn't move. I stepped down off the mound, took my mask off, and whistled and waved, but nothing seemed to be happening in the bull pen.

"Then the center-field fence opens, and here comes the lousy mule again. It walks down the right-field line to the bull pen. Now Catfish has to jump on the mule and ride him to the mound. So Catfish is riding the mule, but the mule spots a guy in the stands with some popcorn, and he wants some. So the mule starts walking the wrong way. Catfish is going nuts. He throws an arm lock on the mule, and the mule's eyes are about popping out of his head because Catfish is squeezing the mule's neck, trying to get him going in the right direction. All this is going on in the ninth inning of a 2–1 ballgame.

"After 1965, I quit. I just had had enough. I tried to come back in the spring of 1967, but I was thirty-four and too far into the jug to be any good."

I remember that John liked his beer.

"You better believe it," he said. "If I went 0 for 4, I drank to forget. If I was 4 for 4, I drank to celebrate. I had a problem when I played, but I didn't admit it. It just kept creeping up on me. And when I was out of baseball, I just couldn't deal with things. I had a liquor store, but it drove me out of my mind to stand in one place for eighteen hours a day. Then I started spinning my wheels. I tried selling cars, selling real estate, recruiting people for insurance companies, and I don't know what else. I must have had seven jobs in ten years. I tried to get back into baseball. I wrote letters to about fourteen different teams. I got nice answers, but no offers.

"I got in a self-pity bag, and I kept drinking. God, I was going downhill and fast. I couldn't find a job I was happy with. I missed baseball, and I couldn't get back in the game. I was lost. The worse it got, the more I drank. Then it got to where I couldn't remember what I had done the night before or where I was. I'd tell myself that I couldn't go on like this, but I'd do the same thing again. My wife, Nancy, was going through hell. I didn't beat her or anything, but I was hardly the perfect husband. I knew I was going to kill somebody unless I died first. I went to see a friend and told him what was happening to me. He said I was having blackouts and I had better get some treatment.

"I went to Abbott Northwestern Hospital in Minneapolis. I was in there for thirty-four days. It kills your ego to think that you have sunk that deep in the booze. But it takes a lot of guts to go in. I know guys who walked right up to the front door but couldn't take that last step. They turned around and left and went right back to the bottle. In the hospital, everyone is in the same boat. That gets your head on straight. I walked out of there in 1975 and haven't had another drink since.

"I've done a complete one-eighty. I just drink water. Once every six months, I give myself a treat and have a Coke. The only time I thought about drinking was six years ago. It was real hot, and I had this taste for a beer. But I was afraid to have one."

John lives in Minnetonka, Minnesota, where he works for the Pettibone Corporation selling switches, turnouts, and cranes to railroads.

"The amazing thing is that I had a job with those people when I went into the hospital, and it was there when I came out," he said. "They stuck with me through that and everything else since 1975."

Falling under the "everything else" heading is cancer.

"We all think that it's somebody else who gets it," said John. "I bet Roger felt the same way. I know I did. In my case, I came home from work on November 16, 1985, and went to the bathroom. I know the date because when they tell you that you have cancer, you never forget when it happened. Anyway, there was blood in my urine. I wondered, what's this. I felt like a million bucks. I hadn't had a drink in ten years. I went to the bathroom a couple more times, and there was even more blood. I called a doctor, and at midnight I went to the emergency room. They did some CAT scans and dye tests. Then the doctor says to me, 'Blanch, I've got some bad news. It's cancer of the kidney.' He wanted to operate the next morning, and I didn't have time to think about it. They had to cut and that was that.

"You can't imagine the mental anguish. I thought about Roger and how cancer was killing him. I thought about all the other people I knew who had had cancer and how they were dead. I thank God that I didn't have too much time to think about it. If I'd had to walk around another day with the thought that there was cancer in me, I don't know if I could have taken it. I was lucky, I was in the hospital for eight days, and tests showed that the cancer was confined to my kidney. There was no aftercare, no chemotherapy, radiation, or anything.

"When I talk about everything, it seems like life has been sort of hell. Not only did I have cancer, but so did my son, Paul. He had been a punter at the University of Minnesota, and his average went from 42 to 35 to 30 yards. It turned out that he had cancer of the lymph glands. He was taking chemotherapy and radiation treatments and still trying to play football. But he's doing okay now. They think they got it all, and Paul is a baseball coach at Northerndale Junior College here in Minnesota.

"Now that I think about it, I guess I do wish I could have played today. I was never much of a catcher, so the DH would have been perfect for me. I never made more than twenty-three grand. In 1963, I hit 16 homers and had 45 RBI in less han 250 at bats. I was making fifteen thousand dollars, and the Yankees wanted to cut me fifteen hundred. Holy criminy, I thought I had a decent year for a utility man, so I didn't sign until I went to Florida for spring training. They told me to sign for the same money I made the year before, and they would keep me around. Like I said, I hated the idea of being traded, so I signed, and a year later they traded me anyway.

"I read the papers and see where some guy goes to arbitration. He had a crap year and he made $150,000. The club offers him $180,000, but no, he wants $250,000. For what? Playing worse than he did the year before. How can you kiss off a thirty-grand raise just like that? If only these guys knew how tough it is to make thirty grand on the outside.

"Ah, I'm really not bitter or anything. I just think about things and get myself worked up over nothing. Let's face it, I was the one who started drinking and had trouble keeping the same job. It's no one's fault that I was born too early. When I calm down, I realize I have beaten the booze. It looks like I've beaten cancer. The same for my son Paul. My wife has stuck by me all these year, and I now work for a good company. Once in a while, somebody recognizes my name, and I get to talk about being with the Yankees. I still get a couple of letters a week from kids wanting autographs. Hey, it ain't all that bad."

Ellie Howard

I was like a lot of guys with the Yankees during the spring of 1961. We stayed at the Hotel Soreno while Hector Lopez and Ellie Howard lived with a family in a black neighborhood of Saint Petersburg. I was aware that Ellie couldn't always eat and stay at the same places as the rest of us in Florida. We would see Ellie at the park and on the team bus. But in spring training, I don't remember any of us inviting him out for dinner. We all liked Ellie. It's not as though we consciously wanted to stay away from him. It was as though no one thought of it, and when I think back on that, it's really sad.

I mentioned this to Ellie's widow, Arlene Howard.

"Tony, that is just how it was back then," she said. "The civil rights bills didn't happen until 1964. Whether we want to admit it or not, until then discrimination was the law of the land. Elston knew it. I knew it. Every black person in Florida lived with it."

Hector Lopez said, "Since they wouldn't let the black and Latin players in the Soreno Hotel, we stayed with black families. This didn't bother me so much, because I was young and just over from Panama. The team bus would go out of its way to drop us off on the other side of town and to pick us up for games. For the most part, the people we stayed with were very nice, and they treated us like kings. But once we had a game in Fort Meyers, and they put us in an undertaker's house. I'll say this much, it was quiet because the five dead bodies they had in that house didn't make much noise."

Arlene Howard said, "Some people said that the Yankees were a big, powerful organization and their dollars were important to the city of Saint Petersburg. Why didn't they demand that blacks get the same accommodations as their white players? The Yankees could have put some pressure on the city fathers, but they weren't about to do that. Let's face it, nothing was going to change until black people got off their behinds. We had to start marching and getting things done for ourselves."

I do remember that Casey Stengel stood up for the black players. We used to take a train from Florida to New York, making stops along the way to play exhibition games in various southern cities. When we got to a small town in Georgia, I think it was Valdosta, we found out that the local officials wouldn't let our black guys play. Casey said if everyone couldn't play, none of us would play, and there was no game there.

But the problems remained.

In 1961, some prominent black players with the Milwaukee Braves—Hank Aaron, Wes Covington, and Billy Bruton—complained when they had to stay at a rooming house in Bradenton instead of the team hotel.

Henry Aaron told the *Sporting News*, "Sometimes the place is so crowded that they have guys sleeping in the hall. They have five guys living in two rooms. They put two beds in one room, two more in the hall and another bed in a smaller room. They got a room over the garage. They call it the penthouse. At the most you can put four people in there and they have eight. They said this place was carefully selected for us to stay. Carefully selected from what? There isn't one decent place in this town for us to stay. . . . We took a bus ride to Miami and we couldn't even eat with the rest of the guys. We had to stay on the bus while the white players bought us sandwiches."

Bob Turley said, "For a while, I remember that Ellie couldn't stay with the rest of us at the hotel in Kansas City. The Yankees put him up with a local black family. Now I realize that Ellie had to be angry, but he never showed it. The other guys didn't think twice about it. There was no attention, and it wasn't on the news until years later. But when you talk about the mood of the country, I remember when I won a big game and afterwards, I hugged Ellie, who was catching. I got several threatening letters, asking me why I'd hug a black man."

Bobby Richardson said, "It's hard for me to believe I played in an era when black and white players weren't allowed to stay in the same hotel. When I think back on it, I'm embarrassed and ashamed that I couldn't do something about it."

This was fourteen years after Jackie Robinson broke the color line, and first-class players were being treated like second-class citizens. For me, it's hard to imagine this because of how we live now, but I was there to see it. Like the rest of the guys, I knew what was happening in Florida wasn't right, but I didn't do anything about it. Later, I went up to Ellie and apologized. I said, "I saw the racism going on. I feel bad. I wish I had done something."

Ellie said, "That's the way things go, and that's how they are. They are changing."

There weren't a lot of racial incidents, but one happened when I was standing in front of a Tampa hotel with Henry Aaron and several other Milwaukee players. We had an exhibition game earlier in the day, and there were about eight of us in front of the hotel, Hank being the only black player. A pickup truck stopped, and there were three guys in the cab and about four in the back. These guys obviously were pretty deep into the beer, and they were loud. In the back of the truck's cab, you could see a shotgun hanging from the rack.

I remember that we were talking about going bowling, and we stopped when we saw the pickup.

The guys in the truck started yelling at us, wondering what we were doing with a black guy. They kept staring at Henry, and you could tell these guys didn't think he should be standing there with us. A couple of guys got out of the truck and approached Henry. They started up with some racial stuff, and things got heated. Henry told one of the guys to take off his coat. Henry took off his own coat. As the other guy got his Levis jacket down to his elbows, Henry nailed him with three quick punches to the face and stomach. The guy fell to the street; his friends picked him up, dropped him in the back of the truck and drove off. Henry had grown up in a tough part of Mobile, Alabama, and he knew how to take care of himself in those situations.

Ellie never thought about being a pioneer, but he was the first black Yankee, and he was selected to break the racial barrier as much for his personality as his talent. Jackie Robinson was outgoing and fiery; Ellie was quiet and reserved. Ellie had an inner toughness and burning desire, but he seldom showed that side. There were other black players in the Yankee farm system before Ellie, and some of them had the talent to play in New York. Vic Power was black and Puerto Rican, and he had great statistics in the minors. He could hit home runs and play first base better than anyone I've seen; it was as if he were a shortstop at first. But the Yankees weren't sold on his personality. The front office was afraid Power might fly off the handle when confronted with the pressure of being the first black Yankee. Eventually, he was traded because the Yankees wanted their first black player to be their kind of guy.

As Dan Daniel wrote in the *Sporting News*, "Howard, the first Negro to gain a place on the Bomber machine, was chosen for that situation *sui generis* because of his quiet demeanor, his gentlemanly habits and instincts, and his lack of aggressive attitudes on race questions. He came to the Yankees determined to achieve the position he now occupies, not as a crusader."

Arlene Howard said, "First of all, Elston knew he was a good player and that the Yankees would have to make room for him. I do think Elston resented the fact that because you're black, you were supposed to be some kind of super human being. To even get an opportunity, you had to be better than anyone else. It was the whole 'credit to your race' business."

I don't think much was made of Ellie coming to the Yankees in 1955 and being the first black Yankee because he fit in so well with the rest of the club. He didn't come to the Yankees until he was twenty-six. He was mature, a great athlete, and an outstanding person. There was no telling how good Ellie could have been if he had gotten to the majors younger and wasn't stuck catching behind Yogi Berra. It wasn't until 1961, when he was thirty-one, that he caught more than a hundred games in a season.

Arlene Howard said, "Elston was frustrated because he wasn't catching as much as he'd like, but he used to say that playing first and the outfield was good experience. I'd tell him that if he were with another team, he'd be a regular catcher. But Elston loved the Yankees so much, he didn't want to leave even if it meant he'd be the regular catcher. Some people told us that it was racist when the Yankees wouldn't let him catch early in his career, but Elston never felt like that. Getting angry wasn't part of his nature."

Bob Turley said, "When I think of Ellie Howard, I think of a great catcher and a beautiful person who never complained about anything."

When Ellie first joined the Yankees, Yogi was estabished as the catcher, and Yogi is a Hall of Famer. So Ellie filled in at first and in the outfield, along with backing up Yogi. By 1961, Ralph Houk wanted

Ellie to catch all the time, so he asked Yogi to switch to left field. A former catcher, Houk appreciated Ellie's amazing throwing arm and how he handled the pitchers. His throws were bullets, but when you caught them at second base, they went into your glove like a feather.

Bill Stafford: "When Ellie caught me, I always felt like I would win, even if I didn't have anything working. There were games when I had absolutely nothing, and Ellie kept me pumped up. No matter how bad things were, Ellie made me think that I'd be okay. Other catchers would say, 'You don't have it today. Just throw the ball in here.' Ellie was always working with me, trying to find a way that we could get people out."

Ralph Terry: "Ellie never gave up on his pitchers. During a bad inning, Ellie would come to the mound and say, 'C'mon, now, make one good pitch, and we'll get out of this thing. Then we'll score a couple runs and win the ball game for you.' He'd tell a pitcher about the great defensive players out there behind you. 'Let them hit the ball, we'll catch it for you,' he'd say. Ellie loved his pitchers. He wasn't a guy who said, 'Give me a fresh horse' because you gave up a couple hits."

Bob Turley: "Some catchers squat back there and fall asleep on you. Ellie was always talking, making sure he gave you a good target and keeping your mind on the game."

Whitey Ford: "Ellie was a much different style of catcher than Yogi. Ellie would get right up on the plate. I sometimes wondered why he never got hit with the bat. Yogi was three or four feet farther back. There was nothing wrong with pitching to Yogi, but when Ellie was that close to the plate, he made me feel like the plate was that much closer to the mound. Since I was throwing a lot of sinkers and curves, Ellie would get me so many low strikes because he caught them before they dropped into the dirt, when it still looked high enough to the umpire."

Jim Coates: "Ellie was the best catcher I ever threw to. He could catch those low pitches and bring them up into the strike zone without the umpire noticing. He stole a lot of strikes for me. And he didn't care if I threw my curveball. 'Just throw it, Jim,' he'd tell me. 'Don't worry if it's in the dirt, I'll catch it.' When Ellie caught, it was great because you could rear back and throw without any care in the world because he could catch any pitch."

It is ironic that Coates would praise Ellie to such lengths. During the spring of 1961, we had an exhibition game at West Point with the Army baseball team. After the game, Mickey and Whitey took us to the gym and divided the guys up in teams, and we played basketball.

When the basketball game was finished, we wandered to the part of the gym where there was a boxing ring. All of a sudden, I looked up, and there were Coates and Ellie in the ring, both wearing gloves. Coates was a rawboned, almost gaunt guy from Virginia, and he had the old-line Southern attitude about race and made no secret about it. He liked to throw at some hitters, and he seemed to come inside more on black players than whites. Jim was sort of an outsider, and some of the guys thought he was a redneck. So when we saw Coates and Ellie in the ring, everybody started yelling, and it seemed everybody was pulling for Ellie. Coates and Ellie weren't messing around. There was no referee, no rules, and no rounds. It was a flat-out brawl, and the punches got harder and harder. The next thing I knew, Coates was face down on the canvas. Ellie took off his gloves, and that was it. He had settled a score, and most of us were glad that he did.

Coates said, "I didn't want to fight, but Ellie kept after me. He taught me a lesson—never put the gloves on with Ellie."

It turned out that Whitey was the one behind the fight. He was tired of Coates giving Ellie a hard time, and he didn't like that kind of stuff going on in the clubhouse. When they got near the ring, Whitey started egging Coates on to have it out with Ellie. This was Whitey's way of getting the two to settle their differences; he knew Ellie would take care of Coates in the ring but probably wouldn't let himself take care of him outside of it.

In the baseball setting, a lot of the guys made a point of being with Ellie. When Ellie first joined the Yankees, it was Moose Skowron who picked him up at the airport. And when he got a hit to win his first game as a Yankee, the veteran players including Whitey and Mickey made a path of towels through the clubhouse to his locker, which is baseball's version of the red carpet treatment.

Ellie was a near Hall of Famer, not making it because his career began so late. He won the MVP award in 1963, hit .274 lifetime, made nine all-star teams, and was one of the best defensive catchers ever. In 1961, he batted .348, which was second highest in the league.

"We found out that to some people, it didn't matter how nice Elston was or how well he played," said Arlene Howard. "We bought our first house in Teaneck, and everything was fine because it was in an integrated neighborhood. They even had an 'Elston Howard

Day' in Teaneck, because the politicians were happy that a member of the Yankees lived in their town. But when we tried to buy a bigger house, Elston was no longer a famous ballplayer. He was just a black trying to get into an all-white neighborhood. We had to have the builder, who was white, buy the property for us. They never would have sold to a black family. Eventually, word got out that the house being built in this nice neighborhood belonged to a black family. I went over there and saw that someone had written 'nigger' all over the house. When we first moved in, our son little Elston had some trouble with the local kids. We had our own friends, so I never socialized much with the neighbors. But Elston was hurt and indignant about the fact that these people showed two sides. They loved you as a ballplayer because you're doing something for them. But when it comes to human decency and buying a house in a neighborhood where you want and can afford to live, it was a different story."

Elston often said that one of the greatest days in his life was when he heard on the radio that Jackie Robinson had been signed by the Brooklyn Dodgers. That's why Elston turned down several college football and basketball scholarships to play baseball in the old Negro Leagues with the Kansas City Blues. His dream of being a big leaguer finally had a chance to happen, and he knew that major-league teams were scouting the Negro Leagues for players to help the various clubs break their respective color lines.

Arlene Howard said, "I was always more furious and militant than Elston. In his own way, he stood up for civil rights. We integrated neighborhoods and so on, but Elston wasn't the kind of guy to get up on a soapbox. He never personalized racism. He realized that when he started playing, segregation was a law, and a lot of people just didn't know better.

"Now, there were some bitter disappointments. He wanted the opportunity to manage, and he did resent the fact that he never got the chance. He had been an outstanding catcher, a leader on the field. The Yankee players all talked about his knowledge of the game. Then he became a coach and learned some more. His dream was to manage the Yankees. We always thought that since they acted like great white liberals, they might give Elston a chance. But they told him, 'You've never managed.' How are you suppose to manage the first time unless someone gives you a job? They suggested that he go to the minors for experience, but a lot of players later became coaches and then managed without being in the minors. Elston wondered why he had to be better than everyone else, why he had to be superman to manage a baseball team. They wanted you to have a Ph.D. to manage if you were black, and about any white guy could manage. To Elston, it was kind of like a slap in the face. The closest we came was when Toronto talked to him about managing its expansion team. We went there for an interview, but nothing came of it. The best shot we had was in 1968. Bill Veeck was going to buy the Washington Senators, and he had offered Elston the job. But Veeck's deal fell through, and that was it."

Ellie Howard and Roger Maris both died on the same date, December 14, Roger in 1985 and Ellie in 1980. They were both fifty-one, and they both had their numbers retired on the same day at Yankee Stadium.

The day Elston died of heart failure, I was going to a Green Bay Packers game. Even though I live only twenty-five miles away from Green Bay, I had never been to a game before. A friend talked me into going. I had just driven into the stadium parking lot, and I heard on the radio that Elston had passed away. I was so upset, I just stayed in the car for a few moments and then drove home.

Arlene Howard still lives in Teaneck, where she is the president of the Elston Howard Printing Company. She is in the office every day and has eight people working under her. She is also very active in the Urban League. Her daughter, Cheryl Howard, has appeared in various musicals on Broadway and in Atlantic City.

"One of Elston's proudest moments was when he took the entire Yankee team to see Cheryl in a show in Chicago," said Arlene Howard. "He liked to talk about that day. Don't think that Elston died bitter. He was disappointed that some things didn't work out, but he was so proud to be a Yankee. He really loved those Yankee teams of the 1950s and 1960s."

Whitey Ford

Whitey Ford always loved being Whitey Ford. By that I mean that he was content with himself and what he accomplished. I'm not saying he just had a big ego, because he was the greatest pitcher in the history of the Yankees.

On the mound, he was so sure of himself, so cocky. But in other ways, he is almost shockingly humble. As a player he was very soft-spoken, and he never liked to talk about himself. He always had a quick wit, and to those who may have read some of Whitey's comments in the newspapers, it was easy to think of him as a wise guy. But Whitey was only like that around his friends. With people on the outside, he is a complete gentleman.

He is almost like two people, a Joe-the-Bartender character. On one level, he is the Irish guy who laughs all the time, tells jokes, and pats everyone on the back. You know, the kind of red-faced guy who isn't afraid to have a few drinks, make everyone laugh, and sing a couple of songs.

But on the other hand, Whitey can be quiet, introspective, and very aware of the feelings of people around him. That is why the guys on the team so admired him. On the field, he was a forceful leader. In the clubhouse, he was even more of a presence. He made a point to spend time not just with the stars or the guys who were having a tough time. He wanted everyone to feel a part of the Yankees, and it meant an awful lot to a young player when Whitey Ford spent some time just making small talk.

Out on the mound, he was amazing. He was so confident out there, and that rubbed off on the rest of us. Moose Skowron, one of the most sensitive players in Yankee history, appreciated Whitey's personality: "I loved playing behind Whitey because he never got on me if I made an error. Whitey liked to try all these pickoff plays, and if I messed one up, I'd feel terrible, but Whitey would say, 'Don't worry, Moose, you'll get the next one.' He wouldn't go slamming the resin bag, kicking the dirt, and doing the other things pitchers do to show up a fielder. With some of these guys, you'd boot one ball behind them, and they'd throw their gloves in the air. Not Whitey. He'd always remember all the big hits you got for him. And after you made an error, he seemed to bear down more to get out of the jam. It was like he wanted to take the pressure off you."

I always considered Whitey the consummate pro. Ellie Howard called him "The Chairman of the Board," and it was an apt nickname. Whitey was in control of every pitch and every situation. If he wanted to have a pickoff play at third base, he'd pick up the resin bag and throw it down toward third. If he wanted to pick a guy off second base, he'd throw the resin bag toward me or Bobby, and then we'd know who was supposed to cover the bag. If he thought the other team was stealing the catcher's signs, Whitey would call the whole game himself. He'd shake his head once for a fastball, twice for a curve, and so on.

There were some hard-hit balls off Whitey, but they usually went right at someone and were caught. That was really frustrating to the guys on the other teams. Sometimes, Whitey would pitch a guy right into his power. In Yankee Stadium, he could get away with it. Whitey would stand behind the mound, rubbing up the ball. He might just catch my eye for a second and move me with his eyes about ten feet toward second base. If he looked to his left, I moved left. To his right, I'd go right. Then a guy would hit a bullet right at me and couldn't believe I was playing in that spot. But Whitey had set the whole thing up.

"I loved playing short behind Whitey," said Joe Demaestri. "For years, I was on pretty lousy teams where most of the guys didn't know where they were throwing the ball. Whitey was incredible. He not only knew where his pitch was going, he knew where the guy was going to hit it. He'd tell you to move a couple of steps to your left, and the guy would hit the ball right at you. I couldn't believe it. I had been in the majors for nine years, and that never happened to me until I came to New York."

"Here is what it was like to catch Whitey," said John Blanchard. "The best thing was that you never had to think about that much because Whitey was calling the game. You didn't have to worry about going to the mound to settle him down, because it seemed he never got upset. There was one time in 1961 when I remember Whitey calling me to the mound. Right away, I started thinking that something was wrong, he must be hurt. Then I was thinking about how much trouble we would be in without Whitey.

"So I asked, 'Whitey, what's wrong?'

"Whitey said, 'Nothing.'

"I said, 'Then why bring me out here?'

"Whitey said, 'I figured you could use a break.'

"Name another pitcher who ever said something like that to a catcher."

Whitey could have won twenty games earlier in his career if he had gone to Casey and said he wanted to start more. But winning twenty wasn't as important to Whitey as winning the pennant. He didn't care about piling up numbers. He felt the same way about complete games. If it was the seventh or eighth inning and he had a good lead, Whitey would just as soon let the bull pen finish up. Then he would be even stronger for his next start. Strikeouts were something else that didn't concern him. He could have racked up a lot more, but he'd rather throw the ball over the plate and get hitters out on fewer pitches, saving his arm for the later innings. He knew he had a good defense behind him. In the infield, Bobby, Clete, and the rest of us would take care of the grounders. In the outfield, Roger and Mickey were there to chase down the fly balls. With Whitey, everything was efficiency, economy, and, in the end, winning. His career record was 236–106, which is a .690 winning percentage.

"Whitey was going for his twentieth win on the last day of the 1956 season," said Mickey. "He got beat 1–0 when I dropped a fly ball in center field. Then I ended the game with Whitey on third. I popped up to the second baseman. I didn't want to go into the clubhouse. Whitey was my best friend, and he could have finally won twenty games, and I blew the damn thing. If there had been a trap door on the field, I would have used it. I finally went into the clubhouse, and Whitey saw how bad I felt. He came up to me and said 'Ah, Mick, the heck with it. We'll get 'em.' And Whitey meant it; that's why the players loved him. They always used to say that 'as Mantle goes, so go the Yankees.' I guess I thought I was an inspirational leader and all that crap, but we all knew that the real leader of the Yankees was Whitey. Line up all the pitchers in the world in front of me, and give me first choice, I'd pick Whitey."

The other Yankee pitchers were astounded by Whitey.

Bud Daley: "It always seemed to me that Whitey was throwing half speed. He never broke a sweat. I never saw a guy who made pitching look so easy."

Ralph Terry: "Whitey was a master. It was like watching a pitching textbook in the flesh. Most guys had curves that broke in the direction of the spin, but Whitey's went down and away. The spin on Whitey's pitches indicated he was throwing a flat curve, when his actually broke right off the table."

Ryan Duren: "Whitey had more going for him than people thought. All pitching starts with the fastball, and Whitey was much quicker than people gave him credit for. He was known for his great curve, and that was the pitch hitters always looked for. But I saw Whitey get power hitters out by throwing three straight belt-high fastballs. It wasn't that he was overpowering, but the hitters were so conscious of the curve. Also, Whitey had just enough on his fastball so that by the time the hitters adjusted, it was by them."

Whitey's personality also had a bearing on his success.

"Everyone liked him," said Duren. "On a professional level, the other teams almost overrated him; when Whitey Ford was pitching, they figured they would lose because Whitey had won so often. Because Whitey never showed up the other team, the opposition wasn't as angry or determined to beat him as they were to beat other pitchers. He also had the good sense to know when he was tired and get the hell off the mound. There were days when he would call me in the bull pen between innings to see how I was feeling because he knew he might need help in the last couple innings. He was so astute that he not only knew how well he did against certain hitters, but how that hitter did against the guys in the bull pen. If the matchup wasn't good for Whitey and he was tired, he would just tell Houk, 'Ralph, I'm done, let Arroyo finish up.' "

Whitey's playful side is what endeared him to his teammates, especially Mickey.

"We started calling each other 'Slick' after Casey called us into his office," said Mickey. "The old man chewed us out for staying up late, and he ended up calling us 'a couple of whiskey slicks.' The name just stuck over the years."

"One day Mickey and I were talking about stupid questions reporters ask," said Whitey. "How such smart guys can ask such dumb questions is beyond me. I remember a reporter coming up to Casey right after Don Larsen threw a perfect game in the World Series. The guy asked Casey, 'Would you say that this game was one of the best Larsen ever pitched?' But my favorite was after Mickey had an awful game, striking out, popping up, and kicking the watercooler. This writer goes up to Mick and asks, 'Hey, Mickey, was that pop-up in the third inning the highest one you ever hit?' The guy was lucky that Mickey didn't pop him in the mouth."

Mickey and Whitey were the only players who roomed alone on the road. But they may as well have roomed together, because they used to get adjoining rooms, and the door between the two suites was almost always open. "And the Yankees pretty much picked up the bills we charged to our rooms," said Whitey.

I also think that Whitey made Mickey a better player. By that, I'm speaking about what happened off the field. Mickey, Whitey, and Billy Martin often ran around town together. Billy took Mickey out and helped Mickey have some very, very long nights. Whitey settled Mickey down.

If Whitey had been an everyday player, he and Mickey would have been out every night. But Whitey being a pitcher, he would take it easy the two nights before he started. He also made sure that Mickey got to bed on those evenings. He kept Mickey straight at least for a couple of days each week.

Whitey's father always worked in the bar business, and that is where Whitey spent much of his time growing up. During the 1961 season, his father could be found behind the Ivy Room bar in Astoria.

Whitey's world was full of wisecracks, practical jokes, and smiles. It's not surprising that he carried this attitude to the mound. Whitey didn't really care about striking out hitters, but he liked to trick them.

"I don't think Ford throws a spitter, I know it," said veteran manager Jimmy Dykes during Whitey's career. "He strikes a guy out on one, they throw it around the field, and by the time it gets back to Whitey, the ball is as dry as the Sahara."

Jimmy Dykes was right. Whitey doctored the ball. But he didn't do it because he had to so much as because he wanted to. It fit in with his New York city-slicker image. Once in a while, he used it just to give the hitters something else to think about and maybe embarrass them a little.

It was fun to watch Whitey on the mound, just to see what he was going to do to the ball. He would waste a pitch or ask the umpire for a new ball. Most umpires liked to show off their arms, and while they turned their backs or threw the ball to Whitey, he'd spit into the pocket of his glove. When Whitey would catch the ball, there would be a splat. Whitey once thanked the umpires for helping him doctor the ball, and this is what he was talking about.

But an ordinary spitter wasn't enough for Whitey. He started devising new illegal pitches and refining those he had heard about from other guys. He picked up the mudball from Warren Spahn and Lou Burdette, who showed it to him during the 1957 World Series. He would take the ball out of the wet spot in his glove, put the ball in his left hand with the wet side facing down, and reach for the resin bag. While picking up the resin bag, he would rub the wet spot of the ball into the dirt. In fact, a rule was changed as a result of Whitey. A pitcher can no longer pick up a resin bag while he has the ball in the same hand.

Whitey also talked about the Bernoulli Principle with Johnny Sain, who was a licensed pilot as well as our pitching coach. One day on a plane, Whitey and I sat and listened to Sain talk, and Whitey applied those principles of aerodynamics to the throwing of the mudball. If Whitey threw with the mud on the top of the ball, the ball sank. When the mud was on the bottom, the ball rose. The foreign substance made the ball move just as airfoils on a plane give it lift.

If the hitter asked the umpire to check the ball, Whitey would fire it into the catcher's mitt, which would rub off the mud, leaving only a smudge by the time the catcher handed it to the umpire.

"That pitch was unbelievable," said John Blanchard. "He'd never throw it unless he had two strikes on a hitter. We had a signal, four fingers with a wiggle. I'd go through the usual pattern of signs. After Whitey would shake me off the third time, I knew what he wanted. After a while, I just called for it when he had two strikes on a hitter because Whitey liked to use it."

Whitey also used his ring.

"It was a ring with a sharp edge, just right to cut up the ball a little bit," said Whitey. "This pitch wasn't like the spitter or the mudball; it just sank slightly more than my ordinary pitches. When Alvin Dark was managing in his home park, he used to save the balls thrown out of the game by the umpire because they were scuffed or too dirty. Dark put all the balls in the bag, and he noticed that they all were scuffed in the same area. He showed the balls to the umpire, I think it was Hank Soar, and Hank asked to look at my glove. I showed him my glove, and he couldn't find anything. Then Hank said, 'What's that ring?' I said it was my wedding ring, I don't think Hank believed me, but he told me not to wear it any more, and that was the end of that."

But when the ring was gone, the cutball remained.

"Ellie Howard would catch my pitch, and then he'd go to work," said Whitey. "On the outside of his right shin guard, he had a rivet which he had sharpened. I never could see exactly how he would do this, but he'd catch the ball and scrape it against that rivet right before he threw it back to me. He did it all in one throwing motion. Some games, it got out of hand. I only wanted the ball cut on one side, but Ellie would nick it on one side. Then a couple pitches later he'd nick the other side, which would counteract the first nick. In other words, a ball with two nicks didn't do anything. Ellie also knew how to get plenty of dirt on the ball, which helped if I wanted to use the mudball."

The rest of us also were willing to lend a hand—actually it was more like a glove—to Whitey's cause. Jimmy Dykes was right about how the ball might start its way around the infield a little wet after a hitter had struck out but would be dry before an umpire could check it. We made sure of that by rubbing it thoroughly in our gloves as we tossed it around the infield.

But sometimes Whitey wanted us to help. So we would throw it around the infield with Clete standing near the mound to receive the ball last. Clete would load up the ball and gently place it in Whitey's glove. Whitey also stopped us from breaking in our gloves with oil, because as we passed the ball around the infield, it would get too slippery. He only wanted one grease spot on the ball, and he was the one who was going to put it there.

"I really didn't throw those pitches that much," said Whitey. "At least not as much as the other teams used to think. They always thought I was up to something. I had a circulation problem with my fingers, and when the weather was cold, I used to keep a little plastic bag of hot water in my back pocket. The trainer put hot water in it every inning. Between pitches, all I did was touch it with my fingertips. If I didn't, I had no feeling of the ball whatsoever. But guys like [Detroit manager] Charlie Dressen used to say I was using that to wet my fingers. I'd tell them it was to keep my hand warm, but they never believed me. How do you figure that?"

Maybe it was because they knew Whitey almost as well as we did.

Whitey never carried that spirit of chicanery over into his off-the-field work.

"From 1959 to 1961, I was a stockbroker," he said. "But I really didn't like it. This was one of the few times in my life when I couldn't sleep at night. I sat up in bed wondering if I gave people the right information on what stocks to buy. I worried so much about losing other people's money that I finally just quit."

But investments have always worked out well for Whitey. Along with Yogi Berra and Bob Turley, he has probably made the most out of his money. He made some great buys in Long Island real estate, and the people he hung around with steered him into some very profitable investments. He is set up very well.

Whitey works for Fundamental Brokers, which deals in government bonds. He also works for the Yankees as a coach in spring training, and for Tele-plus Company. Much of Whitey's work is in public relations—speaking, taking groups to Yankee Stadium, that kind of thing. Whitey is one of those few guys like Mickey Mantle, a superstar who will always be paid extremely well to represent a company. He is great at it because he gets along so well with everyone.

For three years, Whitey was the Yankees' pitching coach (1973–75), but he did it more as a lark. He wanted to stay in uniform for while, and Whitey also wanted to help the Yankees. The team was having a hard time, and they thought this would boost their image. Whitey didn't need the money or the job; he was just being loyal to the organization. He also did some good, and I can recall Catfish Hunter telling me how much he picked up about pitching just by being with Whitey.

His real love now is race horses.

"I've been involved in racing since 1957," he said. "Del Miller was a close friend of mine, and he is the Babe Ruth of harness racing. Another guy I know well is Johnny Nehru, an old neighbor of mine who had trained some Kentucky Derby winners.

"When I'm in Fort Lauderdale for spring training with the Yankees, I wake up real early and go to the track to help out Del Miller. He and I train my own harness horses. I also like to drive them around in the morning, and I've been in about two dozen races.

"Mickey Mantle and I have had eight match harness races, and we're 4–4. We've raced at the Meadowlands, Yonkers, Vernon Downs, Pompano, and Roosevelt."

Today, Whitey is happy, comfortable, and content.

"The only problem I've had was with my heart. It was when I was coaching with the Yankees, and I ended up doing extra duty throwing batting practice. It was a real hot day, and I was out there for about forty-five minutes. Rick Dempsey was batting, and the next thing I knew was that I got really dizzy. I walked off the mound, into the dugout, and down the runway. When I reached the clubhouse, that was it, I blanked out. They took me to the hospital, and Dr. Bobby Brown flew in from Texas to do an angiocardiography. Bobby said that one of my arteries was about 90 percent blocked. It looked like I might need bypass surgery, but they put me on some medication, and it cleared up.

"I've got it really good. I work a little, play some golf, race my horses, and get to see some old friends. To me, that's what a good life is all about."

Mickey Mantle

"You know, I thought I had a chance at the record in '61," said Mickey Mantle. "I had been there in '56 when I hit 52. Roger was having a great year, I was having a great year. That's what it takes, two guys. What everybody forgets is that Ruth hit seventeen in September. So you're ahead of the pace in July and you're still ahead of it in August, and all of sudden, you get to that last month and it seems like you gotta hit one about every day because that's what Ruth did. Man, when I think about what Roger did . . . it was something. The hardest thing in sports is hitting a baseball. That's why I get ticked off when they start saying Roger's record was a fluke and crap like that. All I know is that no one did it before or since, and I know how damn hard it is to do it, because I tried and never made it.

"Some people said I would have got it if I had played in the new Yankee Stadium or in some of these new parks. Whitey used to count some of the balls I hit really deep, like 450 feet, and got caught or at least didn't go out. He figured it was ten a year and said he was being conservative. But I don't think much about what it would have been like if the fences were shorter or if I had played somewhere else. There's no point to it. I will tell you one thing: I do some broadcasting for the Yankees on cable television, and these guys do some stuff we'd never even think of. Can you imagine stealing third when you're seven runs ahead? I've been with the Yankee organization for thirty-five years, and when I see the crap that goes on down there on the field now, it almost makes me want to puke. These guys take forever to get in the batter's box and to throw the ball. Then a guy hits a home run and he stands at home plate, watching the damn thing. I'm proud of the fact that neither me or Roger pulled stunts like that or showed up a pitcher."

I don't think there has ever been a player with Mickey's combination of speed and power, when he was healthy. Go around the American League, and the longest home runs in about half the parks were hit by Mickey Mantle. I've shown some of the modern players where Mickey hit the ball, and they can't believe it. It's impossible for me to imagine a player with more raw physical ability or inner drive. You're talking about Willie Wilson's speed, or maybe a little faster. Consider Mickey going down the first-base line after he drag-bunted out of the left-handed batter's box: Some scouts timed him at 2.9 seconds. Today, they talk about Willie Wilson and Vince Coleman getting down to first at 3.1, and they think that's amazing. Even Willie Mays didn't have Mickey's combination of speed and power. Mickey's arm was also outstanding, although Mays probably threw a little better. But no one could go from first to third base on a single like Mickey, not even Mays.

When Mickey would hit a home run, he'd put his head down and jog around the bases, no great show. But he'd come to the bench with this pleasant smile on his face. At least three times, I saw Mickey hit the ball on the fists or end of the bat and in disgust step out of the batter's box and whack the bat on the ground, breaking it. Then he would look up and start running down to first base just in time to see the ball going out of the park. He was so strong, occasionally he didn't even know when he'd hit a home run. Of course, he also hit the ball five hundred feet. Joe DiMaggio once said, "Reggie Jackson is a lot like Mickey. They think 380-foot homers don't count. They try to hit the ball 500 feet."

As we talked, Mickey said he didn't have much faith in batting coaches. "I just don't think you can teach a guy to hit," he said. But Mickey was, in his own way, a student of hitting. When a new pitcher came into a game, he would kneel in the on-deck circle, intently staring at the guy warming up. Mickey had plenty of help from Bob Turley in calling pitches, but Mickey also called a lot for himself because he watched pitchers so closely and could see if they were tipping their breaking pitches by something they did in their motion.

When I think of Mickey, I think of a player who could do everything—he even had a great knuckleball. Most hitters think they would have made great pitchers, and they throw a curveball or something while playing catch before a game. Mickey's pitch was a knuckleball. Not only do I think it was unhittable, it was uncatchable. He was always showing it to Whitey, saying, "This is something you don't have."

It got to the point that no one would play catch with Mickey if he was going to throw his knuckler. Yogi wouldn't catch him. Neither would Ellie Howard or John Blanchard. Mickey would usually get a rookie and work him over. Right after we signed Jake Gibbs, an All-American quarterback from Ole Miss, he was at the Stadium working out, and Mickey got him to play catch. He'd throw a few soft knuckleballs that didn't do much. Then he'd say, "I'm warmed up now, so maybe you better put on a catcher's mask." Jake wouldn't do it.

Mickey sighed and said, "Okay." Then he uncorked a knuckler that took off, and then we heard this *splat*. That was Gibbs's nose, and it was all over his face. Mickey broke more than one nose with that knuckler.

Casey hated to see Mickey throw his knuckleball, because he thought that was why Mickey's shoulder started to hurt. In fact, Casey barred Mickey from throwing it, but he would sneak off and find someone to catch him when Casey wasn't looking. Mickey used to tell Casey, and later Houk, that he wanted to pitch in a game that was a blowout so he could show everyone his knuckler. Casey would never have done it. I think Ralph gave it some thought, but he didn't want to show up the other team. Also, if Ralph had let Mickey pitch and he got hurt . . . it wasn't something Ralph wanted to risk. But one of the things we'd talk about was if Mickey could throw his knuckler for strikes and if anyone could hit it.

By 1961, there seldom was a day when something wasn't bothering Mickey. It wasn't unusual for him to need help getting out of a cab because his legs were bothering him. He'd sort of brace himself and put out his hand. One of us would grab him by the wrist and literally pull him out of the cab. To fully appreciate Mickey, you would have had to see him after a ball game with his legs taped about from the thigh to the ankle. He wore these awkward rubber wraps, not the sophisticated braces of today. I'd look at the scars on his knees and wonder how he even stood up, much less played.

I once heard the Yankee team doctor, Sidney Gaynor, say that Mickey weighed 210 and none of it was fat. His muscles were like Popeye's. All of his joints—his wrists, his knees, his ankles—were so frail, almost like a girl's. Dr. Gaynor said that there was a conflict between Mickey's muscles and joints. The muscles were so strong; the joints so weak. His muscles were too strong for his bones, and they tore everything apart. I never knew if it was heredity or working in the mines, but Mickey didn't get his solid build from lifting weights. Neither did Roger. Not one of us would touch a weight back then. They were taboo, because there was a fear that you could become too muscle-bound to hit an inside fastball. If you think about it, that was pretty stupid. Either you could hit a fastball or you couldn't. Weights had nothing to do with it.

Pitchers knew where Mickey was vulnerable. They didn't throw at his head; they went for his legs. Especially when Mickey was batting left-handed, he'd see a lot of sliders right at his knees. You knew Mickey hated it, but that wasn't the era when a guy dropped his bat and charged the mound. As for Roger, the pitchers would occasionally throw at his head, but he had such quick reflexes that he would just tilt his chin back, and the ball would zip by maybe an inch from his face. His confidence was so boundless, and he was fearless. Mickey, Roger, and the rest of us retaliated on the bases. If you knocked down enough guys on double plays, the infielders would tell their pitcher to cut out all the inside stuff or else they were going to get killed. And if that didn't work, your pitchers knocked down their hitters.

Mickey drew such respect in the clubhouse. A lot of us were simply in awe of how he played.

Reserve outfielder Jack Reed: "The first time I saw Mickey, I said, 'Good night, old Moses, this is one fine-looking ballplayer.' He was so strong and looked immaculate in that white Yankee uniform. Mickey always seemed like he could run as fast as he wanted. Most guys are pretty fast from home plate to first base, but Mickey seemed even faster legging out a double from first to second."

Bud Daley: "There was an unwritten rule on the club that Mickey didn't steal unless the score was tied or it was a one-run game. What people don't realize is that Mickey could have stolen a hundred bases a year if his legs had been sound."

All of us flinched every time Mickey went down, because we knew that could be the pennant. We also knew that Mickey hated being hurt so much that it sometimes made the situation worse.

"I'd see Mickey start to run, and his knee would just collapse. It was frightening," said Tom Tresh, who came to the Yankees in September of 1961.

Bob Turley: "There were games where Mickey's shoulder bothered him so much that he'd have to swing with one hand, and he'd still get hits. Or else, if it was really bad, I remember him bunting for a hit."

Wally Moses: "Once the weather got warm, Mickey seldom took batting practice. He felt he was in a good groove, and he was more worried about fatigue than anything else. Before games, he'd loosen up his arm a little, stretch a bit, but not too much because he always worried about tearing or pulling a muscle. He didn't do much of anything but play the games."

"Mickey would try to play before one injury was healed, and favoring that, he would hurt something else," said Ralph Houk.

"I hated getting hurt," said Mickey. "That's why I hated doctors. I didn't want to see them because I didn't want to know what they would tell me."

Mickey came to the majors with leg problems and the feeling that the clock was running out on him. He had osteomyelitis in his left leg, which he managed to control with medication. But Mickey sometimes said, "The leg can go, and at any time. If it does, I'm nothing."

So much of it was tied to his background in Commerce, Oklahoma. A lot of guys psychoanalyzed him in magazines, and he was the subject of a few graduate studies. One of the conclusions drawn was that Mickey struck out so often left-handed because he was rebelling against his father, who forced him to switch-hit. A lot of that kind of silly stuff was being said, especially in 1961. Mickey was a natural right-handed hitter. His swing from that side of the plate was perfect, and he could hit the ball to any field. When he batted right-handed, Mickey didn't think anyone should get him out. If he popped up or struck out, it wasn't uncommon for Mickey to come back to the dugout and do something, like maybe rip up the watercooler. If the pitcher got him on some off-speed stuff, Mickey sometimes would go back to the bench, break his bat, and yell at the mound, "Throw the ball in there like a man." He'd really get on the pitcher, and Moose and Ellie Howard would usually help. Left-handed, he had an uppercut swing, and he tried to pull the ball into the short right-field porch in the Stadium. But Mickey became a switch-hitter because he wanted to, and he always said he was glad his father taught him to hit from both sides of the plate.

Actually, Mickey thought his father was the greatest man to ever walk on the face of the earth, and Mickey once told me that he was thankful that his father lived long enough to see him play with the Yankees. That's why his death shattered Mickey.

"My dad died at thirty-nine," said Mickey. "My uncle, both his brothers, and my grandfather all died young. I'm the first male in my family to make it to forty-five since I don't know when. They all had Hodgkin's disease, and that came from working in the zinc mines. You keep breathing all that dust and crap down there. I never believed I'd make forty. Now that I'm fifty-five, I just wish I'd known I was going to be around this long."

When we played together, Mickey told me that at least once a year he had a dream in which a pitch was coming at his head. He would wake up screaming and sweating, "because I didn't know if I got out of the way of the pitch or not." Now, Mickey said he has dreams in which he is back in uniform and there are seventy thousand fans chanting, "We want Mick," but every door he tries to the Stadium is locked. He is in his uniform, everyone is waiting, but he can't get in to play.

Mickey talked a lot about death. The thought of dying scared him, and that's part of the reason he lived the wild life for so long. He was trying to squeeze the most out of every second, yet trying to forget the prospect of dying at the same time. It was an interesting contradiction.

"I know death weighed heavily on Mickey's mind," said Bobby Richardson. "He was always conscious of his age and how much time he thought he had left. I don't think he took the best care of himself because in the back of his mind was the thought, 'What's the use?' He had a big heart and would do a lot of charitable things that people never knew about. When I had Bible services before games, Mickey came more than most people realized. He was very aware of his own mortality."

The Yankee front office knew Mickey's family history, and they knew he was worried about death. One of the reasons I made the Yankees in 1957 was that they were worried about Mickey, and not just his knees and legs. Even though I was a shortstop in the minors, Casey considered me a good athlete and thought I could fill in for Mickey in center. It wouldn't surprise me if the front office thought, 'Maybe we should make some backup plans. Mickey might not be around that long.' And it wouldn't surprise me if that thinking went into their search for another outfielder, which led to the deal for Roger.

Now that I think about it, I suppose there had to be times when Mickey doubted his greatness. But he knew that he was a great player. I once asked him why he played on some days when he couldn't even get out of a cab.

Mickey said, "When I grew up, we didn't have any money, and I never saw a big-league game. I keep thinking that there might be a father out there who can afford to take his kid to only one game all year. And maybe that kid wanted to see me play. Tony, I just hated disappointing people, especially kids."

Ralph Terry grew up in the same part of Oklahoma as Mickey.

"Both of our high schools were in the same league in Northeast Oklahoma," said Terry. "It was called the Lucky Seven Conference. Mickey was three years ahead of me, but I saw him play all three sports. He was a great football player, but he already had bad legs. He'd take off on a fifty-yard run and then have to go to the sidelines for a while. Next thing you knew, he was back in the game, running fifty yards again. In baseball, we had a state championship team, and I was the catcher. We played Commerce High, and I remember that we struck Mickey out twice, but he also hit two doubles off the concrete wall in left field, which was 375 feet from the plate. Mickey wasn't very big, but he still hit the ball a mile. After one of the doubles, I remember he said to someone on the bench, 'I wish that ball had gone foul.' I guess he figured he might have hit a homer if he had another shot."

By the time Mickey was twenty, he was with Yankees.

"A kid in bad need of a haircut with a sport coat that barely came down to his wrists," according to Dan Daniel

Like most young players, Mickey idolized DiMaggio. Mickey would go by DiMaggio's locker and make a point to be seen by Joe D., but Joe D. seldom spoke to him. I think this hurt Mickey, and it was something he never forgot. As Mickey got older, he realized that Joe D. wasn't being cruel; it was just his personality to be sort of aloof and quiet.

But Mickey always went out of his way to greet rookies. When a new player came into the clubhouse, Mickey was usually the first guy to shake his hand. In my first year with the Yankees, I was given number 34 in spring training. Mickey took me into the clubhouse and said to Pete Sheehy, "You better give Tony a lower number because he is going to be with us for a long time." Mickey felt you gave number 34 to a ballplayer the way you gave 99 to a tackle; the higher the number, the lower the esteem. That's how I ended up with number 10.

"As a young player, I worshiped Mickey," said Tom Tresh. "I was an outfielder and a switch-hitter, and I found myself imitating him. I couldn't run as fast, but I could run like him. I couldn't hit like Mickey, but I stood at the plate like he did. I even named my son after him. When I came up in 1961, I found myself staring at Mickey. I just wanted to watch him, to learn from him. And he was one of the first guys who talked to me. The following year, I opened with the Yankees, and I never found out until late in the season that Mickey had made a bet with [sportswriter] Phil Pepe that I would hit twenty homers. I had never hit more than fourteen in the minors. That was his way of showing confidence in me."

With the help of Ralph Houk, Mickey became more assertive. It was as if the wraps had been taken off him when Houk replaced Casey. He seemed relieved and more verbal. Mickey always talked, but under Ralph he came to the forefront. Mickey didn't hold pep talks, but he led by how he played. Mickey was determined to get off fast in 1961 to take the pressure off Ralph.

"I never believed in captains," said Houk. "But you do need leaders. I always was a Mantle man. Who wouldn't be? After I got the job, I went to Mickey and said, 'You're the leader of this ball club.' I did it because of his talent and his competitiveness. He wanted to win so bad. I told Mickey, 'I'm going to the press and telling them you're the guy.'

"Mickey said, 'Well, Ralph, I just don't know.'

"I said, 'Mickey, this is what I'm going to do.'

"Mickey said, 'What do I do?'

"I said, 'Just be yourself. The guys get fired up just watching you go all out.'

"Mickey said, 'If you want me to be the leader, then I guess I gotta be the leader. At least, I'll try to do it for you.'

"It seemed that Mickey was kind of awed by the whole thing. I thought he'd be ideal for the younger players. What I loved about Mickey was if he had a bad day and we won, he still was happy. If he had a good day and we lost, in his heart Mickey wished he could have done more. And Mickey always backed my decisions."

One of the most moving moments of the 1961 season was at West Point, where we always played an exhibition game with Army's baseball team. We ate lunch at the West Point mess hall. When it came time for the orders of the day the cadets began chanting, "We want Mickey, we want Mickey." Mickey was embarrassed, his head down. He didn't know what he was supposed to do. The cadets came to his table, picked him up, and carried him on their shoulders to the balcony of the mess hall. Mickey couldn't understand why the cadets wanted him, a civilian who was classified 4-F because of his leg problems during the Korean War. Only the most elite among the cadets were singled out for this honor. Others given it were Patton, Eisenhower, and MacArthur.

The military was a difficult subject for Mickey, who once said, "I remember a guy writing that there was no reason I should be 4-F. I wasn't supposed to go to Korea and kick guys to death."

This also was one of the sources of Mickey's loyalty to Ralph. When Mickey was receiving mail about being a draft dodger, it was Houk, the war hero, who comforted him. And it was Houk who made Mickey the leader.

"I remember that day at West Point very well," said Bill Stafford. "Before we went to eat, Mickey and Whitey had stolen my shoes and socks. I went to the lunch in my best suitcoat, shirt, pants, and in bare feet."

Practical jokes by Mickey and Whitey were legendary.

A lot of Mickey's humor was the kind that would work only in a baseball setting. We once had a big doubleheader with the Indians, and there was supposed to be a crowd of seventy thousand in Cleveland. Mickey showed up at the park that day wearing one of those phony arrows through his head. Or before an important game, Mickey would get the guys together and say, "Let's set up Ellie." Right before the game, we would be in the dugout, and Mickey would start talking about how this was an important game and so on. Then Mickey would say, "Let's go get 'em." We'd all fake running on the field, and then stop on the top step. Only Ellie, or whomever Mickey had set up that day, would be on the field, alone, with all the fans wondering what that player was doing.

"One day in spring training, I was sitting against a fence in Bradenton," said Bill Stafford. "Mickey had a pipe that was two feet long, and he was messing around with it. Mickey knew I hated bugs and reptiles.

"Mickey said, 'Billy, I'm going to tap you on the knee with this pipe, and an animal will jump on your leg.'

"So he hit me on the leg and one of those little lizards jumped on me. I couldn't shake it off because it had its claws in me. I was jumping up and down because those things scare the hell out of me. I thought I was going to have a heart attack before I knocked it off my leg."

Mickey used to make up hillbilly songs. He'd get our batting practice pitcher, Spud Murray, to play his harmonica, and Mickey would get us to sing. His voice had an awful twang. He sang this song called "Cowtown" that was so terrible, it was hilarious. It was dumb, made no sense, and we all liked to hear Mickey sing it. That was a side of Mickey that few people got to see, because he would sort of go into a shell around fans and writers.

"Here is a story Mickey always loved," said Bill Kane, who was the Yankee statistician in 1961. "Occasionally, I was mistaken for Mickey, especially if I was out with some of the other Yankee players. One night I was in a bar with Whitey, and a fan came up wanting an autograph. Whitey signed right away; then the guy asked me if I would sign. I made sure I was polite, but I turned him down, saying I wasn't Mickey.

"Then Whitey said, 'Come on, Mick, sign for the guy.'

"I could see that the fan was going to stand there until I signed, and since I didn't want him around all night, I signed Mickey's name. Then the guy got real excited and started talking about Mickey's legs. The guy wanted to see my legs.

"Whitey said, 'Come on, Mick, show the guy your legs.'

"As a kid, I'd had polio, and one of my legs was much thinner than the other. Whitey knew this, which is why he wanted me to show the guy my legs. Finally, I just lifted up my pants leg and told the guy, 'This leg isn't so bad, it's coming along.'

"The guy stared at my thin leg, shook his head, and said, 'Mickey, you've got more guts than any guy I've ever seen.'

"Whitey laughed so hard he almost fell down, and he and Mickey roared about it the next day."

Mickey's least favorite umpire was Bill Valentine, who came into the league arrogant and cocky, determined to make a reputation as being the boss. One way to do that was to challenge Mickey, and Valentine relished calling Mickey out on strikes, even if it was on a bad pitch.

Instead of arguing with Valentine and eventually getting thrown out, Mickey came to me, and we devised a plan to retaliate. It was Mickey's version of umpire dodgeball. We waited until Valentine was working at second base, then Mickey went into action. On a fly ball to center, it is the job of the second base umpire to go out and make sure the ball is caught cleanly. Valentine would trot out to short center field, and Mickey would have me line up with Valentine directly between me and him, putting Valentine right in the line of Mickey's throw to the infield. Mickey would throw the ball right at Valentine's head, but it was also going right to me. Usually, Valentine saw it coming and ducked on his own. But a few times, he had his back to Mickey. I'd yell at Valentine to get out of the way, and he'd flop to the ground as though someone were shooting at him. It took Valentine a couple series to figure out this wasn't a coincidence, and when he did, he ejected Mickey. Can you imagine Valentine's report to the league office? "I thumbed the great Mantle for throwing the ball to the infield." The funny part was that a couple members of Valentine's umpiring crew knew what was going on but didn't say anything. In the end, this did get Mickey better calls at the plate.

One of my favorite Mickey stories was of a night in Baltimore when eight or ten of us went out to dinner after a flash flood had washed away the game. We left the restaurant, and on the way back to the Lord Baltimore Hotel, Mickey said we should play follow the leader. It was still pouring, and the water was rushing down the cobblestone streets and flooding out of the gutters and onto the sidewalk. Mickey and Whitey flipped a coin to see who would be leader. Whitey won and off we went. It was about 1:00 A.M., and we were chasing Whitey through alleys and leaping over garbage cans and fire hydrants. Whitey vaulted over the railing of a row house and lost his balance, landing on some cement steps directly on his left shoulder. Whitey was hurting and rubbing his shoulder. Mickey was laughing, and he sent Whitey to the end of the line.

Mickey led us to the Lord Baltimore, which had a marble floor in the lobby. We were all soaked, and water was dripping off us onto the floor. Suddenly, Mickey decided it was time for the grand finale. He took off and slid headfirst across the lobby in his Nieman-Marcus suit. Since it was so late, there was no one operating the elevator. The door was open, and Mickey's slide didn't stop until he went through the lobby and headlong into the back of the elevator. He got up holding his head and rubbing his right shoulder. He was a ghostly pale, and we realized that the game was over and we were lucky that none of us got killed.

Whitey pulled one of the best practical jokes I've ever seen, and he did it to Mickey. Before and after every game, Mickey's routine was to take a whirlpool bath for his sore legs. As soon as this one game ended, Whitey took two quarts of rubbing alcohol and poured it into the whirlpool. Then Mickey climbed into the whirlpool, and you can imagine how the hot water opened his pores and the alcohol went directly into his system. About a half hour later, Whitey called a bunch of us over to the whirlpool to watch Mickey try to get out. Mickey wasn't very steady as he stepped out of the whirlpool; then he fell right into the wall.

And no matter what anyone else tells you, that was the biggest drunk Mickey ever had—and he hadn't even taken a drink.

The fact that Mickey and Whitey were such close friends intrigued me. Mickey, the kid from rural Oklahoma, and Whitey, the kid who grew up in a New York tavern. Mickey was shy and quiet, Whitey sharp and outgoing. On one level, it was a case of opposites attracting. But there was more to it. I think Whitey recognized Mickey's greatness. Whitey never got the superstar treatment that Mickey did, but Whitey also felt somewhat responsible for him. Whitey always handled the press so well, while Mickey's relationship with the writers ran hot and cold. I think Whitey tried to help Mickey in that area. Whitey also would take Mickey under his wing and make sure he got in at a reasonable hour, at least on the nights before Whitey pitched. Their families also got along well, and they had mutual admiration for each other as people and players.

It's true that Mickey liked to go out and have a few drinks. He was one of the few athletes I've seen who had superhuman strength, and he could maintain his tremendous intensity level. When he did go out, it really didn't affect his performance much. But if Mickey had done all the things they say he did, he wouldn't have been able to walk, let alone play. I ran with Mickey often enough to know that he'd have dinner, a couple of drinks, and stay out for a while and talk. But he didn't stay out all night, every night. A lot of that was a myth created by the writers, in much the same way Joe Namath and Ruth had the reputation. Whitey and Mickey were seen around town quite a bit, but it was in celebrity places, where you couldn't act that badly. That's where they would be seen by Walter Winchell and Earl Wilson, and that led to them getting their names in the gossip columns. These guys weren't out tearing down the town, as some people would like you to believe.

Mickey and Whitey also had an agreement whereby they'd take the money they made from endorsements, such as commercials for Gillette, and not give it to their wives. Instead, they'd stash the five hundred dollars from here, the thousand dollars from there, in the Yankee valuables box in the clubhouse. When it finally got up to eight or ten thousand dollars, they'd say, "Hey, guys, we're all going out tonight," and they'd buy. I don't think Joannie Ford or Merlyn Mantle ever found out about it.

That valuables trunk had little compartments for everyone on the team. Each guy had a key for his own slot, and that's where you stored your watch, wallet, and World Series ring. It was the same trunk that Ruth and Gehrig had used. At the end of one season, Mickey put an eight-thousand-dollar check in there. When he came back from spring training the next year, the check was still in the trunk. He never even missed the eight thousand all winter, and this was back when the average salary was about twelve thousand dollars and meal money was seven-fifty a day.

Mickey made a lot of money and spent a lot. He never seemed to worry about it much. On the other hand, Whitey also made quite a bit, but he invested well.

"That's basically true," said Whitey. "Unless I went into something with Mickey. Then we both usually lost. In 1961, it was Canadian Bomb Shelters. Bob Feller introduced us to this guy who said, 'I'm going to make both of you millionaires. We're going to put a bomb shelter in every home in Canada. Then we'll move into the U.S.' This was during the cold war, and people were worried about being attacked by the Russians. Some people were even building their own shelters, so it seemed like a good idea. Mickey and I each put in ten thousand dollars. We were going to be on the board of directors, and we had a certificate for forty-three thousand shares. The guy cashed our checks, and we never saw him again.

"Mickey went into a business called Mantle Men and Namath Women, an employment agency, which was a bust. Mickey also had a bowling alley that didn't do well. Mickey used his first World Series check to buy into something called the Will Rogers Insurance Company, and the guy who sold him that stock was once in Leavenworth for fraud. We did go into a Holiday Inn in Joplin, Missouri, that was great, but it seemed like Mickey was pretty unlucky with some of his investments."

Mickey said, "There are a lot of things I wish I could do over. Hey, if I knew I was still going to be alive now, I'd have taken care of myself. When I had knee surgery in 1951, I never did the exercises. Maybe if I had, my legs would have lasted longer. I don't know. I was young, I figured it was never going to end. Because, what the hell, I figured I was a dead man by forty. But you look at the guys who are at the top of the stats—Pete Rose, Stan Musial, Hank Aaron, and Willie Mays—those guys kept in condition all the time. I had two big disappointments in baseball. The first was losing to Pittsburgh in the 1960 World Series. That still makes me mad to think about it. And it makes me damn sick every time I think that I didn't end up with a .300 lifetime batting average. I missed by two points, and I still know I was a .300 hitter. It's funny, I think I was a .300 hitter even though I never swung at a ball that I didn't try to hit out of the park. I do a lot of jokes about striking out 1,710 time, but that eats at me, all that striking out."

As I listened to Mickey, I reminded him that he was there to hit home runs. That was one of the things that we needed him to do.

Being honest as always, Mickey said, "I can't say I swung hard for the good of the team. What the hell, I just did it to hit home runs."

Mickey was the one constant with the Yankees, coming to New York when DiMaggio was in his last season in 1951. A year later, Mickey was twenty and under the gun as he replaced Joe D. in center field. His career ended in 1968 as a thirty-seven-year-old first baseman. He was there for the best and worst times, a great player through it all. Yet you have to wonder how much better he could have been if it weren't for all his injuries.

"They keep talking about me getting hurt," said Mickey. "I still played eighteen years. I went to the plate more than anyone else in Yankee history. I saw a lot of changes. When I was a kid, I was afraid to even say hello to Joe D. But in the mid-sixties, these kid players would come up to me and say, 'Hey, Mick, let's go get a drink.' In the fifties and early sixties, the players took care of each other. We paid our dues, getting beers for the veterans, learning from them. Then these guys like Joe Pepitone and Jim Bouton came along, that was the start of the change. You couldn't treat them like rookies should be treated. If you had told them to get you a beer, they would have laughed in your face."

Mickey returned to the Yankees briefly as a coach in August of 1970.

"I wasn't a fool; I knew why the Yankees did it," said Mickey. "They thought I might bring in a few extra fans. I coached the middle three innings. It was dumb. I didn't feel like part of the team. I felt like a sideshow. After a couple of weeks, I quit."

There were rumors that Mickey might have managed the Rangers when Bob Short owned them.

"Short did call me and said he wanted to talk to me about managing," said Mickey. "I got pretty excited, because I had Mickey Mantle Country Cooking at the time and it wasn't doing that well. Hell, I was used to making a hundred thousand dollars a year, and that was even for a couple years after I quit. But all of a sudden, the money stopped coming in. So I got worked up, and I told Merlyn, and she said, 'Mickey, that sounds great. I know you'll make a good manager.'

"Short told me to meet him for an early breakfast, and I had to get up at six in the morning to meet him. We settled down and Short says, 'Mickey, I need a new manager, and I wondered if you had anyone in mind.'

"It was kind of disappointing, because I realized he wasn't interested in me. So I told him to hire Billy Martin, and that was it, the closest I ever got to managing, and it wasn't all that close. When I think about it, I suppose guys like me wouldn't be good managers. Everything I did came naturally. I never knew when I was supposed to bunt, and I don't think I ever hit-and-run in my life. I just played, you know?"

Mickey's son, Mickey Jr., did play a year of minor league ball with the Yankees. But being Mickey Mantle, Jr., was tough. Mickey said he went to see his son at a high school track meet. When they announced that Mickey Mantle, Jr., was at the starting blocks, the fans booed. Mickey felt so bad that he left the meet. Later, his son quit. Mickey Jr. took up golf and plays pretty well, because it is something he can do himself without being under all the pressure.

"I think Mickey Jr. could have been a pretty good player," said Mickey. "But no one spent the time with him. My father worked with me every day after he came home from the mines. Me, I wasn't around for Mickey Jr. That was a big difference."

Mickey works for the Claridge Hotel and casino in Atlantic City. He will turn fifty-six in October, but the prospect of death lingers in his family.

"My son Billy has Hodgkin's disease," said Mickey. "He had a big lump on his throat, and we took him to a doctor. It turned out it was the same thing my dad had, and it was what I was supposed to get. He was nineteen, and they gave him only a 25 percent chance of survival. As a kid, he had dyslexia, which is a pretty bad reading disability. I wonder why the disease skipped me and hit Billy. They took out Billy's spleen. They gave him radiation treatments and later chemotherapy. Nothing helped until we took him to the Anderson Clinic in Houston. They put him on some medication, and it knocked out those lumps. That's why I wanted Roger to go to that clinic, but by the time he got there, he was too far gone. Billy has been in remission for three years and they think he will beat it."

Mickey was loved when he was with the Yankees, but he is even more popular today.

"It started in '61 when I lost the home run thing to Roger," said Mickey. "Before that, I got the boos. From that point, no matter what I did or where I was, everybody was great to me. I guess it was sixty-one that turned everyone to me. Maybe if I had beaten Roger, everyone would have been on my case. They would have kept booing me and made Roger the hero. Who knows? But I do know I get more mail today than ever before."

Mickey's book, *The Mick,* was a bestseller a few years ago. He also likes his job with the Claridge.

"I do more charity work now than I ever dreamed of doing," said Mickey. "People found out they could call the hotel and get the Claridge to send me places for a good cause, and it wouldn't cost them a cent. It's a great way to raise money. I've been to Boston for the Jimmy Fund, to Philadelphia for the Special Olympics, and to a lot of benefit golf tournaments. I hardly go into the casino.

"When Peter Ueberroth brought me back into baseball, it made me feel great. He looked into my job and saw it was a good one. That's why I got teed off when Bowie Kuhn banned me from baseball. He didn't even check what I was doing. I'm in public relations, not gambling. I never knocked Kuhn, because I knew I was going to get banned when I took the job. Actually, it wasn't like he was taking anything away from me. I wasn't in baseball, except to do some instruction in spring training. But what the hell, I don't want to be banned from anything. I used to think that twenty years from now when I'm dead, I'll have a grandson and he'll be reading something about me and see that I was kicked out of baseball. Then he'll ask his mother, 'What did Grandpa do to get banned from baseball?' Who wants a kid thinking about you like that, especially when I'd never do anything to hurt the game I love?"

Tony Kubek

In many ways, a brown envelope I received before the fifth game of the 1961 World Series changed my life.

It was about 3½ hours before the game, and when I arrived at Crosley Field there was a guy in a military uniform waiting for me. I was a member of the U.S. Army Reserves, so I could tell that the guy was a specialist fifth class. He handed me the envelope, and I signed for it. I knew they were some sort of orders. I opened it, and my face went absolutely white. Standing next to me was Frank Slocum, who was working for the baseball commissioner's office.

I said, "Hey, Frank, look at this."

Frank asked, "What's the problem?"

I handed him the papers and said, "I've just been recalled to active military duty for a year."

Frank read the papers and said, "Don't say a word about this to anyone."

I nodded.

Frank said, "We'll see if anything can be done. Maybe it's a mistake."

I was planning to get married about a month after the season, but I was supposed to report to duty at Fort Lewis in Washington State in two weeks. The Berlin Crisis was heating up, and I also think the draft boards wanted to crack down on ballplayers, who were supposedly getting too many breaks and exemptions. It seemed they wanted to make examples out of some of us. Anyway, it turned out that Frank Slocum and the Yankees had no influence with the draft board. You could be in the World Series one day and have a sergeant screaming at you the next.

Margaret Timmel and I had been dating for four years. Margaret's father, Kurt, was a Lutheran minister, and he married us at Trinity Church in Watertown. Then it was off to Washington.

When I got to Fort Lewis, it was obvious that they had called up too many guys, and there wasn't anything for us to do. That first week, we played a lot of touch football. I remember going out for a pass, and I got upended. Something didn't feel right in my neck and back. For three days, I went to the base clinic, but the lines were so long that I never got in. After a while, I just stopped going.

It wasn't until much later that I realized the extent of what I had done to myself in that touch football game. When I returned to the Yankees, there were days when my left hand felt numb, and it would fly off the bat as I swung. Other days, I had trouble bending over for grounders. My father would come to games in Chicago and ask me what happened. I didn't know. Things just kept getting worse, although it was a gradual process. It wasn't like being in a car wreck and ending up in the hospital staring at the ceiling for a month.

I went to a lot of doctors, who couldn't find much wrong. But I was having back problems. One of our trainers, Gus Soares, knew a few chiropractic techniques, and he used to pop my neck and my back. For a while, that gave me some relief, but it didn't help in the long run. Furthermore, he wasn't supposed to do it, but I talked him into it.

Finally in 1965, the Mayo Clinic discovered that I had broken my neck when I was playing touch football. It had healed wrong. There was some nerve damage and some vertebrae putting stress and pressure on the spinal cord. The doctors said there was a good chance I could end up paralyzed if I kept playing and slid headfirst or made an abrupt move. So that was it. I quit at twenty-nine. I had no choice.

I was like most of the guys in sixty one; I didn't think about what would happen to me after baseball. Eventually, I knew I'd have to stop playing. And eventually, that meant getting a job, or maybe staying around as a coach or minor-league manager.

But perhaps the last thing I could have imagined doing was being on television, doing the "Game of the Week" for NBC.

With the Yankees, I was the only player who wouldn't do radio or television interviews. I had nothing against Red Barber and the other sportscasters, but there was just something that bothered me. I don't know if it was the microphone, or the fact that I didn't want people to hear my voice, or exactly what the problem was. I always tried to cooperate with the sportswriters, and there was never any trouble in that area.

But the radio and the television interviews. . . .

Well, it reached the point that former Yankee general manager George Weiss ordered me to do one interview a year. The way I handled it was for Bobby Richardson to interview me, and the two of us would just talk about the team. I don't know if it goes back to high school when I hated to answer questions in class, but the fact was that I never liked talking about myself.

I ended up in television because of David Kennedy, the son of former NBA Commissioner Walter Kennedy. David was working for NBC as a page, and I ran into him at a restaurant called Mr. Laffs, which was owned by former Yankees' shortstop Phil Linz. I was just saying good-bye to Phil, and David and I got to talking about my back trouble, and he asked me what I was going to do. I said I had an interest in a cheese company, and I also might have some possibilities to stay in baseball. That's when David mentioned that NBC was looking for a color commentator for the "Game of the Week." He said it could be a good opportunity, and he convinced me to talk with Chet Simmons and Carl Lindemann, who were in charge of NBC Sports.

Chet gave me a six-week trial. That was in 1966, and I've been working for them ever since.

Margaret and I have been married for twenty-five years, and we have four children—Tony, Jimmy, Anne, and Margaret. There are a couple of reasons that our marriage has worked out. One is that I never had a normal nine-to-five life-style. Since I was seventeen, I had played pro baseball and traveled around the country. That's what I was doing when we were married, so Margaret grew accustomed to the schedule.

But Margaret deserves most of the credit. She had to sacrifice more than I did, often being father and mother while I was gone. She has a master's degree in social work, and she probably would have stayed in it if I had had a regular job. But she quit, because she knew she would have to spend more time with the kids. Her life was changed far more than mine.

Between working for NBC and doing the Toronto Blue Jays games, I'm on the air for about a hundred games a year, and that means a lot of travel. The closest big-league team to our home in Appleton, Wisconsin, is the Milwaukee Brewers, who are ninety miles away.

People sometimes ask me if I get bored after all these years. With the game, not at all. But I get a little tired of the travel, and I really do get sick of listening to myself talk. Sometimes, I'm on the air and I'm babbling away and I think, "Gee, why don't you just keep quiet, give the people a break, already."

In fact, there are days when I take an index card up to the booth that says, "Shut up, already."

But if I did that for too long, I'd be out of a job. So I'll just keep going to games and keep on talking for as long as they let me.

One of the ironies of my job is that it brought me to Yankee Stadium on the twenty-fifth anniversary of Roger's sixty-first homer. It was a quirk of the schedule, the simple fact that the Blue Jays were playing the Yankees that day. I'm not one to continually walk back through the past, but during this trip to Yankee Stadium I couldn't stop myself.

The first day of this three-game Series was a Monday, and I was on the field about four hours before the game talking to some of the Blue Jay players. Then Mickey Mantle showed up, since this was one of the games Mickey was doing for cable television. As usual, Mickey attracted some autograph-seekers, but this time it wasn't the fans but the Blue Jay players and coaches. Toronto third-base coach John McLaren had bought a life-sized poster of Mickey just in the hope that he might see him and get an autograph. Buck Martinez had a Mantle baseball card from 1961 that he wanted Mickey to sign. Other players had balls for him to autograph.

Mickey was only on the field for a few minutes, then went back to the booth. I stayed down and talked with two of the Toronto players, Garth Iorg and Rance Mulliniks. They started asking me about how the old Yankee Stadium looked, where Mickey hit some of his longest homers, and where Roger's sixty-first landed. They were under the impression that Roger's homer was a high fly ball into the short right-field porch. But I told them it was like most of Roger's homers—more of a line drive than a fly ball and it was hit really hard.

Later, I went up to the press box and talked with Mickey. It was mostly general conversation; Mickey was impressed by the fact that Dave Winfield was going for his fifth 100-RBI season. "You know, I only had four of those," he said. But as we talked, I could tell that Mickey was worried about something.

Finally, Mickey told me that his son, Billy, had come out of remission and it seemed that cancer had once again gotten a hold on his system. Of course, cancer was the one thing that Mickey feared the most, the disease that killed most of the male members of his family, and the sickness Mickey was sure would one day kill him. He left the Stadium early that night.

The next day was Tuesday, and there was no real reason for me to go to the Stadium. We weren't broadcasting the game, the pennant races were over, and it was the last week of the season. Some friends had invited me out for dinner, but I just wanted to go to the park. I said I thought it might be nice to watch Don Mattingly hit, but once I got there, I knew Mattingly had nothing to do with why I was back.

There were some players on the field taking early hitting, and I wandered around. The next thing I knew, I was in the outfield, heading toward the monuments. When I played for the Yankees the monuments were on the field, and I never really looked at them. During batting practice, a ball might roll out there and I'd pick it up and maybe glance at one of the plaques. Now, the monuments are behind the fence, in a nice little park area.

I started looking at the plaques, and saw the lines that stretch through the history of the Yankees, from the first great owner and general manager of the Yankees—Jacob Ruppert and Ed Barrow—to people like Ruth, Lou Gehrig, and Joe DiMaggio. There were also plaques for Mickey, Roger, and Ellie Howard. I thought of Rupert and Barrow, and how they gave way to men like Del Webb and Dan Topping, who kept the dynasty going. Then there were all the great outfielders, from Ruth to DiMaggio to Mickey. I thought of the similarities between Roger and Thurman Munson. The two men never really knew each other, but they were so alike in that they were portrayed as stubborn and surly, but at the same time they were loved by their teammates. I mentioned this to Thurman one time and he smiled. I could tell he liked the idea of being from the same mold as Roger.

After a while, I almost laughed. I had been out there with the monuments for over an hour. It wasn't like it was the shrine at Lourdes, but there was something about being there, something that made me read everything that was on every plaque. I was overwhelmed by the idea that I played with some of these guys, even if it was at the end of the dynasty.

Next, I went into the clubhouse. That's where I found Pete Sheehy's plaque. I sat at the old wooden table, the one constant for so many generations of Yankee players. It was hard not to remember guys like Pete, Bob Fishel, Joe Soares, Gus Mauch, Spud Murray, and the rest of the people behind the scenes.

That night, I ended up watching the game with Tracy Stallard. He was in New York to appear on the "Today" show and talk about the pitch he threw to Roger for the sixty-first homer. Tracy is a distinguished looking guy now, with silver hair and a silver moustache. He looks good in a suit.

Tracy runs a strip-mining company in Virginia. I told him that I had read he was a cab driver in London for five years.

"I heard about that, too," he said. "I have no idea where that come from."

We talked about our families and the game. A reporter stopped by and asked Tracy if he ever regretted throwing the pitch to Roger.

"If I hadn't, no one back in Virginia would know that I once played baseball," he said.

But I detected a little uneasiness with the whole thing. I don't think Tracy was very comfortable with the publicity. We talked a little about things that are written about us. He mentioned the London cab story again, and I said that there's a book out that says that after the last game of the 1960 World Series, Mickey walked into the trainer's room and saw me on the table, blood gushing out of my throat, and then he cried.

It makes for a good story, except that it never happened. I never bled from the throat, and by the end of the last game of that World Series I was on my way to the hospital. So there we were—Tracy Stallard, the guy who threw the pitch, and Tony Kubek, the guy who got hit in the throat with a ground ball.

The third day was the anniversary of Roger's homer. I bought several newspapers to see how they treated the event. *Newsday* devoted its back page to a picture of Roger swinging and a nice story about the home run. The New York *Daily News* had nothing on it, but Howard Cosell did write a column about Bobby Thomson's famous homer. Another paper just had a couple of lines about it, under "This Day In Baseball History."

I went to the park that day and walked toward the right-field bleachers. I was trying to remember exactly where Roger's homer landed, but it was difficult because the Stadium has been remodeled. Finally, I just sat down as close as I could to where Sal Durante caught the ball. Next, I went into the Yankee dugout and stood exactly where I was when Roger hit No. 61. I can still see everything: the swing, where everyone else was, and Roger rounding the bases.

During the Yankee–Blue Jay game that day, they showed a tape of Roger's sixty-first homer on the scoreboard before the fourth inning. As I looked at the field, I saw that all the players in both dugouts were standing on the front step watching, just as another set of players had twenty-five years ago.

I suppose that Roger's homer means so much to me because it was the end of my most enjoyable season. It wasn't just being a part of history; we were part of a tradition, and we knew it. I'm proud to have been on the '61 Yankees, and I'm proud to call these guys my friends.

APPENDIX

The Career Record of Everyone Who Played for the 1961 Yankees

Yogi Berra

BERRA, LAWRENCE PETER BL TR 5'7½" 185 lbs.
Father of Dale Berra.
B. May 12, 1925, St. Louis, Mo.
Manager 1964, 1972-75, 1984-85.
Hall of Fame 1971.

	G	AB	H	2B	3B	HR	HR %	R	RBI	BB	SO	SB	BA	SA	Pinch Hit AB	Pinch Hit H	G by POS
1946 NY A	7	22	8	1	0	2	9.1	3	4	1	1	0	.364	.682	1	0	C-6
1947	83	293	82	15	3	11	3.8	41	54	13	12	0	.280	.464	8	2	C-51, OF-24
1948	125	469	143	24	10	14	3.0	70	98	25	24	3	.305	.488	10	5	C-71, OF-50
1949	116	415	115	20	2	20	4.8	59	91	22	25	2	.277	.480	7	3	C-109
1950	151	597	192	30	6	28	4.7	116	124	55	12	4	.322	.533	3	1	C-148
1951	141	547	161	19	4	27	4.9	92	88	44	20	5	.294	.492	0	0	C-141
1952	142	534	146	17	1	30	5.6	97	98	66	24	2	.273	.478	3	0	C-140
1953	137	503	149	23	5	27	5.4	80	108	50	32	0	.296	.523	10	4	C-133
1954	151	584	179	28	6	22	3.8	88	125	56	29	0	.307	.488	1	0	C-149, 3B-1
1955	147	541	147	20	3	27	5.0	84	108	60	20	1	.272	.470	4	1	C-145
1956	140	521	155	29	2	30	5.8	93	105	65	29	3	.298	.534	4	0	C-135, OF-1
1957	134	482	121	14	2	24	5.0	74	82	57	25	1	.251	.438	10	1	C-121, OF-6
1958	122	433	115	17	3	22	5.1	60	90	35	35	3	.266	.471	10	3	C-85, OF-21, 1B-2
1959	131	472	134	25	1	19	4.0	64	69	43	38	1	.284	.462	11	3	C-116, OF-7
1960	120	359	99	14	1	15	4.2	46	62	38	23	2	.276	.446	24	5	C-63, OF-36
1961	119	395	107	11	0	22	5.6	62	61	35	28	2	.271	.466	19	5	OF-87, C-15
1962	86	232	52	8	0	10	4.3	25	35	24	18	0	.224	.388	23	6	C-31, OF-28
1963	64	147	43	6	0	8	5.4	20	28	15	17	1	.293	.497	28	5	C-35
1965 NY N	4	9	2	0	0	0	0.0	1	0	0	3	0	.222	.222	2	0	C-2
19 yrs.	2120	7555	2150	321	49	358	4.7	1175	1430	704	415	30	.285	.482	178	44	C-1696, OF-260, 1B-2, 3B-1
WORLD SERIES																	
1947 NY A	6	19	3	0	0	1	5.3	2	2	1	2	0	.158	.316	1	1	C-4
1949	4	16	1	0	0	0	0.0	2	1	1	3	0	.063	.063	0	0	C-4
1950	4	15	3	0	0	1	6.7	2	2	2	1	0	.200	.400	0	0	C-4
1951	6	23	6	1	0	0	0.0	4	0	2	1	0	.261	.304	0	0	C-6
1952	7	28	6	1	0	2	7.1	2	3	2	4	0	.214	.464	0	0	C-7
1953	6	21	9	1	0	1	4.8	3	4	3	3	0	.429	.619	0	0	C-6
1955	7	24	10	1	0	1	4.2	5	2	3	1	0	.417	.583	0	0	C-7
1956	7	25	9	2	0	3	12.0	5	10	4	1	0	.360	.800	0	0	C-7
1957	7	25	8	1	0	1	4.0	5	2	4	0	0	.320	.480	0	0	C-7
1958	7	27	6	3	0	0	0.0	3	2	1	0	0	.222	.333	0	0	C-7
1960	7	22	7	0	0	1	4.5	6	8	2	0	0	.318	.455	1	0	C-3
1961	4	11	3	0	0	1	9.1	2	3	5	1	0	.273	.545	0	0	OF-4
1962	2	2	0	0	0	0	0.0	0	0	2	0	0	.000	.000	0	0	C-1
1963	1	1	0	0	0	0	0.0	0	0	0	0	0	.000	.000	1	0	
14 yrs.	75	259	71	10	0	12	4.6	41	39	32	17	0	.274	.452	3	1	C-63, OF-4
	1st	1st	1st	1st		3rd		2nd	2nd	3rd							

Johnny Blanchard

BLANCHARD, JOHN EDWIN BL TR 6'1" 193 lbs.
B. Feb. 26, 1933, Minneapolis, Minn.

	G	AB	H	2B	3B	HR	HR %	R	RBI	BB	SO	SB	BA	SA	Pinch Hit AB	Pinch Hit H	G by POS
1955 NY A	1	3	0	0	0	0	0.0	0	0	1	0	0	.000	.000	0	0	C-1
1959	49	59	10	1	0	2	3.4	6	4	7	12	0	.169	.288	28	2	C-12, OF-8, 1B-1
1960	53	99	24	3	1	4	4.0	8	14	6	17	0	.242	.414	23	4	C-28
1961	93	243	74	10	1	21	8.6	38	54	27	28	1	.305	.613	26	7	C-48, OF-15
1962	93	246	57	7	0	13	5.3	33	39	28	32	0	.232	.419	25	3	OF-47, C-15, 1B-2
1963	76	218	49	4	0	16	7.3	22	45	26	30	0	.225	.463	14	1	OF-64
1964	77	161	41	8	0	7	4.3	18	28	24	24	1	.255	.435	31	8	C-25, OF-14, 1B-3
1965 3 teams NY A (12G – .147) KC A (52G – .200) MIL N (10G – .100)																	
" total	74	164	30	3	0	4	2.4	12	16	17	20	0	.183	.274	30	4	C-26, OF-21
8 yrs.	516	1193	285	36	2	67	5.6	137	200	136	163	2	.239	.441	177	29	OF-169, C-155, 1B-6
WORLD SERIES																	
1960 NY A	5	11	5	2	0	0	0.0	2	2	0	0	0	.455	.636	3	1	C-2
1961	4	10	4	1	0	2	20.0	4	3	2	0	0	.400	1.100	2	1	OF-2
1962	1	1	0	0	0	0	0.0	0	0	0	1	0	.000	.000	1	0	
1963	1	3	0	0	0	0	0.0	0	0	0	0	0	.000	.000	0	0	OF-1
1964	4	4	1	1	0	0	0.0	0	0	0	1	0	.250	.500	4	1	
5 yrs.	15	29	10	4	0	2	6.9	6	5	2	2	0	.345	.690	10	3	OF-3, C-2
															1st	1st	

Clete Boyer

BOYER, CLETIS LEROY BR TR 6' 165 lbs.
Brother of Ken Boyer. Brother of Cloyd Boyer.
B. Feb. 8, 1937, Cassville, Mo.

	G	AB	H	2B	3B	HR	HR %	R	RBI	BB	SO	SB	BA	SA	Pinch Hit AB	Pinch Hit H	G by POS
1955 KC A	47	79	19	1	0	0	0.0	3	6	3	17	0	.241	.253	9	0	SS-12, 3B-11, 2B-10
1956	67	129	28	3	1	1	0.8	15	4	11	24	1	.217	.279	5	1	2B-51, 3B-7
1957	10	0	0	0	0	0	–	0	0	0	0	0	–	–	0	0	3B-1, 2B-1
1959 NY A	47	114	20	2	0	0	0.0	4	3	6	23	1	.175	.193	6	0	SS-26, 3B-16
1960	124	393	95	20	1	14	3.6	54	46	23	85	2	.242	.405	2	0	3B-99, SS-33
1961	148	504	113	19	5	11	2.2	61	55	63	83	1	.224	.347	0	0	3B-141, SS-12, OF-1
1962	158	566	154	24	1	18	3.2	85	68	51	106	3	.272	.413	0	0	3B-157
1963	152	557	140	20	3	12	2.2	59	54	33	91	4	.251	.363	0	0	3B-141, SS-9, 2B-1
1964	147	510	111	10	5	8	1.6	43	52	36	93	6	.218	.304	3	0	3B-123, SS-21
1965	148	514	129	23	6	18	3.5	69	58	39	79	4	.251	.424	1	0	3B-147, SS-2
1966	144	500	120	22	4	14	2.8	59	57	46	48	6	.240	.384	0	0	3B-85, SS-59
1967 ATL N	154	572	140	18	3	26	4.5	63	96	39	81	6	.245	.423	2	0	3B-150, SS-6
1968	71	273	62	7	2	4	1.5	19	17	16	32	2	.227	.311	2	0	3B-69
1969	144	496	124	16	1	14	2.8	57	57	55	87	3	.250	.371	3	0	3B-141
1970	134	475	117	14	1	16	3.4	44	62	41	71	2	.246	.381	2	1	3B-126, SS-5
1971	30	98	24	1	0	6	6.1	10	19	8	11	0	.245	.439	3	1	3B-25, SS-1
16 yrs.	1725	5780	1396	200	33	162	2.8	645	654	470	931	41	.242	.372	38	3	3B-1439, SS-186, 2B-63, OF-1
LEAGUE CHAMPIONSHIP SERIES																	
1969 ATL N	3	9	1	0	0	0	0.0	0	3	2	3	0	.111	.111	0	0	3B-3

Clete Boyer continued

	G	AB	H	2B	3B	HR	HR %	R	RBI	BB	SO	SB	BA	SA	Pinch Hit AB	Pinch Hit H	G by POS
WORLD SERIES																	
1960 NY A	4	12	3	2	1	0	0.0	1	1	0	1	0	.250	.583	0	0	3B-4
1961	5	15	4	2	0	0	0.0	0	3	4	0	0	.267	.400	0	0	3B-5
1962	7	22	7	1	0	1	4.5	2	4	1	3	0	.318	.500	0	0	3B-7
1963	4	13	1	0	0	0	0.0	0	0	1	6	0	.077	.077	0	0	3B-4
1964	7	24	5	1	0	1	4.2	2	3	1	5	1	.208	.375	0	0	3B-7
5 yrs.	27	86	20	6	1	2	2.3	5	11	7	15	1	.233	.395	0	0	3B-27

Bob Cerv

CERV, ROBERT HENRY
B. May 5, 1926, Weston, Neb.

BR TR 6' 200 lbs.

	G	AB	H	2B	3B	HR	HR %	R	RBI	BB	SO	SB	BA	SA	Pinch Hit AB	Pinch Hit H	G by POS
1951 NY A	12	28	6	1	0	0	0.0	4	2	4	6	0	.214	.250	3	0	OF-9
1952	36	87	21	3	2	1	1.1	11	8	9	22	0	.241	.356	9	2	OF-27
1953	8	6	0	0	0	0	0.0	0	0	1	1	0	.000	.000	6	0	
1954	56	100	26	6	0	5	5.0	14	13	11	17	0	.260	.470	28	9	OF-24
1955	55	85	29	4	2	3	3.5	17	22	7	16	4	.341	.541	33	11	OF-20
1956	54	115	35	5	6	3	2.6	16	25	18	13	0	.304	.530	10	0	OF-44
1957 KC A	124	345	94	14	2	11	3.2	35	44	20	57	1	.272	.420	41	9	OF-89
1958	141	515	157	20	7	38	7.4	93	104	50	82	3	.305	.592	6	2	OF-136
1959	125	463	132	22	4	20	4.3	61	87	35	87	3	.285	.479	5	2	OF-119
1960 2 teams KC A (23G – .256) NY A (87G – .250)																	
" total	110	294	74	12	2	14	4.8	46	40	40	53	0	.252	.449	30	8	OF-72, 1B-3
1961 2 teams LA A (18G – .158) NY A (57G – .271)																	
" total	75	175	41	8	1	8	4.6	20	26	13	25	1	.234	.429	22	8	OF-45, 1B-3
1962 2 teams NY A (14G – .118) HOU N (19G – .226)																	
" total	33	48	9	1	0	2	4.2	3	3	4	13	0	.188	.333	20	4	OF-9
12 yrs.	829	2261	624	96	26	105	4.6	320	374	212	392	12	.276	.481	213	55	OF-594, 1B-6
WORLD SERIES																	
1955 NY A	5	16	2	0	0	1	6.3	1	1	0	4	0	.125	.313	1	1	OF-4
1956	1	1	1	0	0	0	0.0	0	0	0	0	0	1.000	1.000	1	1	
1960	4	14	5	0	0	0	0.0	1	0	0	3	0	.357	.357	1	1	OF-3
3 yrs.	10	31	8	0	0	1	3.2	2	1	0	7	0	.258	.355	3	3	OF-7
																1st	

Joe DeMaestri

DeMAESTRI, JOSEPH PAUL (Oats)
B. Dec. 9, 1928, San Francisco, Calif.

BR TR 6' 170 lbs.

	G	AB	H	2B	3B	HR	HR %	R	RBI	BB	SO	SB	BA	SA	Pinch Hit AB	Pinch Hit H	G by POS
1951 CHI A	56	74	15	0	2	1	1.4	8	3	5	11	0	.203	.297	6	1	SS-27, 2B-11, 3B-8
1952 STL A	81	186	42	9	1	1	0.5	13	18	8	25	0	.226	.301	1	0	SS-77, 3B-1, 2B-1
1953 PHI A	111	420	107	17	3	6	1.4	53	35	24	39	0	.255	.352	0	0	SS-108
1954	146	539	124	16	3	8	1.5	49	40	20	63	1	.230	.315	3	0	SS-142, 3B-1, 2B-1
1955 KC A	123	457	114	14	1	6	1.3	42	37	20	47	3	.249	.324	1	1	SS-122
1956	133	434	101	16	1	6	1.4	41	39	25	73	3	.233	.316	1	0	SS-132, 2B-2
1957	135	461	113	14	6	9	2.0	44	33	22	82	6	.245	.360	1	0	SS-134
1958	139	442	97	11	1	6	1.4	32	38	16	84	1	.219	.290	2	1	SS-137
1959	118	352	86	16	5	6	1.7	31	34	28	65	1	.244	.369	2	0	SS-115
1960 NY A	49	35	8	1	0	0	0.0	8	2	0	9	0	.229	.257	7	1	2B-19, SS-17
1961	30	41	6	0	0	0	0.0	1	2	0	13	0	.146	.146	0	0	SS-18, 2B-5, 3B-4
11 yrs.	1121	3441	813	114	23	49	1.4	322	281	168	511	15	.236	.325	24	4	SS-1029, 2B-39, 3B-14
WORLD SERIES																	
1960 NY A	4	2	1	0	0	0	0.0	1	0	0	1	0	.500	.500	0	0	SS-3

Billy Gardner

GARDNER, WILLIAM FREDERICK (Shotgun)
B. July 19, 1927, Waterford, Conn.
Manager 1981-85.

BR TR 6' 170 lbs.

	G	AB	H	2B	3B	HR	HR %	R	RBI	BB	SO	SB	BA	SA	Pinch Hit AB	Pinch Hit H	G by POS
1954 NY N	62	108	23	5	0	1	0.9	10	7	6	19	0	.213	.287	3	1	3B-30, 2B-13, SS-5
1955	59	187	38	10	1	3	1.6	26	17	13	19	0	.203	.316	8	0	SS-38, 3B-10, 2B-4
1956 BAL A	144	515	119	16	2	11	2.1	53	50	29	53	5	.231	.334	1	0	2B-132, SS-25, 3B-6
1957	154	**644**	169	**36**	3	6	0.9	79	55	53	67	10	.262	.356	0	0	2B-148, SS-9
1958	151	560	126	28	2	3	0.5	32	33	34	53	2	.225	.298	0	0	2B-151, SS-13
1959	140	401	87	13	2	6	1.5	34	27	38	61	2	.217	.304	0	0	2B-139, SS-1, 3B-1
1960 WAS A	145	592	152	26	5	9	1.5	71	56	43	76	0	.257	.363	0	0	2B-145, SS-13
1961 2 teams MIN A (45G – .234) NY A (41G – .212)																	
" total	86	253	57	14	0	2	0.8	24	13	16	32	0	.225	.304	3	1	2B-47, 3B-35
1962 2 teams NY A (4G – .000) BOS A (53G – .271)																	
" total	57	200	54	9	2	0	0.0	23	12	10	40	0	.270	.335	3	1	2B-39, 3B-8, SS-4
1963 BOS A	36	84	16	2	1	0	0.0	4	1	4	19	0	.190	.238	12	2	2B-21, 3B-2
10 yrs.	1034	3544	841	159	18	41	1.2	356	271	246	439	19	.237	.327	30	5	2B-839, SS-108, 3B-92
WORLD SERIES																	
1961 NY A	1	1	0	0	0	0	0.0	0	0	0	0	0	.000	.000	1	0	

Jesse Gonder

GONDER, JESSE LEMAR
B. Jan. 20, 1936, Monticello, Ark.

BL TR 5'10" 180 lbs.

	G	AB	H	2B	3B	HR	HR %	R	RBI	BB	SO	SB	BA	SA	Pinch Hit AB	Pinch Hit H	G by POS
1960 NY A	7	7	2	0	0	1	14.3	1	3	1	1	0	.286	.714	5	1	C-1
1961	15	12	4	1	0	0	0.0	2	3	3	1	0	.333	.417	12	4	
1962 CIN N	4	4	0	0	0	0	0.0	0	0	0	3	0	.000	.000	4	0	
1963 2 teams CIN N (31G – .313) NY N (42G – .302)																	
" total	73	158	48	6	0	6	3.8	17	20	7	37	1	.304	.456	34	10	C-38
1964 NY N	131	341	92	11	1	7	2.1	28	35	29	65	0	.270	.370	43	8	C-97
1965 2 teams NY N (53G – .238) MIL N (31G – .151)																	
" total	84	158	33	6	0	5	3.2	8	14	15	29	0	.209	.342	**52**	13	C-44
1966 PIT N	59	160	36	3	1	7	4.4	13	16	12	39	0	.225	.388	12	2	C-52
1967	22	36	5	1	0	0	0.0	4	3	5	9	0	.139	.167	5	1	C-18
8 yrs.	395	876	220	28	2	26	3.0	73	94	72	184	1	.251	.377	167	39	C-250

	G	AB	H	2B	3B	HR	HR %	R	RBI	BB	SO	SB	BA	SA	Pinch Hit AB	Pinch Hit H	G by POS

Bob Hale

HALE, ROBERT HOUSTON
B. Nov. 7, 1933, Sarasota, Fla.
BL TL 5'10" 195 lbs.

	G	AB	H	2B	3B	HR	HR %	R	RBI	BB	SO	SB	BA	SA	Pinch Hit AB	Pinch Hit H	G by POS
1955 **BAL A**	67	182	65	7	1	0	0.0	13	29	5	19	0	.357	.407	26	10	1B-44
1956	85	207	49	10	1	1	0.5	18	24	11	10	0	.237	.309	36	6	1B-51
1957	42	44	11	0	0	0	0.0	2	7	2	2	0	.250	.250	35	9	1B-5
1958	19	20	7	2	0	0	0.0	2	3	2	1	0	.350	.450	15	5	1B-2
1959	40	54	10	3	0	0	0.0	2	7	2	6	0	.185	.241	30	7	1B-8
1960 **CLE A**	70	70	21	7	0	0	0.0	2	12	3	6	0	.300	.400	**63**	**19**	1B-5
1961 **2 teams**	**CLE A** (42G – .167) **NY A** (11G – .154)																
" **total**	53	49	8	0	0	1	2.0	2	7	1	7	0	.163	.224	44	6	1B-5
7 yrs.	376	626	171	29	2	2	0.3	41	89	26	51	0	.273	.335	249	62	1B-120

Elston Howard

HOWARD, ELSTON GENE (Ellie)
B. Feb. 23, 1929, St. Louis, Mo. D. Dec. 14, 1980, New York, N. Y.
BR TR 6'2" 196 lbs.

	G	AB	H	2B	3B	HR	HR %	R	RBI	BB	SO	SB	BA	SA	Pinch Hit AB	Pinch Hit H	G by POS
1955 **NY A**	97	279	81	8	7	10	3.6	33	43	20	36	0	.290	.477	21	4	OF-75, C-9
1956	98	290	76	8	3	5	1.7	35	34	21	30	0	.262	.362	12	5	OF-65, C-26
1957	110	356	90	13	4	8	2.2	33	44	16	43	2	.253	.379	9	3	OF-71, C-32, 1B-2
1958	103	376	118	19	5	11	2.9	45	66	22	60	1	.314	.479	9	5	C-67, OF-24, 1B-5
1959	125	443	121	24	6	18	4.1	59	73	20	57	0	.273	.476	11	3	1B-50, C-43, OF-28
1960	107	323	79	11	3	6	1.9	29	39	28	43	3	.245	.353	14	5	C-91, OF-1
1961	129	446	155	17	5	21	4.7	64	77	28	65	0	.348	.549	14	4	C-111, 1B-9
1962	136	494	138	23	5	21	4.3	63	91	31	76	1	.279	.474	7	1	C-129
1963	135	487	140	21	6	28	5.7	75	85	35	68	0	.287	.528	5	1	C-132
1964	150	550	172	27	3	15	2.7	63	84	48	73	1	.313	.455	6	1	C-146
1965	110	391	91	15	1	9	2.3	38	45	24	65	0	.233	.345	12	2	C-95, 1B-5, OF-1
1966	126	410	105	19	2	6	1.5	38	35	37	65	0	.256	.356	12	2	C-100, 1B-13
1967 **2 teams**	**NY A** (66G – .196) **BOS A** (42G – .147)																
" **total**	108	315	56	9	0	4	1.3	22	28	21	60	0	.178	.244	19	2	C-89, 1B-1
1968 **BOS A**	71	203	49	4	0	5	2.5	22	18	22	45	1	.241	.335	3	0	C-68
14 yrs.	1605	5363	1471	218	50	167	3.1	619	762	373	786	9	.274	.427	154	38	C-1138, OF-265, 1B-85
WORLD SERIES																	
1955 **NY A**	7	26	5	0	0	1	3.8	3	3	1	8	0	.192	.308	0	0	OF-7
1956	1	5	2	1	0	1	20.0	1	1	0	0	0	.400	1.200	0	0	OF-1
1957	6	11	3	0	0	1	9.1	2	3	1	3	0	.273	.545	3	1	1B-3
1958	6	18	4	0	0	0	0.0	4	2	1	4	1	.222	.222	1	0	OF-6
1960	5	13	6	1	1	1	7.7	4	4	1	4	0	.462	.923	1	1	C-4
1961	5	20	5	3	0	1	5.0	5	1	2	3	0	.250	.550	0	0	C-5
1962	6	21	3	1	0	0	0.0	1	1	1	4	0	.143	.190	0	0	C-6
1963	4	15	5	0	0	0	0.0	0	1	0	3	0	.333	.333	0	0	C-4
1964	7	24	7	1	0	0	0.0	5	2	4	6	0	.292	.333	0	0	C-7
1967 **BOS A**	7	18	2	0	0	0	0.0	0	1	1	2	0	.111	.111	0	0	C-7
10 yrs.	54	171	42	7	1	5	2.9	25	19	12	37	1	.246	.386	5	2	C-33, OF-14, 1B-3
	3rd	**8th**	**10th**	**9th**				**7th**			**2nd**						

Deron Johnson

JOHNSON, DERON ROGER
B. July 17, 1938, San Diego, Calif.
BR TR 6'2" 200 lbs.

	G	AB	H	2B	3B	HR	HR %	R	RBI	BB	SO	SB	BA	SA	Pinch Hit AB	Pinch Hit H	G by POS
1960 **NY A**	6	4	2	1	0	0	0.0	0	0	0	0	0	.500	.750	1	0	3B-5
1961 **2 teams**	**NY A** (13G – .105) **KC A** (83G – .216)																
" **total**	96	302	63	11	3	8	2.6	32	44	16	49	0	.209	.344	10	2	OF-59, 3B-27, 1B-3
1962 **KC A**	17	19	2	1	0	0	0.0	1	0	3	8	0	.105	.158	9	0	OF-2, 3B-2, 1B-2
1964 **CIN N**	140	477	130	24	4	21	4.4	63	79	37	98	4	.273	.472	13	5	1B-131, OF-10, 3B-1
1965	159	616	177	30	7	32	5.2	92	**130**	52	97	0	.287	.515	0	0	3B-159
1966	142	505	130	25	3	24	4.8	75	81	39	87	1	.257	.461	5	1	OF-106, 1B-71, 3B-18
1967	108	361	81	18	1	13	3.6	39	53	22	104	0	.224	.388	10	3	1B-81, 3B-24
1968 **ATL N**	127	342	71	11	1	8	2.3	29	33	35	79	0	.208	.316	13	3	1B-97, 3B-21
1969 **PHI N**	138	475	121	19	4	17	3.6	51	80	60	111	4	.255	.419	6	1	OF-72, 3B-50, 1B-18
1970	159	574	147	28	3	27	4.7	66	93	72	132	0	.256	.456	5	2	1B-154, 3B-3
1971	158	582	154	29	0	34	5.8	74	95	72	146	0	.265	.490	3	1	1B-136, 3B-22
1972	96	230	49	4	1	9	3.9	19	31	26	69	0	.213	.357	30	6	1B-62
1973 **2 teams**	**PHI N** (12G – .167) **OAK A** (131G – .246)																
" **total**	143	500	120	16	2	20	4.0	64	86	64	126	0	.240	.400	3	0	DH-107, 1B-33
1974 **3 teams**	**OAK A** (50G – .195) **MIL A** (49G – .151) **BOS A** (11G – .120)																
" **total**	110	351	60	4	2	13	3.7	30	43	32	84	2	.171	.305	6	0	DH-77, 1B-30
1975 **2 teams**	**CHI A** (148G – .232) **BOS A** (3G – .600)																
" **total**	151	565	135	25	1	19	3.4	68	75	50	117	0	.239	.388	3	2	DH-94, 1B-57
1976 **BOS A**	15	38	5	1	1	0	0.0	3	0	5	11	0	.132	.211	3	0	OF-5
16 yrs.	1765	5941	1447	247	33	245	4.1	706	923	585	1318	11	.244	.420	120	26	1B-875, 3B-332, DH-278, OF-254
LEAGUE CHAMPIONSHIP SERIES																	
1973 **OAK A**	4	10	1	0	0	0	0.0	0	0	0	0	0	.100	.100	0	0	DH-4
WORLD SERIES																	
1973 **OAK A**	6	10	3	1	0	0	0.0	0	0	1	4	0	.300	.400	3	2	1B-2

Tony Kubek

KUBEK, ANTHONY CHRISTOPHER
B. Oct. 12, 1936, Milwaukee, Wis.
BL TR 6'3" 190 lbs.

	G	AB	H	2B	3B	HR	HR %	R	RBI	BB	SO	SB	BA	SA	Pinch Hit AB	Pinch Hit H	G by POS
1957 **NY A**	127	431	128	21	3	3	0.7	56	39	24	48	6	.297	.381	8	1	OF-50, SS-41, 3B-38, 2B-1
1958	138	559	148	21	1	2	0.4	66	48	25	57	5	.265	.317	1	0	SS-134, OF-3, 2B-1, 1B-1
1959	132	512	143	25	7	6	1.2	67	51	24	46	3	.279	.391	4	1	SS-67, OF-53, 3B-17, 2B-1
1960	147	568	155	25	3	14	2.5	77	62	31	42	3	.273	.401	6	2	SS-136, OF-29
1961	153	617	170	38	6	8	1.3	84	46	27	60	3	.276	.395	8	2	SS-145
1962	45	169	53	6	1	4	2.4	28	17	12	17	2	.314	.432	2	1	SS-35, OF-6
1963	135	557	143	21	3	7	1.3	72	44	28	68	4	.257	.343	1	1	SS-132, OF-1
1964	106	415	95	16	3	8	1.9	46	31	26	55	4	.229	.340	2	0	SS-99

	G	AB	H	2B	3B	HR	HR %	R	RBI	BB	SO	SB	BA	SA	Pinch Hit AB	Pinch Hit H	G by POS

Tony Kubek continued

	G	AB	H	2B	3B	HR	HR %	R	RBI	BB	SO	SB	BA	SA	Pinch Hit AB	Pinch Hit H	G by POS
1965	109	339	74	5	3	5	1.5	26	35	20	48	1	.218	.295	12	4	SS-93, OF-3, 1B-1
9 yrs.	1092	4167	1109	178	30	57	1.4	522	373	217	441	29	.266	.364	44	12	SS-882, OF-145, 3B-55, 2B-3, 1B-2
WORLD SERIES																	
1957 NY A	7	28	8	0	0	2	7.1	4	4	0	4	0	.286	.500	0	0	OF-5
1958	7	21	1	0	0	0	0.0	0	1	1	7	0	.048	.048	0	0	SS-7
1960	7	30	10	1	0	0	0.0	6	3	2	2	0	.333	.367	0	0	SS-7
1961	5	22	5	0	0	0	0.0	3	1	1	4	0	.227	.227	0	0	SS-5
1962	7	29	8	1	0	0	0.0	2	1	1	3	0	.276	.310	0	0	SS-7
1963	4	16	3	0	0	0	0.0	1	0	0	3	0	.188	.188	0	0	SS-4
6 yrs.	37	146	35	2	0	2	1.4	16	10	5	23	0	.240	.295	0	0	SS-30, OF-5
											10th						

Hector Lopez

LOPEZ, HECTOR HEADLEY BR TR 5'11½" 174 lbs.
B. July 8, 1932, Colon, Panama

	G	AB	H	2B	3B	HR	HR %	R	RBI	BB	SO	SB	BA	SA	Pinch Hit AB	Pinch Hit H	G by POS
1955 KC A	128	483	140	15	2	15	3.1	50	68	33	58	1	.290	.422	1	0	3B-93, 2B-36
1956	151	561	153	27	3	18	3.2	91	69	63	73	4	.273	.428	5	2	3B-121, OF-20, 2B-8, SS-4
1957	121	391	115	19	4	11	2.8	51	35	41	66	1	.294	.448	8	3	3B-111, 2B-4, OF-3
1958	151	564	147	28	4	17	3.0	84	73	49	61	2	.261	.415	4	1	2B-96, 3B-55, OF-1, SS-1
1959 2 teams	KC A (36G – .281)				NY A (112G – .283)												
" total	148	541	153	26	5	22	4.1	82	93	36	77	4	.283	.471	5	0	3B-76, OF-35, 2B-33
1960 NY A	131	408	116	14	6	9	2.2	66	42	46	64	1	.284	.414	26	2	OF-106, 2B-5, 3B-1
1961	93	243	54	7	2	3	1.2	27	22	24	38	1	.222	.305	16	4	OF-72
1962	106	335	92	19	1	6	1.8	45	48	33	53	0	.275	.391	24	5	OF-84, 3B-1, 2B-1
1963	130	433	108	13	4	14	3.2	54	52	35	71	1	.249	.395	9	2	OF-124, 2B-1
1964	127	285	74	9	3	10	3.5	34	34	24	54	1	.260	.418	22	7	OF-103, 3B-1
1965	111	283	74	12	2	7	2.5	25	39	26	61	0	.261	.392	28	5	OF-75, 1B-2
1966	54	117	25	4	1	4	3.4	14	16	8	20	0	.214	.368	20	7	OF-29
12 yrs.	1451	4644	1251	193	37	136	2.9	623	591	418	696	16	.269	.415	168	38	OF-652, 3B-459, 2B-184, SS-5, 1B-2
WORLD SERIES																	
1960 NY A	3	7	3	0	0	0	0.0	0	0	0	0	0	.429	.429	2	2	OF-1
1961	4	9	3	0	1	1	11.1	3	7	2	3	0	.333	.889	0	0	OF-3
1962	2	2	0	0	0	0	0.0	0	0	0	0	0	.000	.000	2	0	
1963	3	8	2	2	0	0	0.0	1	0	0	1	0	.250	.500	1	0	OF-2
1964	3	2	0	0	0	0	0.0	0	0	0	2	0	.000	.000	2	0	OF-1
5 yrs.	15	28	8	2	1	1	3.6	4	7	2	6	0	.286	.536	7	2	OF-7
															6th		

Mickey Mantle

MANTLE, MICKEY CHARLES (The Commerce Comet) BB TR 5'11½" 195 lbs.
B. Oct. 20, 1931, Spavinaw, Okla.
Hall of Fame 1974.

	G	AB	H	2B	3B	HR	HR %	R	RBI	BB	SO	SB	BA	SA	Pinch Hit AB	Pinch Hit H	G by POS
1951 NY A	96	341	91	11	5	13	3.8	61	65	43	74	8	.267	.443	8	1	OF-86
1952	142	549	171	37	7	23	4.2	94	87	75	**111**	4	.311	.530	1	0	OF-141, 3B-1
1953	127	461	136	24	3	21	4.6	105	92	79	90	8	.295	.497	8	4	OF-121, SS-1
1954	146	543	163	17	12	27	**5.0**	**129**	102	102	**107**	5	.300	.525	1	0	OF-144, SS-4, 2B-1
1955	147	517	158	25	**11**	**37**	7.2	121	99	**113**	97	8	.306	**.611**	3	1	OF-145, SS-2
1956	150	533	188	22	5	**52**	**9.8**	**132**	**130**	112	99	10	**.353**	**.705**	4	1	OF-144
1957	144	474	173	28	6	34	7.2	**121**	94	**146**	75	16	.365	.665	4	1	OF-139
1958	150	519	158	21	1	**42**	8.1	**127**	97	**129**	**120**	18	.304	.592	0	0	OF-150
1959	144	541	154	23	4	31	5.7	104	75	94	**126**	21	.285	.514	0	0	OF-143
1960	153	527	145	17	6	**40**	7.6	**119**	94	111	**125**	14	.275	.558	2	0	OF-150
1961	153	514	163	16	6	54	**10.5**	**132**	128	**126**	112	12	.317	**.687**	2	0	OF-150
1962	123	377	121	15	1	30	8.0	96	89	**122**	78	9	.321	.605	6	1	OF-117
1963	65	172	54	8	0	15	8.7	40	35	40	32	2	.314	.622	10	3	OF-52
1964	143	465	141	25	2	35	7.5	92	111	99	102	6	.303	.591	11	2	OF-132
1965	122	361	92	12	1	19	5.3	44	46	73	76	4	.255	.452	14	0	OF-108
1966	108	333	96	12	1	23	6.9	40	56	57	76	1	.288	.538	11	2	OF-97
1967	144	440	108	17	0	22	5.0	63	55	107	113	1	.245	.434	12	5	1B-131
1968	144	435	103	14	1	18	4.1	57	54	106	97	6	.237	.398	9	4	1B-131
18 yrs.	2401	8102	2415	344	72	536	6.6	1677	1509	1734	1710	153	.298	.557	106	25	OF-2019, 1B-262, SS-7, 3B-1, 2B-1
						6th	**7th**			**5th**	**6th**						
WORLD SERIES																	
1951 NY A	2	5	1	0	0	0	0.0	1	0	2	1	0	.200	.200	0	0	OF-2
1952	7	29	10	1	1	2	6.9	5	3	3	4	0	.345	.655	0	0	OF-7
1953	6	24	5	0	0	2	8.3	3	7	3	8	0	.208	.458	0	0	OF-6
1955	3	10	2	0	0	1	10.0	1	1	0	2	0	.200	.500	1	0	OF-2
1956	7	24	6	1	0	3	12.5	6	4	6	5	1	.250	.667	0	0	OF-7
1957	6	19	5	0	0	1	5.3	3	2	3	1	0	.263	.421	0	0	OF-5
1958	7	24	6	0	1	2	8.3	4	3	7	4	0	.250	.583	0	0	OF-7
1960	7	25	10	1	0	3	12.0	8	11	8	9	0	.400	.800	0	0	OF-7
1961	2	6	1	0	0	0	0.0	0	0	0	2	0	.167	.167	0	0	OF-2
1962	7	25	3	1	0	0	0.0	2	0	4	5	2	.120	.160	0	0	OF-7
1963	4	15	2	0	0	1	6.7	1	1	1	5	0	.133	.333	0	0	OF-4
1964	7	24	8	2	0	3	12.5	8	8	6	8	0	.333	.792	0	0	OF-7
12 yrs.	65	230	59	6	2	18	7.8	42	40	43	54	3	.257	.535	1	0	OF-63
	2nd	**2nd**	**2nd**			**1st**	**8th**	**1st**	**1st**	**1st**	**1st**						

Roger Maris

MARIS, ROGER EUGENE BL TR 6' 197 lbs.
B. Sept. 10, 1934, Fargo, N. D. D. Dec. 14, 1985, Houston, Tex.

	G	AB	H	2B	3B	HR	HR %	R	RBI	BB	SO	SB	BA	SA	Pinch Hit AB	Pinch Hit H	G by POS
1957 CLE A	116	358	84	9	5	14	3.9	61	51	60	79	8	.235	.405	5	2	OF-112
1958 2 teams	CLE A (51G – .225)				KC A (99G – .247)												
" total	150	583	140	19	4	28	4.8	87	80	45	85	4	.240	.431	6	0	OF-146
1959 KC A	122	433	118	21	7	16	3.7	69	72	58	53	2	.273	.464	5	2	OF-117

	G	AB	H	2B	3B	HR	HR %	R	RBI	BB	SO	SB	BA	SA	Pinch Hit AB	Pinch Hit H	G by POS

Roger Maris continued

	G	AB	H	2B	3B	HR	HR %	R	RBI	BB	SO	SB	BA	SA	PH AB	PH H	G by POS
1960 NY A	136	499	141	18	7	39	**7.8**	98	**112**	70	65	2	.283	**.581**	4	1	OF-131
1961	161	590	159	16	4	**61**	10.3	**132**	**142**	94	67	0	.269	.620	1	0	OF-160
1962	157	590	151	34	1	33	5.6	92	100	87	78	1	.256	.485	3	0	OF-154
1963	90	312	84	14	1	23	7.4	53	53	35	40	1	.269	.542	5	2	OF-86
1964	141	513	144	12	2	26	5.1	86	71	62	78	3	.281	.464	6	1	OF-137
1965	46	155	37	7	0	8	5.2	22	27	29	29	0	.239	.439	4	1	OF-43
1966	119	348	81	9	2	13	3.7	37	43	36	60	0	.233	.382	20	6	OF-95
1967 STL N	125	410	107	18	7	9	2.2	64	55	52	61	0	.261	.405	19	2	OF-118
1968	100	310	79	18	2	5	1.6	25	45	24	38	0	.255	.374	21	6	OF-84
12 yrs.	1463	5101	1325	195	42	275	5.4	826	851	652	733	21	.260	.476	99	23	OF-1383
WORLD SERIES																	
1960 NY A	7	30	8	1	0	2	6.7	6	2	2	4	0	.267	.500	0	0	OF-7
1961	5	19	2	1	0	1	5.3	4	2	4	6	0	.105	.316	0	0	OF-5
1962	7	23	4	1	0	1	4.3	4	5	5	2	0	.174	.348	0	0	OF-7
1963	2	5	0	0	0	0	0.0	0	0	0	1	0	.000	.000	0	0	OF-2
1964	7	30	6	0	0	1	3.3	4	1	1	4	0	.200	.300	0	0	OF-7
1967 STL N	7	26	10	1	0	1	3.8	3	7	3	1	0	.385	.538	0	0	OF-7
1968	6	19	3	1	0	0	0.0	5	1	3	3	0	.158	.211	1	0	OF-5
7 yrs.	41	152	33	5	0	6	3.9	26	18	18	21	0	.217	.368	1	0	OF-40
	10th	**10th**						**6th**									

Jack Reed

REED, JOHN BURWELL BR TR 6'1" 185 lbs.
B. Feb. 2, 1933, Silver City, Miss.

	G	AB	H	2B	3B	HR	HR %	R	RBI	BB	SO	SB	BA	SA	PH AB	PH H	G by POS
1961 NY A	28	13	2	0	0	0	0.0	4	1	1	1	0	.154	.154	0	0	OF-27
1962	88	43	13	2	1	1	2.3	17	4	4	7	2	.302	.465	2	0	OF-75
1963	106	73	15	3	1	0	0.0	18	1	9	14	5	.205	.274	6	0	OF-89
3 yrs.	222	129	30	5	2	1	0.8	39	6	14	22	7	.233	.326	8	0	OF-191
WORLD SERIES																	
1961 NY A	3	0	0	0	0	0	–	0	0	0	0	0	–	–	0	0	OF-3

Bobby Richardson

RICHARDSON, ROBERT CLINTON BR TR 5'9" 170 lbs.
B. Aug. 19, 1935, Sumter, S. C.

	G	AB	H	2B	3B	HR	HR %	R	RBI	BB	SO	SB	BA	SA	PH AB	PH H	G by POS
1955 NY A	11	26	4	0	0	0	0.0	2	3	2	0	1	.154	.154	0	0	2B-6, SS-4
1956	5	7	1	0	0	0	0.0	1	0	0	1	0	.143	.143	0	0	2B-5
1957	97	305	78	11	1	0	0.0	36	19	9	26	1	.256	.298	1	0	2B-93
1958	73	182	45	6	2	0	0.0	18	14	8	5	1	.247	.302	0	0	2B-51, 3B-13, SS-2
1959	134	469	141	18	6	2	0.4	53	33	26	20	5	.301	.377	0	0	2B-109, SS-14, 3B-12
1960	150	460	116	12	3	1	0.2	45	26	35	19	6	.252	.298	1	0	2B-141, 3B-11
1961	162	662	173	17	5	3	0.5	80	49	30	23	9	.261	.316	1	0	2B-161
1962	161	**692**	**209**	38	5	8	1.2	99	59	37	24	11	.302	.406	0	0	2B-161
1963	151	**630**	167	20	6	3	0.5	72	48	25	22	15	.265	.330	1	0	2B-150
1964	159	**679**	181	25	4	4	0.6	90	50	28	36	11	.267	.333	2	1	2B-157, SS-1
1965	160	664	164	28	2	6	0.9	76	47	37	39	7	.247	.322	3	0	2B-158
1966	149	610	153	21	3	7	1.1	71	42	25	28	6	.251	.330	2	0	2B-147, 3B-2
12 yrs.	1412	5386	1432	196	37	34	0.6	643	390	262	243	73	.266	.335	11	1	2B-1339, 3B-38, SS-21
WORLD SERIES																	
1957 NY A	2	0	0	0	0	0	–	0	0	0	0	0	–	–	0	0	2B-1
1958	4	5	0	0	0	0	0.0	0	0	0	0	0	.000	.000	0	0	3B-4
1960	7	30	11	2	2	1	3.3	8	12	1	1	0	.367	.667	0	0	2B-7
1961	5	23	9	1	0	0	0.0	2	0	0	0	1	.391	.435	0	0	2B-5
1962	7	27	4	0	0	0	0.0	3	0	3	1	0	.148	.148	0	0	2B-7
1963	4	14	3	1	0	0	0.0	0	0	1	3	0	.214	.286	0	0	2B-4
1964	7	32	13	2	0	0	0.0	3	3	0	2	1	.406	.469	0	0	2B-7
7 yrs.	36	131	40	6	2	1	0.8	16	15	5	7	2	.305	.405	0	0	2B-31, 3B-4

Bill Skowron

SKOWRON, WILLIAM JOSEPH (Moose) BR TR 5'11" 195 lbs.
B. Dec. 18, 1930, Chicago, Ill.

	G	AB	H	2B	3B	HR	HR %	R	RBI	BB	SO	SB	BA	SA	PH AB	PH H	G by POS
1954 NY A	87	215	73	12	9	7	3.3	37	41	19	18	2	.340	.577	22	7	1B-61, 3B-5, 2B-2
1955	108	288	92	17	3	12	4.2	46	61	21	32	1	.319	.524	35	6	1B-74, 3B-3
1956	134	464	143	21	6	23	5.0	78	90	50	60	4	.308	.528	12	2	1B-120, 3B-2
1957	122	457	139	15	5	17	3.7	54	88	31	60	3	.304	.470	9	3	1B-115
1958	126	465	127	22	3	14	3.0	61	73	28	69	1	.273	.424	7	3	1B-118, 3B-2
1959	74	282	84	13	5	15	5.3	39	59	20	47	1	.298	.539	3	1	1B-72
1960	146	538	166	34	3	26	4.8	63	91	38	95	2	.309	.528	6	1	1B-142
1961	150	561	150	23	4	28	5.0	76	89	35	108	0	.267	.472	1	0	1B-149
1962	140	478	129	16	6	23	4.8	63	80	36	99	0	.270	.473	12	4	1B-135
1963 LA N	89	237	48	8	0	4	1.7	19	19	13	49	0	.203	.287	24	6	1B-66, 3B-1
1964 2 teams	WAS A (73G – .271)				CHI A (73G – .293)												
" total	146	535	151	21	3	17	3.2	47	79	30	92	0	.282	.428	13	3	1B-136
1965 CHI A	146	559	153	24	3	18	3.2	63	78	32	77	1	.274	.424	1	1	1B-145
1966	120	337	84	15	2	6	1.8	27	29	26	45	1	.249	.359	23	3	1B-98
1967 2 teams	CHI A (8G – .000)				CAL A (62G – .220)												
" total	70	131	27	2	1	1	0.8	8	11	4	19	0	.206	.260	37	7	1B-32
14 yrs.	1658	5547	1566	243	53	211	3.8	681	888	383	870	16	.282	.459	205	47	1B-1463, 3B-13, 2B-2
WORLD SERIES																	
1955 NY A	5	12	4	2	0	1	8.3	2	3	0	1	0	.333	.750	2	0	1B-3
1956	3	10	1	0	0	1	10.0	1	4	0	3	0	.100	.400	1	0	1B-2
1957	2	4	0	0	0	0	0.0	0	0	0	0	0	.000	.000	1	0	1B-2
1958	7	27	7	0	0	2	7.4	3	7	1	4	0	.259	.481	0	0	1B-7
1960	7	32	12	2	0	2	6.3	7	6	0	6	0	.375	.625	0	0	1B-7
1961	5	17	6	0	0	1	5.9	3	5	3	4	0	.353	.529	0	0	1B-5
1962	6	18	4	0	1	0	0.0	1	1	1	5	0	.222	.333	0	0	1B-6

Bill Skowron continued

	G	AB	H	2B	3B	HR	HR %	R	RBI	BB	SO	SB	BA	SA	Pinch Hit AB	Pinch Hit H	G by POS
1963 LA N	4	13	5	0	0	1	7.7	2	3	1	3	0	.385	.615	0	0	1B-4
8 yrs.	39	133	39	4	1	8	6.0	19	29	6	26	0	.293	.519	4	0	1B-36
						7th			6th		6th						

Lee Thomas

THOMAS, JAMES LEROY
B. Feb. 5, 1936, Peoria, Ill.
BL TL 6'2" 195 lbs.

	G	AB	H	2B	3B	HR	HR %	R	RBI	BB	SO	SB	BA	SA	Pinch Hit AB	Pinch Hit H	G by POS
1961 2 teams	NY A (2G – .500) LA A (130G – .284)																
" total	132	452	129	11	5	24	5.3	77	70	47	74	0	.285	.491	18	5	OF-86, 1B-34
1962 LA A	160	583	169	21	2	26	4.5	88	104	55	74	6	.290	.467	3	0	1B-90, OF-74
1963	149	528	116	12	6	9	1.7	52	55	53	82	6	.220	.316	6	2	1B-104, OF-43
1964 2 teams	LA A (47G – .273) BOS A (107G – .257)																
" total	154	573	150	27	3	15	2.6	58	66	52	51	3	.262	.398	1	0	OF-154, 1B-2
1965 BOS A	151	521	141	27	4	22	4.2	74	75	72	42	6	.271	.464	9	1	1B-127, OF-20
1966 2 teams	ATL N (39G – .198) CHI N (75G – .242)																
" total	114	275	61	5	1	7	2.5	26	24	24	30	1	.222	.324	33	9	1B-56, OF-17
1967 CHI N	77	191	42	4	1	2	1.0	16	23	15	22	1	.220	.283	22	4	OF-43, 1B-10
1968 HOU N	90	201	39	4	0	1	0.5	14	11	14	22	2	.194	.229	39	7	OF-48, 1B-2
8 yrs.	1027	3324	847	111	22	106	3.2	405	428	332	397	25	.255	.397	131	28	OF-485, 1B-425

Earl Torgeson

TORGESON, CLIFFORD EARL (The Earl of Snohomish)
B. Jan. 1, 1924, Snohomish, Wash.
BL TL 6'3" 180 lbs.

	G	AB	H	2B	3B	HR	HR %	R	RBI	BB	SO	SB	BA	SA	Pinch Hit AB	Pinch Hit H	G by POS
1947 BOS N	128	399	112	20	6	16	4.0	73	78	82	59	11	.281	.481	11	1	1B-117
1948	134	438	111	23	5	10	2.3	70	67	81	54	19	.253	.397	4	2	1B-129
1949	25	100	26	5	1	4	4.0	17	19	13	4	4	.260	.450	0	0	1B-25
1950	156	576	167	30	3	23	4.0	**120**	87	119	69	15	.290	.472	0	0	1B-156
1951	155	581	153	21	4	24	4.1	99	92	102	70	20	.263	.437	0	0	1B-155
1952	122	382	88	17	0	5	1.3	49	34	81	38	11	.230	.314	12	2	1B-105, OF-5
1953 PHI N	111	379	104	25	8	11	2.9	58	64	53	57	7	.274	.470	6	1	1B-105
1954	135	490	133	22	6	5	1.0	63	54	75	52	7	.271	.371	1	0	1B-133
1955 2 teams	PHI N (47G – .267) DET A (89G – .283)																
" total	136	450	125	15	4	10	2.2	87	67	93	49	11	.278	.396	9	3	1B-126
1956 DET A	117	318	84	9	3	12	3.8	61	42	78	47	6	.264	.425	27	10	1B-83
1957 2 teams	DET A (30G – .240) CHI A (86G – .295)																
" total	116	301	86	13	3	8	2.7	58	51	61	54	7	.286	.429	28	8	1B-87, OF-1
1958 CHI A	96	188	50	8	0	10	5.3	37	30	48	29	7	.266	.468	24	9	1B-73
1959	127	277	61	5	3	9	3.2	40	45	62	55	7	.220	.357	24	5	1B-103
1960	68	57	15	2	0	2	3.5	12	9	21	8	1	.263	.404	41	12	1B-10
1961 2 teams	CHI A (20G – .067) NY A (22G – .111)																
" total	42	33	3	0	0	0	0.0	4	1	11	8	0	.091	.091	23	2	1B-9
15 yrs.	1668	4969	1318	215	46	149	3.0	848	740	980	653	133	.265	.417	210	55	1B-1416, OF-6
WORLD SERIES																	
1948 BOS N	5	18	7	3	0	0	0.0	2	1	2	1	1	.389	.556	0	0	1B-5
1959 CHI A	3	1	0	0	0	0	0.0	1	0	1	0	0	.000	.000	1	0	1B-1
2 yrs.	8	19	7	3	0	0	0.0	3	1	3	1	1	.368	.526	1	0	1B-6

Tom Tresh

TRESH, THOMAS MICHAEL
Son of Mike Tresh.
B. Sept. 20, 1937, Detroit, Mich.
BB TR 6'1" 180 lbs.

	G	AB	H	2B	3B	HR	HR %	R	RBI	BB	SO	SB	BA	SA	Pinch Hit AB	Pinch Hit H	G by POS
1961 NY A	9	8	2	0	0	0	0.0	1	0	0	1	0	.250	.250	3	1	SS-3
1962	157	622	178	26	5	20	3.2	94	93	67	74	4	.286	.441	2	0	SS-111, OF-43
1963	145	520	140	28	5	25	4.8	91	71	83	79	3	.269	.487	1	0	OF-144
1964	153	533	131	25	5	16	3.0	75	73	73	110	13	.246	.402	7	1	OF-146
1965	156	602	168	29	6	26	4.3	94	74	59	92	5	.279	.477	2	0	OF-154
1966	151	537	125	12	4	27	5.0	76	68	86	89	5	.233	.421	3	1	OF-84, 3B-64
1967	130	448	98	23	3	14	3.1	45	53	50	86	1	.219	.377	10	1	OF-118
1968	152	507	99	18	3	11	2.2	60	52	76	97	10	.195	.308	6	1	SS-119, OF-27
1969 2 teams	NY A (45G – .182) DET A (94G – .224)																
" total	139	474	100	18	3	14	3.0	59	46	56	70	4	.211	.350	10	1	SS-118, OF-11, 3B-1
9 yrs.	1192	4251	1041	179	34	153	3.6	595	530	550	698	45	.245	.411	44	6	OF-727, SS-351, 3B-65
WORLD SERIES																	
1962 NY A	7	28	9	1	0	1	3.6	5	4	1	4	2	.321	.464	0	0	OF-7
1963	4	15	3	0	0	1	6.7	1	2	1	6	0	.200	.400	0	0	OF-4
1964	7	22	6	2	0	2	9.1	4	7	6	7	0	.273	.636	0	0	OF-7
3 yrs.	18	65	18	3	0	4	6.2	10	13	8	17	2	.277	.508	0	0	OF-18

	W	L	PCT	ERA	G	GS	CG	IP	H	BB	SO	ShO	Relief Pitching W	L	SV	BATTING AB	H	HR	BA

Luis Arroyo

ARROYO, LUIS ENRIQUE (Yo-Yo)
B. Feb. 18, 1927, Penuelas, Puerto Rico
BL TL 5'8½" 178 lbs.

	W	L	PCT	ERA	G	GS	CG	IP	H	BB	SO	ShO	Relief W	Relief L	SV	AB	H	HR	BA
1955 STL N	11	8	.579	4.19	35	24	9	159	162	63	68	1	1	0	0	56	13	1	.232
1956 PIT N	3	3	.500	4.71	18	2	1	28.2	36	12	17	0	2	2	0	4	2	0	.500
1957	3	11	.214	4.68	54	10	0	130.2	151	31	101	0	3	5	1	32	5	0	.156
1959 CIN N	1	0	1.000	3.95	10	0	0	13.2	17	11	8	0	1	0	0	2	0	0	.000
1960 NY A	5	1	.833	2.88	29	0	0	40.2	30	22	29	0	5	1	7	5	0	0	.000
1961	15	5	.750	2.19	**65**	0	0	119	83	49	87	0	**15**	5	29	25	7	0	.280
1962	1	3	.250	4.81	27	0	0	33.2	33	17	21	0	1	3	7	4	2	0	.500
1963	1	1	.500	13.50	6	0	0	6	12	3	5	0	1	1	0	0	0	0	–
8 yrs.	40	32	.556	3.93	244	36	10	531.1	524	208	336	1	29	17	44	128	29	1	.227
WORLD SERIES																			
1960 NY A	0	0	–	13.50	1	0	0	.2	2	0	1	0	0	0	0	1	0	0	.000
1961	1	0	1.000	2.25	2	0	0	4	4	2	3	0	1	0	0	0	0	0	–
2 yrs.	1	0	1.000	3.86	3	0	0	4.2	6	2	4	0	1	0	0	1	0	0	.000

Tex Clevenger

CLEVENGER, TRUMAN EUGENE
B. July 9, 1932, Visalia, Calif.
BR TR 6'1" 180 lbs.

	W	L	PCT	ERA	G	GS	CG	IP	H	BB	SO	ShO	Relief W	Relief L	SV	AB	H	HR	BA
1954 BOS A	2	4	.333	4.79	23	8	1	67.2	67	29	43	0	1	0	0	14	3	0	.214
1956 WAS A	0	0	–	5.40	20	1	0	31.2	33	21	17	0	0	0	0	2	0	0	.000
1957	7	6	.538	4.19	52	9	2	139.2	139	47	75	0	5	4	8	33	7	0	.212
1958	9	9	.500	4.35	**55**	4	0	124	119	50	70	0	0	3	6	22	3	0	.136
1959	8	5	.615	3.91	50	7	2	117.1	114	51	71	2	5	2	8	23	4	0	.174
1960	5	11	.313	4.20	53	11	1	128.2	150	49	49	0	3	4	7	22	2	0	.091
1961 2 teams LA A (12G 2–1) NY A (21G 1–1)																			
" total	3	2	.600	3.78	33	0	0	47.2	48	34	25	0	3	2	1	7	1	0	.143
1962 NY A	2	0	1.000	2.84	21	0	0	38	36	17	11	0	2	0	0	4	0	0	.000
8 yrs.	36	37	.493	4.18	307	40	6	694.2	706	298	361	2	19	15	30	127	20	0	.157

Jim Coates

COATES, JAMES ALTON
B. Aug. 4, 1932, Farnham, Va.
BR TR 6'4" 192 lbs.

	W	L	PCT	ERA	G	GS	CG	IP	H	BB	SO	ShO	Relief W	Relief L	SV	AB	H	HR	BA
1956 NY A	0	0	–	13.50	2	0	0	2	1	4	0	0	0	0	0	0	0	0	–
1959	6	1	.857	2.87	37	4	2	100.1	89	36	64	0	4	1	3	21	2	0	.095
1960	13	3	.813	4.28	35	18	6	149.1	139	66	73	2	4	0	1	48	12	0	.250
1961	11	5	.688	3.44	43	11	4	141.1	128	53	80	1	6	2	5	35	1	0	.029
1962	7	6	.538	4.44	50	6	0	117.2	119	50	67	0	7	5	6	32	4	0	.125
1963 2 teams WAS A (20G 2–4) CIN N (9G 0–0)																			
" total	2	4	.333	5.34	29	2	0	60.2	72	28	42	0	2	4	0	9	0	0	.000
1965 CAL A	2	0	1.000	3.54	17	0	0	28	23	16	15	0	2	0	3	1	0	0	.000
1966	1	1	.500	3.98	9	4	1	31.2	32	10	16	1	0	0	0	11	1	0	.091
1967	1	2	.333	4.30	25	1	0	52.1	47	23	39	0	1	1	0	3	1	0	.333
9 yrs.	43	22	.662	4.00	247	46	13	683.1	650	286	396	4	26	13	18	160	21	0	.131
WORLD SERIES																			
1960 NY A	0	0	–	5.68	3	0	0	6.1	6	1	3	0	0	0	0	1	0	0	.000
1961	0	0	–	0.00	1	0	0	4	1	1	2	0	0	0	1	1	0	0	.000
1962	0	1	.000	6.75	2	0	0	2.2	1	1	3	0	0	1	0	0	0	0	–
3 yrs.	0	1	.000	4.15	6	0	0	13	8	3	8	0	0	1	1	2	0	0	.000

Bud Daley

DALEY, LEAVITT LEO
B. Oct. 7, 1932, Orange, Calif.
BL TL 6'1" 185 lbs.

	W	L	PCT	ERA	G	GS	CG	IP	H	BB	SO	ShO	Relief W	Relief L	SV	AB	H	HR	BA
1955 CLE A	0	1	.000	6.43	2	1	0	7	10	1	2	0	0	0	0	2	0	0	.000
1956	1	0	1.000	6.20	14	0	0	20.1	21	14	13	0	1	0	0	2	0	0	.000
1957	2	8	.200	4.43	34	10	1	87.1	99	40	54	0	0	2	2	20	4	0	.200
1958 KC A	3	2	.600	3.31	26	5	1	70.2	67	19	39	0	2	0	0	16	2	0	.125
1959	16	13	.552	3.16	39	29	12	216.1	212	62	125	2	1	2	1	78	23	0	.295
1960	16	16	.500	4.56	37	35	13	231	234	96	126	1	1	1	0	75	12	0	.160
1961 2 teams KC A (16G 4–8) NY A (23G 8–9)																			
" total	12	17	.414	4.28	39	27	9	193.1	211	73	119	0	1	3	1	63	8	0	.127
1962 NY A	7	5	.583	3.59	43	6	0	105.1	105	21	55	0	5	3	4	27	5	0	.185
1963	0	0	–	0.00	1	0	0	1	2	0	0	0	0	0	1	0	0	0	–
1964	3	2	.600	4.63	13	3	0	35	37	25	16	0	0	2	1	8	2	0	.250
10 yrs.	60	64	.484	4.03	248	116	36	967.1	998	351	549	3	11	13	10	291	56	0	.192
WORLD SERIES																			
1961 NY A	1	0	1.000	0.00	2	0	0	7	5	0	3	0	1	0	0	1	0	0	.000
1962	0	0	–	0.00	1	0	0	1	1	1	0	0	0	0	0	0	0	0	–
2 yrs.	1	0	1.000	0.00	3	0	0	8	6	1	3	0	1	0	0	1	0	0	.000

Art Ditmar

DITMAR, ARTHUR JOHN
B. Apr. 3, 1929, Winthrop, Mass.
BR TR 6'2" 185 lbs.

	W	L	PCT	ERA	G	GS	CG	IP	H	BB	SO	ShO	Relief W	Relief L	SV	AB	H	HR	BA
1954 PHI A	1	4	.200	6.41	14	5	0	39.1	50	36	14	0	0	2	0	8	1	0	.125
1955 KC A	12	12	.500	5.03	35	22	7	175.1	180	86	79	1	3	2	1	62	13	0	.210
1956	12	**22**	.353	4.42	44	34	14	254.1	254	108	126	2	3	1	1	91	13	1	.143
1957 NY A	8	3	.727	3.25	46	11	0	127.1	128	35	64	0	6	1	6	35	7	0	.200
1958	9	8	.529	3.42	38	13	4	139.2	124	38	52	0	4	4	4	44	11	0	.250
1959	13	9	.591	2.90	38	25	7	202	156	52	96	1	1	1	1	76	15	1	.197
1960	15	9	.625	3.06	34	28	8	200	195	56	65	1	1	2	0	69	11	0	.159
1961 2 teams NY A (12G 2–3) KC A (20G 0–5)																			
" total	2	8	.200	5.15	32	13	1	108.1	119	37	43	0	0	2	1	31	3	0	.097
1962 KC A	0	2	.000	6.65	6	5	0	21.2	31	13	13	0	0	0	0	6	1	0	.167
9 yrs.	72	77	.483	3.98	287	156	41	1268	1237	461	552	5	18	15	14	422	75	2	.178
WORLD SERIES																			
1957 NY A	0	0	–	0.00	2	0	0	6	2	0	2	0	0	0	0	1	0	0	.000
1958	0	0	–	0.00	1	0	0	3.2	2	0	2	0	0	0	0	1	0	0	.000
1960	0	2	.000	21.60	2	2	0	1.2	6	1	0	0	0	0	0	0	0	0	–
3 yrs.	0	2	.000	3.18	5	2	0	11.1	10	1	4	0	0	0	0	2	0	0	.000

	W	L	PCT	ERA	G	GS	CG	IP	H	BB	SO	ShO	Relief Pitching W	L	SV	BATTING AB	H	HR	BA

Al Downing

DOWNING, ALPHONSO ERWIN
B. June 28, 1941, Trenton, N. J.

BR TL 5'11" 175 lbs.

	W	L	PCT	ERA	G	GS	CG	IP	H	BB	SO	ShO	Relief W	Relief L	SV	AB	H	HR	BA
1961 NY A	0	1	.000	8.00	5	1	0	9	7	12	12	0	0	0	0	1	0	0	.000
1962	0	0	–	0.00	1	0	0	1	0	0	1	0	0	0	0	0	0	0	–
1963	13	5	.722	2.56	24	22	10	175.2	114	80	171	4	0	1	0	58	6	0	.103
1964	13	8	.619	3.47	37	35	11	244	201	**120**	**217**	1	0	0	2	85	15	0	.176
1965	12	14	.462	3.40	35	32	8	212	185	105	179	2	0	0	0	74	8	1	.108
1966	10	11	.476	3.56	30	30	1	200	178	79	152	0	0	0	0	70	7	0	.100
1967	14	10	.583	2.63	31	28	10	201.2	158	61	171	4	2	0	0	66	8	1	.121
1968	3	3	.500	3.52	15	12	1	61.1	54	20	40	0	0	0	0	17	3	0	.176
1969	7	5	.583	3.38	30	15	5	130.2	117	49	85	1	1	1	0	44	6	0	.136
1970 2 teams OAK A (10G 3–3) MIL A (17G 2–10)																			
" total	5	13	.278	3.52	27	22	2	135.1	118	81	79	0	0	0	0	35	4	0	.114
1971 LA N	20	9	.690	2.68	37	36	12	262	245	84	136	**5**	0	0	0	92	16	0	.174
1972	9	9	.500	2.98	31	30	7	202.2	196	67	117	4	0	0	0	66	8	0	.121
1973	9	9	.500	3.31	30	28	5	193	155	68	124	2	1	0	0	57	5	0	.088
1974	5	6	.455	3.67	21	16	1	98	94	45	63	1	0	0	0	29	5	0	.172
1975	2	1	.667	2.88	22	6	0	75	59	28	39	0	2	1	1	16	0	0	.000
1976	1	2	.333	3.86	17	3	0	46.2	43	18	30	0	1	1	0	6	0	0	.000
1977	0	1	.000	6.75	12	1	0	20	22	16	23	0	0	1	0	1	0	0	.000
17 yrs.	123	107	.535	3.22	405	317	73	2268	1946	933	1639	24	7	5	3	717	91	2	.127
LEAGUE CHAMPIONSHIP SERIES																			
1974 LA N	0	0	–	0.00	1	0	0	4	1	1	0	0	0	0	0	1	0	0	.000
WORLD SERIES																			
1963 NY A	0	1	.000	5.40	1	1	0	5	7	1	6	0	0	0	0	1	0	0	.000
1964	0	1	.000	8.22	3	1	0	7.2	9	2	5	0	0	0	0	2	0	0	.000
1974 LA N	0	1	.000	2.45	1	1	0	3.2	4	4	3	0	0	0	0	1	0	0	.000
3 yrs.	0	3	.000	6.06	5	3	0	16.1	20	7	14	0	0	0	0	4	0	0	.000

Ryne Duren

DUREN, RINOLD GEORGE
B. Feb. 22, 1929, Cazenovia, Wis.

BR TR 6'2" 190 lbs.

	W	L	PCT	ERA	G	GS	CG	IP	H	BB	SO	ShO	Relief W	Relief L	SV	AB	H	HR	BA
1954 BAL A	0	0	–	9.00	1	0	0	2	3	1	2	0	0	0	0	0	0	0	–
1957 KC A	0	3	.000	5.27	14	6	0	42.2	37	30	37	0	0	0	1	14	1	0	.071
1958 NY A	6	4	.600	2.02	44	1	0	75.2	40	43	87	0	6	4	20	13	1	0	.077
1959	3	6	.333	1.88	41	0	0	76.2	49	43	96	0	3	6	14	14	0	0	.000
1960	3	4	.429	4.96	42	1	0	49	27	49	67	0	3	4	9	6	0	0	.000
1961 2 teams NY A (4G 0–1) LA A (40G 6–12)																			
" total	6	13	.316	5.19	44	14	1	104	89	79	115	1	4	9	2	25	1	0	.040
1962 LA A	2	9	.182	4.42	42	3	0	71.1	53	57	74	0	2	8	8	15	1	0	.067
1963 PHI N	6	2	.750	3.30	33	7	1	87.1	65	52	84	0	3	1	2	21	3	0	.143
1964 2 teams PHI N (2G 0–0) CIN N (26G 0–2)																			
" total	0	2	.000	3.09	28	0	0	46.2	46	16	44	0	0	2	1	5	0	0	.000
1965 2 teams PHI N (6G 0–0) WAS A (16G 1–1)																			
" total	1	1	.500	5.56	22	0	0	34	34	22	24	0	1	1	0	1	0	0	.000
10 yrs.	27	44	.380	3.83	311	32	2	589.1	443	392	630	1	22	35	57	114	7	0	.061
WORLD SERIES																			
1958 NY A	1	1	.500	1.93	3	0	0	9.1	7	6	14	0	1	1	1	3	0	0	.000
1960	0	0	–	2.25	2	0	0	4	2	1	5	0	0	0	0	0	0	0	–
2 yrs.	1	1	.500	2.03	5	0	0	13.1	9	7	19	0	1	1	1	3	0	0	.000

Whitey Ford

FORD, EDWARD CHARLES (The Chairman of the Board)
B. Oct. 21, 1928, New York, N. Y.
Hall of Fame 1974.

BL TL 5'10" 178 lbs.

	W	L	PCT	ERA	G	GS	CG	IP	H	BB	SO	ShO	Relief W	Relief L	SV	AB	H	HR	BA
1950 NY A	9	1	.900	2.81	20	12	7	112	87	52	59	2	0	1	1	36	7	0	.194
1953	18	6	.750	3.00	32	30	11	207	187	110	110	3	0	0	0	75	20	0	.267
1954	16	8	.667	2.82	34	28	11	210.2	170	101	125	3	2	2	1	62	10	0	.161
1955	**18**	7	.720	2.63	39	33	**18**	253.2	188	113	137	5	0	1	2	86	14	1	.163
1956	19	6	**.760**	**2.47**	31	30	18	225.2	187	84	141	2	0	0	1	78	17	0	.218
1957	11	5	.688	2.57	24	17	5	129.1	114	53	84	0	3	0	0	42	6	0	.143
1958	14	7	.667	**2.01**	30	29	15	219.1	174	62	145	**7**	0	0	1	73	15	0	.205
1959	16	10	.615	3.04	35	29	9	204	194	89	114	2	2	2	1	65	15	1	.231
1960	12	9	.571	3.08	33	29	8	192.2	168	65	85	**4**	0	0	0	53	8	0	.151
1961	**25**	4	**.862**	3.21	39	**39**	11	**283**	242	92	209	3	0	0	0	96	17	0	.177
1962	17	8	.680	2.90	38	37	7	257.2	243	69	160	0	0	0	0	85	10	0	.118
1963	**24**	7	**.774**	2.74	38	**37**	13	**269.1**	240	56	189	3	0	0	1	92	13	1	.141
1964	17	6	.739	2.13	39	36	12	244.2	212	57	172	8	0	0	1	67	8	0	.119
1965	16	13	.552	3.24	37	36	9	244.1	241	50	162	2	0	0	1	82	15	0	.183
1966	2	5	.286	2.47	22	9	0	73	79	24	43	0	2	1	0	18	0	0	.000
1967	2	4	.333	1.64	7	7	2	44	40	9	21	1	0	0	0	13	2	0	.154
16 yrs.	236	106	.690	2.75	498	438	156	3170.1	2766	1086	1956	45	9	7	10	1023	177	3	.173
			4th																
WORLD SERIES																			
1950 NY A	1	0	1.000	0.00	1	1	0	8.2	7	1	7	0	0	0	0	3	0	0	.000
1953	0	1	.000	4.50	2	2	0	8	9	2	7	0	0	0	0	3	1	0	.333
1955	2	0	1.000	2.12	2	2	1	17	13	8	10	0	0	0	0	6	0	0	.000
1956	1	1	.500	5.25	2	2	1	12	14	2	8	0	0	0	0	4	0	0	.000
1957	1	1	.500	1.13	2	2	1	16	11	5	7	0	0	0	0	5	0	0	.000
1958	0	1	.000	4.11	3	3	0	15.1	19	5	16	0	0	0	0	4	0	0	.000
1960	2	0	1.000	0.00	2	2	2	18	11	2	8	2	0	0	0	8	2	0	.250
1961	2	0	1.000	0.00	2	2	1	14	6	1	7	1	0	0	0	5	0	0	.000
1962	1	1	.500	4.12	3	3	1	19.2	24	4	12	0	0	0	0	7	0	0	.000
1963	0	2	.000	4.50	2	2	0	12	10	3	8	0	0	0	0	3	0	0	.000
1964	0	1	.000	8.44	1	1	0	5.1	8	1	4	0	0	0	0	1	1	0	1.000
11 yrs.	10	8	.556	2.71	22	22	7	146	132	34	94	3	0	0	0	49	4	0	.082
	1st	**1st**			**1st**	**1st**	**4th**	**1st**	**1st**	**1st**	**1st**	**2nd**							

Johnny James

JAMES, JOHN PHILLIP BL TR 5'10" 160 lbs.
B. July 23, 1933, Bonner's Ferry, Ida.

	W	L	PCT	ERA	G	GS	CG	IP	H	BB	SO	ShO	Relief Pitching W	Relief Pitching L	Relief Pitching SV	Batting AB	Batting H	Batting HR	BA
1958 NY A	0	0	–	0.00	1	0	0	3	2	4	1	0	0	0	0	1	0	0	.000
1960	5	1	.833	4.36	28	0	0	43.1	38	26	29	0	5	1	2	3	0	0	.000
1961 2 teams NY A (1G 0–0) LA A (36G 0–2)																			
" total	0	2	.000	5.20	37	3	0	72.2	67	54	43	0	0	1	0	13	0	0	.000
3 yrs.	5	3	.625	4.76	66	3	0	119	107	84	73	0	5	2	2	17	0	0	.000

Duke Maas

MAAS, DUANE FREDERICK BR TR 5'10" 170 lbs.
B. Jan. 31, 1929, Utica, Mich. D. Dec. 7, 1976, Mt. Clemens, Mich.

	W	L	PCT	ERA	G	GS	CG	IP	H	BB	SO	ShO	Relief Pitching W	Relief Pitching L	Relief Pitching SV	Batting AB	Batting H	Batting HR	BA
1955 DET A	5	6	.455	4.88	18	16	5	86.2	91	50	42	2	0	0	0	30	5	0	.167
1956	0	7	.000	6.54	26	7	0	63.1	81	32	34	0	0	1	0	16	3	0	.188
1957	10	14	.417	3.28	45	26	8	219.1	210	65	116	2	1	2	6	71	6	1	.085
1958 2 teams KC A (10G 4–5) NY A (22G 7–3)																			
" total	11	8	.579	3.85	32	20	5	156.2	142	49	69	2	2	2	1	51	6	0	.118
1959 NY A	14	8	.636	4.43	38	21	3	138	149	53	67	1	5	0	4	40	5	0	.125
1960	5	1	.833	4.09	35	1	0	70.1	70	35	28	0	5	0	4	6	0	0	.000
1961	0	0	–	54.00	1	0	0	.1	2	0	0	0	0	0	0	0	0	0	–
7 yrs.	45	44	.506	4.19	195	91	21	734.2	745	284	356	7	13	5	15	214	25	1	.117
WORLD SERIES																			
1958 NY A	0	0	–	81.00	1	0	0	.1	2	1	0	0	0	0	0	0	0	0	–
1960	0	0	–	4.50	1	0	0	2	2	0	1	0	0	0	0	0	0	0	–
2 yrs.	0	0	–	15.43	2	0	0	2.1	4	1	1	0	0	0	0	0	0	0	–

Danny McDevitt

McDEVITT, DANIEL EUGENE BL TL 5'10" 175 lbs.
B. Nov. 18, 1932, New York, N. Y.

	W	L	PCT	ERA	G	GS	CG	IP	H	BB	SO	ShO	Relief Pitching W	Relief Pitching L	Relief Pitching SV	Batting AB	Batting H	Batting HR	BA
1957 BKN N	7	4	.636	3.25	22	17	5	119	105	72	90	2	0	0	0	39	6	0	.154
1958 LA N	2	6	.250	7.45	13	10	2	48.1	71	31	26	0	0	0	0	15	2	0	.133
1959	10	8	.556	3.97	39	22	6	145	149	51	106	2	1	0	4	46	5	0	.109
1960	0	4	.000	4.25	24	7	0	53	51	42	30	0	0	2	0	10	2	0	.200
1961 2 teams NY A (8G 1–2) MIN A (16G 1–0)																			
" total	2	2	.500	4.08	24	3	0	39.2	38	27	23	0	2	0	1	4	0	0	.000
1962 KC A	0	3	.000	5.82	33	1	0	51	47	41	28	0	0	2	2	9	2	0	.222
6 yrs.	21	27	.438	4.40	155	60	13	456	461	264	303	4	3	4	7	123	17	0	.138

Hal Reniff

RENIFF, HAROLD EUGENE (Porky) BR TR 6' 215 lbs.
B. July 2, 1938, Warren, Ohio

	W	L	PCT	ERA	G	GS	CG	IP	H	BB	SO	ShO	Relief Pitching W	Relief Pitching L	Relief Pitching SV	Batting AB	Batting H	Batting HR	BA
1961 NY A	2	0	1.000	2.58	25	0	0	45.1	31	31	21	0	2	0	2	5	0	0	.000
1962	0	0	–	7.36	2	0	0	3.2	6	5	1	0	0	0	0	0	0	0	–
1963	4	3	.571	2.62	48	0	0	89.1	63	42	56	0	4	3	18	15	0	0	.000
1964	6	4	.600	3.12	41	0	0	69.1	47	30	38	0	6	4	9	10	1	0	.100
1965	3	4	.429	3.80	51	0	0	85.1	74	48	74	0	3	4	3	2	0	0	.000
1966	3	7	.300	3.21	56	0	0	95.1	80	49	79	0	3	7	9	14	4	0	.286
1967 2 teams NY A (24G 0–2) NY N (29G 3–3)																			
" total	3	5	.375	3.80	53	0	0	83	82	37	45	0	3	5	4	6	0	0	.000
7 yrs.	21	23	.477	3.27	276	0	0	471.1	383	242	314	0	21	23	45	52	5	0	.096
WORLD SERIES																			
1963 NY A	0	0	–	0.00	3	0	0	3	0	1	1	0	0	0	0	0	0	0	–
1964	0	0	–	0.00	1	0	0	.1	2	0	0	0	0	0	0	0	0	0	–
2 yrs.	0	0	–	0.00	4	0	0	3.1	2	1	1	0	0	0	0	0	0	0	–

Rollie Sheldon

SHELDON, ROLAND FRANK BR TR 6'4" 185 lbs.
B. Dec. 17, 1936, Putnam, Conn.

	W	L	PCT	ERA	G	GS	CG	IP	H	BB	SO	ShO	Relief Pitching W	Relief Pitching L	Relief Pitching SV	Batting AB	Batting H	Batting HR	BA
1961 NY A	11	5	.688	3.60	35	21	6	162.2	149	55	84	2	2	0	0	56	7	0	.125
1962	7	8	.467	5.49	34	16	2	118	136	28	54	0	3	1	1	26	2	0	.077
1964	5	2	.714	3.61	19	12	3	102.1	92	18	57	0	0	0	1	34	3	0	.088
1965 2 teams NY A (3G 0–0) KC A (32G 10–8)																			
" total	10	8	.556	3.86	35	29	4	193.1	185	57	112	1	0	0	0	52	4	0	.077
1966 2 teams KC A (14G 4–7) BOS A (23G 1–6)																			
" total	5	13	.278	4.12	37	23	2	148.2	179	49	64	1	0	2	0	41	4	0	.098
5 yrs.	38	36	.514	4.08	160	101	17	725	741	207	371	4	5	3	2	209	20	0	.096
WORLD SERIES																			
1964 NY A	0	0	–	0.00	2	0	0	2.2	0	2	2	0	0	0	0	0	0	0	–

Bill Stafford

STAFFORD, WILLIAM CHARLES BR TR 6'1" 188 lbs.
B. Aug. 13, 1939, Catskill, N. Y.

	W	L	PCT	ERA	G	GS	CG	IP	H	BB	SO	ShO	Relief Pitching W	Relief Pitching L	Relief Pitching SV	Batting AB	Batting H	Batting HR	BA
1960 NY A	3	1	.750	2.25	11	8	2	60	50	18	36	1	0	0	0	22	1	0	.045
1961	14	9	.609	2.68	36	25	8	195	168	59	101	3	0	2	2	67	12	0	.179
1962	14	9	.609	3.67	35	33	7	213.1	188	77	109	2	0	1	0	78	17	0	.218
1963	4	8	.333	6.02	28	14	0	89.2	104	42	52	0	2	1	3	24	7	0	.292
1964	5	0	1.000	2.67	31	1	0	60.2	50	22	39	0	5	0	4	13	1	0	.077
1965	3	8	.273	3.56	22	15	1	111.1	93	31	71	0	0	1	0	29	0	0	.000
1966 KC A	0	4	.000	4.99	9	8	0	39.2	42	12	31	0	0	0	0	11	0	0	.000
1967	0	1	.000	1.69	14	0	0	16	12	9	10	0	0	1	0	1	0	0	.000
8 yrs.	43	40	.518	3.52	186	104	18	785.2	707	270	449	6	7	6	9	245	38	0	.155
WORLD SERIES																			
1960 NY A	0	0	–	1.50	2	0	0	6	5	1	2	0	0	0	0	1	0	0	.000
1961	0	0	–	2.70	1	1	0	6.2	7	2	5	0	0	0	0	2	0	0	.000
1962	1	0	1.000	2.00	1	1	1	9	4	2	5	0	0	0	0	3	0	0	.000
3 yrs.	1	0	1.000	2.08	4	2	1	21.2	16	5	12	0	0	0	0	6	0	0	.000

Ralph Terry

TERRY, RALPH WILLARD BR TR 6'3" 195 lbs.
B. Jan. 9, 1936, Big Cabin, Okla.

	W	L	PCT	ERA	G	GS	CG	IP	H	BB	SO	ShO	Relief Pitching W	Relief Pitching L	Relief Pitching SV	Batting AB	Batting H	Batting HR	BA
1956 NY A	1	2	.333	9.45	3	3	0	13.1	17	11	8	0	0	0	0	6	1	0	.167
1957 2 teams NY A (7G 1–1) KC A (21G 4–11)																			
" total	5	12	.294	3.33	28	21	4	151.1	137	55	87	2	0	1	0	46	7	0	.152
1958 KC A	11	13	.458	4.24	40	33	8	216.2	217	61	134	3	0	0	2	71	14	0	.197

Ralph Terry continued

Year	Team	W	L	PCT	ERA	G	GS	CG	IP	H	BB	SO	ShO	Relief Pitching W	Relief Pitching L	Relief Pitching SV	BATTING AB	BATTING H	BATTING HR	BA
1959	2 teams KC A (9G 2–4) NY A (24G 3–7)																			
"	total	5	11	.313	3.89	33	23	7	173.2	186	49	90	1	0	0	0	58	7	0	.121
1960	NY A	10	8	.556	3.40	35	23	7	166.2	149	52	92	3	1	1	1	49	6	0	.122
1961		16	3	.842	3.15	31	27	9	188.1	162	42	86	2	1	0	0	66	15	0	.227
1962		**23**	12	.657	3.19	43	**39**	14	**298.2**	257	57	176	3	1	0	2	106	20	0	.189
1963		17	15	.531	3.22	40	**37**	**18**	268	246	39	114	3	0	0	1	87	7	0	.080
1964		7	11	.389	4.54	27	14	2	115	130	31	77	1	2	3	4	35	7	0	.200
1965	CLE A	11	6	.647	3.69	30	26	6	165.2	154	23	84	2	0	0	0	49	7	1	.143
1966	2 teams KC A (15G 1–5) NY N (11G 0–1)																			
"	total	1	6	.143	4.06	26	11	0	88.2	92	26	47	0	0	1	1	20	4	0	.200
1967	NY N	0	0	–	0.00	2	0	0	3.1	1	0	5	0	0	0	0	0	0	0	–
12 yrs.		107	99	.519	3.62	338	257	75	1849.1	1748	446	1000	20	5	6	11	593	95	1	.160
WORLD SERIES																				
1960	NY A	0	2	.000	5.40	2	1	0	6.2	7	1	5	0	0	1	0	2	0	0	.000
1961		0	1	.000	4.82	2	2	0	9.1	12	2	7	0	0	0	0	3	0	0	.000
1962		2	1	.667	1.80	3	3	2	25	17	2	16	1	0	0	0	8	1	0	.125
1963		0	0	–	3.00	1	0	0	3	3	1	0	0	0	0	0	0	0	0	–
1964		0	0	–	0.00	1	0	0	2	2	0	3	0	0	0	0	0	0	0	–
5 yrs.		2	4	.333	2.93	9	6	2	46	41	6	31	1	0	1	0	13	1	0	.077
			7th																	

Bob Turley

TURLEY, ROBERT LEE (Bullet Bob)
B. Sept. 19, 1930, Troy, Ill.

BR TR 6'2" 215 lbs.

Year	Team	W	L	PCT	ERA	G	GS	CG	IP	H	BB	SO	ShO	Relief Pitching W	Relief Pitching L	Relief Pitching SV	BATTING AB	BATTING H	BATTING HR	BA
1951	STL A	0	1	.000	7.36	1	1	0	7.1	11	3	5	0	0	0	0	2	0	0	.000
1953		2	6	.250	3.28	10	7	3	60.1	39	44	61	1	1	1	0	18	5	1	.278
1954	BAL A	14	15	.483	3.46	35	35	14	247.1	178	**181**	**185**	0	0	0	0	81	11	0	.136
1955	NY A	17	13	.567	3.06	36	34	13	246.2	168	**177**	210	6	0	0	1	82	11	0	.134
1956		8	4	.667	5.05	27	21	5	132	138	103	91	1	0	0	1	46	8	0	.174
1957		13	6	.684	2.71	32	23	9	176.1	120	85	152	4	1	0	3	57	5	0	.088
1958		**21**	7	**.750**	2.97	33	31	**19**	245.1	178	**128**	168	6	0	0	1	88	12	2	.136
1959		8	11	.421	4.32	33	22	7	154.1	141	83	111	3	0	0	0	46	4	0	.087
1960		9	3	.750	3.27	34	24	4	173.1	138	87	87	1	1	0	5	55	4	0	.073
1961		3	5	.375	5.75	15	12	1	72	74	51	48	0	0	0	0	21	2	0	.095
1962		3	3	.500	4.57	24	8	0	69	68	47	42	0	3	0	1	12	0	0	.000
1963	2 teams LA A (19G 2–7) BOS A (11G 1–4)																			
"	total	3	11	.214	4.20	30	19	3	128.2	113	79	105	2	0	1	0	39	7	1	.179
12 yrs.		101	85	.543	3.64	310	237	78	1712.2	1366	1068	1265	24	6	2	12	547	69	4	.126
WORLD SERIES																				
1955	NY A	0	1	.000	8.44	3	1	0	5.1	7	4	7	0	0	0	0	1	0	0	.000
1956		0	1	.000	0.82	3	1	1	11	4	8	14	0	0	0	0	4	0	0	.000
1957		1	0	1.000	2.31	3	2	1	11.2	7	6	12	0	0	0	0	4	0	0	.000
1958		2	1	.667	2.76	4	2	1	16.1	10	7	13	1	1	0	1	5	1	0	.200
1960		1	0	1.000	4.82	2	2	0	9.1	15	4	0	0	0	0	0	4	1	0	.250
5 yrs.		4	3	.571	3.19	15	8	3	53.2	43	29	46	1	1	0	1	18	2	0	.111
						3rd	10th				5th	10th								

INDEX